THE WAY WE ATE

THE WAY WE ATE

memories of maltese meals

MATTY CREMONA

midsea BOOKS

By the same author
Cooking with Maltese Olive Oil
A Year in the Country – Life and Food in Rural Malta

First published in 2010 by Midsea Books
3a Strait Street, Valletta, Malta
www.midseabooks.com

Design & Layout: Ramon Micallef
Printers: Gutenberg Press
Food Photography: Pippa Zammit Cutajar
General Photography: Joe P. Borg

ISBN: 978-99932-7-326-4

CONTENTS

RECIPE INDEX

MEMORIES OF MALTESE MEALS

What is Maltese Food? Like the food of all nations it moves with the times and food fashions or fads are quick to come and go. It is the signature dishes – the tried and tested dishes – that endure to become "traditional". But even these are subject to change and availability. Imagine if food purists sneered when potatoes were woven into the tapestry of Maltese food? What then of our famous *patata Maltija*, *patata fgat* or *patata fil-forn*? Or our perfect *ħobż biż-żejt* that was probably first made with oil and a few olives – if traditionalists had sniffed at the tomato and said, "what's this strange foreign fruit?", where would our national dish be today?

So it is far more interesting to trace the evolution of our nation's favourite dishes; why we eat what we eat and how we eat it. Even, when we eat it. All of these play a part in stitching together a multi flavoured backdrop to our history because eating is something people have to (and want to) do every day and always have. The foods they chose to eat were the result of the environment they were living in. The foods we choose to eat today are conditioned by their choices and influenced by our situation today. Therefore our meals are a tiny, if slightly cloudy, window onto the past, kindly held open by recipes handed on down through the generations, making us the eaters we are today.

This book traces the history of some of our popular dishes, meals and festivals and I enjoyed writing it very much. I am grateful to the authors of the many books I read about Malta and its history that are listed in the bibliography. The information found therein created a wonderful picture of the past that I enjoyed slotting the food into.

I am also indebted to the many people who have been kind enough to answer all my endless questions about what they remembered about the food and meals they ate or cooked. These include Mrs Tina Agius, Mrs Joan Bonello, Mrs Maria Bondi, Mrs Josephine Burridge, Mrs Molly Caruana Dingli, Mr Alex Caruana Soler, Mrs Ġuża Cremona, Miss Margaret Ferro, Mrs Rita Ferro, Ms Greta Gatt, Ms Blanche Gatt, Mr Adrian Mercieca, Mrs Yvonne Pisani, Mrs Laura Pullicino, Mrs Antoinette Samut, Dr and Mrs Mario Sant Cassia, Captain and Mrs Harry Sullivan, Mrs Clara Testaferrata Moroni Viani, Mrs Jane Testaferrata Moroni Viani and everyone else generous enough to bother to share their food memories with me.

Successful cookery depends to a certain degree on excellent ingredients and in turn reliable suppliers. I buy all my meat from Charles Butcher in

Naxxar and I must thank Victor and Leli Grech for their patience in providing me with so much information and meeting my many strange requests. Their extensive knowledge and experience with meat is a family thing; their grandmother started off the business in St Lucy Street, Naxxar before the war and 54 years ago their father moved the shop to the main square in Naxxar where Victor and Leli are today. Pippa Zammit Cutajar and I spent most of one night at Joseph Cassar's bakery in Triq San Silvestru, Mosta and while she photographed the baking session I followed the baker round, asking him all about his work. It was great fun and he kindly explained and showed us the whole baking process. All the fish and vegetables I use, except on the odd occasion, are local as the taste and texture of Maltese fish, vegetables and fruit is vastly superior, far fresher and healthier than imported produce. I use Maltese Extra Virgin Olive Oil and honey produced by my husband, Sam Cremona in all my cooking because they are delicious, enhance food beautifully and are full of beneficial qualities.

An author can only get so far with a manuscript. Once it is written and is simply a bulky sheaf of papers, the experts step in and transform it into a book. In this case Ramon Micallef not only designed the book but helped tie up the loose ends with amazing tolerance and kindness. Pippa Zammit Cutajar took all the wonderful photographs of the food I cooked that bring the text to life so beautifully. Nicholas de Piro read through my book, gently pointed out the errors and omissions and supplied the corrections as well as helping me find the paintings and illustrations I needed. Michael Ferro meticulously proofread my book and indicated all the mistakes, typos and semi colons with great humour and all the accuracy and consistency my grammar and spelling lacks. Blanche Gatt and Antoinette Micallef checked the text for still more inconsistencies and messy grammer. Daphne Caruana Galizia kindly gave permission for photographs of my food and excerpts from my articles previously published in *Taste Magazine* to be reproduced here. To them all an inadequate thank you for all their time, patience and generosity in sharing their expertise. Any remaining errors are certainly mine.

I would like to thank Timmy Gambin for introducing me to Joseph Mizzi of Midsea Books and for encouraging me to carry on writing this book. And finally, my enduring gratitude and love to my beloved daughter Lizzie and husband Sammy for being there.

FOREWORD

Matty Cremona has given birth to something spectacular. Her book 'The Way We Ate' is so special that my enthusiasm for it may well harm the credibility of my good intentions to praise it to high Heaven. As I paged through this large book of cookery and its history I soon realised that this was not just another recipe book. It is an education backed by a great deal of research, nostalgia and anthropology so deep and so moving that were I to read it on some desert island there is no doubt that tears of longing would flow and my heart would break.

The book exudes the pride of a nation: perhaps that sounds too grand. Truly I should say that it makes me happy to be Maltese. The historical notes around each subject are separate from the recipes and are mostly sheer delight. There are lots of good stories salvaged from the past – from parents, aunts and uncles and further back into earlier generations not to mention historical archives. Whoever does not read this book may be missing out on the grand and perhaps unique experience of being Maltese.

The earliest, the mediaeval, the grandeur of the knights' cuisine, and, most interestingly, the stringencies to which the poor were subjected at various times are dealt with. Historically, bread shortages and feeding the population have been Malta's Achilles' heel. The Knights' granaries are an important monument to their charitable and hospitaller rule.

Procurator of Wheat was a vital appointment during the period of the Order and it was often held by a Maltese subject, an important post needed to sustain the whole structure of our little sovereign society. Under the British, the last great crisis before World War II was in 1919 when bread riots erupted with grievous consequences, and the clear need for a bread subsidy by government was at this time finally established. Hunger, once again, during World War II became a reality and there is a good description surrounding wartime 'Victory Kitchens' and the shortage of cats!

The relationship of the people of Gozo vis-à-vis those who live on the island of Malta can easily be compared to the Scots and the English. Traditionally the Gozitans are renowned for being careful with their money and are both astute and thrifty. It was to the people of his diocese, mainly a farming community, that the late Bishop Michael Gonzi turned to for help when the pangs of hunger on the two islands really got bad. His appeal to the Gozo farmers to share their stores for the common good was accepted by them because of their Christian faith. And so it was that the people of Gozo saved the Maltese.

There is, of course, more than bread alone: Matty Cremona deals with all the nostalgia surrounding Maltese cuisine. From granita to rosolin, from rabbit, fish, pork and beef to puddings, ices and dates (just imagine – stuffed with walnuts, rolled in salt and fried in honey – caramelised). By the way, her description of seasonal cooking is really worth reading. There is so much more which I must not mention – I am not analysing the book I am just recommending it to you and this I do without second thoughts.

I never cease to wonder how this little speck of an island of ours could possibly have such a definite and vital identity. Matty Cremona describes mouth-watering local specialities on 273 pages excellently illustrated by Pippa Zammit Cutajar. An extra word of praise here for Pippa whose pictures of Maltese delicacies have not been surpassed. If I were to criticise the book I would say that it has created a yearning in me, more than that, a passion to eat everything in it.

Nicholas De Piro

Memories carved in stone

Olives crushed to oily pulp in an old Roman stone olive press, ancient grains ground to coarse flour on a Neolithic stone quern, bee hives stored in stone apiaries, festivals celebrated round old stone chapels. These are all memories carved into stone structures that bring food to life. These are the memories that are explored in the four chapters that make up this section.

12

Joseph Cassar – Maltese baker in Mosta

BREAD*ħobż*

Il-forn

I*l-Forn* is the huge, wood burning, stone and metal oven that is the dominant feature of a traditional Maltese bakery. It is built into a wall with an indented metal door that opens on to a massive stone space within, heated to 275C/550F by a fire burning in a stone chamber next to the oven. This chamber, called a *gali* (gully), is connected to the main oven by an opening so that the heat can flow directly into the oven while keeping it clear of any cinders or ashes that may contaminate the bread. The base of the gully is a grate so that as the firewood burns down into ashes, they simply fall through the grate into the catchment space below called *is-sentina.* An eight pointed cross is hammered into the top metal frame of traditional ovens, indicating that the Knights of St John brought these ovens to Malta.

The art of making Maltese bread has changed little over the centuries and produces an inimitable loaf that is the emperor of the bread world. The crown of a genuine Maltese loaf is the dark brown crust, a crunchy covering for bread that is springy, full of air holes and softly chewy. The base of the bread, which cooks directly on the stone base of the oven, is hard and satisfyingly chewy.

A Maltese bakery, also called *Il-Forn*, runs along simple lines. The baker's assistant, *il-lavrant,* arrives first at about nine p.m. and starts to heat the oven by filling the *gali* with firewood and setting it alight. The temperature in the oven would only have fallen to about 200ºC/400F throughout the day, as the fire-brick walls and special Gozitan stone floor of the oven retain much of the heat from the previous night's baking session.

The next and most important stage is the dough. This is the key to the delicious taste and texture of Maltese bread. Only flour, salt, and *it-tinsila* (a lump of dough from the previous days' baking session) are used, although nowadays many bakers use a little commercial yeast to boost the process.

All these ingredients are kneaded together to make massive mounds of dough that are then left to prove for about 3 hours, less when the weather is hot and humid. In the meantime most bakeries prepare other types of bread such as *ħobż tal-Franċiż* or French bread. Some bakeries also produce *galletti* or sweet biscuits that they specialise in, like *biskuttini tar-raħal* or delicious *qagħaq tal-ħmira*, a favourite of mine.

The baker and his assistant then work together shaping the dough into loaves. The speed they work at is incredible – it is almost impossible to actually see what their hands are doing. The assistant cuts the dough into chunks, weighs each piece and puts it onto the wooden table and the baker rolls and twists the dough into a perfect sphere so fast that the movement is a complete blur. Working in this way they fill trays with neat rows of dough – three loaves to a row and each row is referred to as a *triq* or road – many, of course, are called *toroq*.

The filled trays are stacked and left to rise again for an hour. In the meantime the bakers roll some of the dough into small bread rolls called *panini* and long loaves called *bziezen tal-Malti*. The *bziezen* or long rolls are made by flattening a piece of dough into a disc, folding in the sides and then rolling it up. *Ftajjar* are shaped last of all using some risen loaves or small rolls – these are completely flattened into a disc and a hole is torn into the centre. These are left to rise briefly for about half an hour – a period known as *it-tiswija* or correction.

The thrilling business of loading up the oven begins once all the bread dough is ready and the oven has reached 275C/550F. The baker first wipes the stone floor of the oven clean with a wet cloth tied around a baker's peel, to make sure it is free of cinders that may spoil the bread. Immediately afterwards, the *ftajjar* go into the searing hot oven to cook while the rest of the prepared loaves are loaded into the oven. The baker uses an enormous baker's peel called a *palun*. The one used to fill the oven, called *Il-Palun tal-ħabża*, looks like a massive oar and the baker loads the blade of the *palun* with a row of 12 loaves. He carefully slides it into the oven and, with a quick flick of the wrist, slips them perfectly into place on the stone bottom of the oven. He does this until all the loaves are in the oven, then he fills the blade with *Panini* which he slits with a very sharp knife – sharpened at intervals on the metal frame of the oven itself – does the same to the *bziezen*, then removes the *ftajjar* and the first *fornata* or baking of the night is in the oven.

While the bread cooks the baker and his assistant repeat the whole process; shaping the Maltese bread dough into loaves, leaving them to rise and working the dough for French bread – *tal-Franċiż* – which is made from ordinary yeast to make a variety of rolls and then finishes off any of the specialities he makes. The bread is taken out of the oven using the *palun tal-ħruġ* and loaded on to trays where they are left to cool down- the loaves make the most amazing sound as they cool – a sort of crackling that almost sounds as though the loaves are laughing, relieved to be out of the oven.

The baker re-heats and reloads the oven in the same way and finishes off the night's baking. Then he fills his van with the fruit of his labour and he then drives round the towns and villages delivering the loaves to households.

Bread has been the backbone of the Maltese diet for thousands of years and archaeological remains suggest that it goes as far back as the New Stone Age. Neolithic farmers in Malta harvested the club wheat they grew and crushed or ground the grains into rough flour using stone querns. Querns are rectangular or oval slabs of hard coralline limestone that have a concave hollow carved into the top. This is where "the grains were ground to flour

Ftajjar (singular: Ftira) straight out of the oven.

QAGĦAQ TAL-ĦMIRA

Qagħaq tal-ħmira are sweet ring cakes made from enriched, sweetened bread dough and probably originated in bakeries when there was some extra bread dough. The flavours added to the bread dough are typically Maltese and include crushed aniseeds, grated orange and lemon peel. Some cooks like to add some ground cloves for a pleasant warm flavour that is especially good in winter.

The method below involves first making yeasty bread dough/batter that is enriched with buttery, sweet dough after the first proving. The two different types of dough are then kneaded well to mix them together and work the gluten in the flour.

600g plain flour
1 sachet instant yeast
100g butter
100g castor sugar
2 heaped teaspoons aniseeds
– lightly crushed
½ teaspoon ground cloves (optional)
The grated rind of 1 orange
and 2 tangerines

To finish
1 egg
Sesame seeds

Put 300g of the flour into a large bowl and stir in the yeast. Make a well in the centre, pour in 400ml tepid water and beat to make a thick, smooth batter. Leave this to rise and bubble for about 1 ½ hours in a warmish, draught free place. In the meantime, rub the butter into the rest of the flour, stir in the sugar, aniseeds, grated peel and the ground cloves (if using). Put this to one side.

After at least an hour and a half, add the buttery, flavoured and sweetened flour to the sloppy dough and knead in to make a smooth elastic dough. If it is too dry add a little juice from the zested fruits, whereas if is too sticky to knead, simply add a little more flour and carry on kneading for about 10 minutes. Then dust the dough lightly in a little flour and leave it to rise in a warm place.

Once the dough has doubled in size (about an hour to an hour and a half), knock it back and knead till the dough is elastic again. Then break off Ping-Pong ball sized pieces of dough, roll each one into a thin sausage and press the ends together to make a ring. Lightly beat the egg with a tablespoon of water and brush each ring with it, then sprinkle them quite generously with the sesame seeds.

Preheat the oven to gas mark 6/200 C. Leave the little rings to rise in a warm place till doubled in size – about half an hour. Then bake them in the preheated oven for about 15 minutes or till golden brown.

N.B. Make the hole in the middle of the rings of raw dough quite big otherwise it will close up in the oven.

16

with the help of a smaller hard stone"[1]. A number of these querns were found in the excavated remains of the Neolithic hamlet of Skorba among which was one very old one dating back to the Għar Dalam Period (approximately 4850 B.C.), and eleven other querns from a later time were found in what is called "The Hut of Querns". In fact one of the earliest compound dishes was a crude paste, similar to pulmentum of the Roman legions, made by mixing the crushed kernels of these early grains with water into a thick paste and made into a porridge-like stew. Perhaps this was sometimes dropped onto a hot stone and toasted to a delicious crunchiness instead of stewing the mixture, for a bit of variety. This was probably the first step towards the earliest form of the bread that has formed the basis of the Mediterranean diet since then; just as Virgil describes in the Georgics, translated by Ernle Bradford: "The grain first of all being toasted, and then crushed between stones or in a pestle and mortar." He carries on to say that "the dough was then probably laid on a flat or convex shaped stone; this was placed over a fire, and the dough covered with hot ashes. Bread of this type had been made since prehistoric times." [2]

This first form of bread must have been fibrous and chewy and it left its mark on Neolithic people in "the high degree of attrition or wear of the teeth suggests a rough diet with a low proportion of fermentable carbohydrate in a sticky form"[3]. That is, until the Ancient Egyptians improved this crude form of bread when an error led to the discovery of leaven. A piece of this simple dough must have been forgotten or left aside until it fermented. The baker added it to a fresh batch of dough and the dough rose. This led to the development of sour-dough bread because incorporating a piece of sour dough makes bread rise, aerating it and making it more palatable. They invented a technique still used in many parts of the world; in Malta the piece of old or mother dough is called *it-tinsila* or *ħmira* and traditional Maltese bakers still use this system to give our bread its special taste and texture.

Throughout Maltese history a significant part of everyday life revolved around the wheat harvest, the success or failure of which meant survival or famine. Malta rarely, if ever, produced enough wheat to be self sufficient, even though the total population up to the Middle Ages was a tiny fraction of what it is today. As a result large shipments of wheat and other cereals and pulses were imported annually from Sicily, free of Sicilian export duties. "The privilege of the *tratte*, as it was called, was unequivocally obtained soon after the 1429 invasion. The concession dated 5th June 1431 specifically cites the Muslim attack, as well as mortality from disease as urgent reasons justifying the Island's tax free wheat import."[4] Sicilian traders were paid with money earned from the export of Malta's cash crops, cotton and cumin; two crops that yielded high enough profits to pay for vital grains, thus encouraging farmers to cultivate cotton and cumin at the expense of other crops.

1   David H. Trump, *Malta Prehistory and Temples*
2   Ernle Bradford, *Mediterranean, Portrait of a sea*
3   C. Savona-Ventura, *Outlines of Maltese Medical History.*
4   Charles Dalli, *Malta, The Medieval Millennium*

GRILLED BREAD

Cooking bread dough like this makes a tasty change and is delicious served with a simple dish of crushed olives and salad or boiled wild greens dressed with olive oil and salt. The smoky flavour of the bread takes one back to the times when man cooked over an open fire. Try cooking it this way; you will need

100g whole-grain flour
250g plain flour
½ tbs instant yeast,
A pinch of salt and one of sugar,
4 tbs olive oil + extra for brushing
200 ml warm water

Mix the dry ingredients together, stir in the olive oil and add the water and mix to bind it all into dough. Knead it all very well, until it is smooth and pliable, about 10 minutes. Coat the dough lightly with some olive oil and leave to rise for about an hour to an hour and a half in a covered bowl. The dough should double in size. Once the dough has risen, divide it into about 20 pieces, roll them into balls and flatten them into little discs. Brush them lightly with olive oil and cook these on a very hot griddle pan – a few at a time until golden brown, about 4 minutes on each side. Serve immediately.

The main occupation of our early form of self government known as the *Università* (municipal council) was the business of grain imports and price regulation. Letters flew between Maltese *Jurats* and the Viceroy living in Sicily, and Sicilian *Jurats*. For example on the 7th November 1431 the Viceroy Johannes de Ventimiglia in Palermo wrote to the harbour officials that in view of the extreme poverty prevalent in Malta he commanded them to allow all exportation of food necessities to Malta as well as the "usual exportation of wheat, free of all payment and of all excise duties"[5]. Merchant shippers built companies around trading grains and a few other commodities, a risky living in those days when the Mediterranean was pirate infested and Malta plagued by a series of attacks by the Moors. These were all conditions that made life in Malta far less predictable than it is today.

Once the grain arrived in Malta it was stored and distributed by officials of the *Università*. Concern about the condition of the grain was great – wet grain was a preoccupation that was combated with various laws and proclamations throughout the ages – one issued by Grand Master Lascaris in 1641, for example ordered that to ensure a supply of dry grain shippers had to make certain their grain laden ships were well sealed before returning to Malta. Grain was stored in *magazzeni* or warehouses in Mdina and later in the specially built underground granaries in Valletta and Floriana. *Contestabili*, grain distributors chosen by the parish priest and villagers of each parish, distributed grain in the villages. This was milled and baked into bread – that essential food that was the staple food of the Maltese people for centuries.

The grain problem persisted throughout the rule of the knights – home grown grain could, at best, feed one third of the population. The knights did their best to avert shortages; they had large store houses for grain built in various localities in Sicily and in Marseille, some grain came from the Order's European estates and new sources like Sardinia. Production of barley and *mischiato*, a hardy mixed grain, was encouraged on substandard and marginal land to be eaten by the poorer people.

Another serious problem in islands like Malta was that there wasn't enough wood to go round to fuel ovens. Peasants solved this by gathering thistles and scrub to be used as fuel for the ovens. This system went on for hundreds of years and was first referred to in 1536 by Jean Quintin d'Autun who wrote, "The inhabitants make use of certain kinds of thistles instead of wood, which together with dried cows dung, is used for the bakers' ovens."

In rural areas bread was often made at home and simply taken to the bakery to bake, as home ovens were as scarce as fuel. Country women started the bread making process by first going to the millers to have their home-grown grains ground into flour. They kneaded their flour into dough and when it was ready they gave it to the bakers to be baked. They paid for this with the thistles gathered as fuel for the oven. As this was a lengthy process, it took place just once a week, but the bread was much better quality and kept well. This system came to an end when rationing was enforced during World War Two and was never revived.

5   Julio Del Amo Garcia, Stanley Fiorini and Godfrey Wettinger, *Documentary Sources of Maltese History Part III Documents of the Maltese Universitas*

Ħobż Malti – Maltese Bread

The price of grain and bread fluctuated in Malta as it did everywhere; but never as infamously as it did in 1919. The price skyrocketed when trade was disrupted by the First World War and the Russian Revolution and this was one of the main reasons for the *Sette Giugno* bread riots that took place in Malta on 7th June 1919. The people's dependence on their daily loaf of bread provoked and wholly justified their reaction to this shocking price hike; people protested the price increase in bread prices with demonstrations and riots in Valletta. Tragically British Troops panicked and fired on the crowd, wounding and killing Maltese civilians. Carmel Cassar wrote that "Sette Giugno, with its tragic associations, has since become a symbolic date in the genesis of Maltese nationalism" that led, two years later, to a form of self-government under the British.

There seem to have been at least four types of bread common in Malta during the time of the Knights. One was called *alla Francese* – probably the same as the bread we still call *Tal-Franċiż* to this day; there were two sorts popular in towns called *pane d'albergo* made from super fine semolina and white bread made exclusively from flour; while the peasants and poor people made and ate bread made from *maħlut*, a hardy mixed grain obtained when wheat and barley are grown together.

On certain feast days bread was distributed to the poor; *Ħobż Ta' San Nikola* for example was given out by the Augustinians in honour of Saint Nicholas, *Ħobż ta' Sant Antnin* were very small loaves devoted to Saint Anthony given to sick people to help them regain their health quickly.[6] Nowadays certain breads are eaten on particular feast days like *qagħaq tal-appostli* on Maundy Thursday. This sort of bread is made with the finest flour available and left to rise for longer than usual. Bread was often flavoured with sweet cumin or anise in the past – this gave it a delicious flavour. Nowadays bread is more likely to be sprinkled with a few sesame seeds.

Ġużè Cassar Pullicino noted that bakers recited certain rhymes such as the one below, to encourage the dough to rise

Itla' u fur
Bħalma Kristu
Tela' minn ġol-qbur.
Itla' u thenna
U thallix 'il min jistenna.
Itla' u thenna
Bħal meta Kristu
Tela' l-Ġenna.
Itla' u rendi
W imla l-lenbi.
Itla' u strieħ
Bħal meta d-dqieq
Ikun ġewwa s-siegħ.
Itla' fil-friex
Biex toħroġ bħal tan-nies

Step 1. Shaping the dough into loaves

Step 2. Weighing the bread

Step 3. The bread rises before going into the oven

---

6   Joseph Aquilina, *Maltese–English Dictionary*

Step 4. Sprinkling Sesame Seeds on the bread

Step 5. Loading the bread into the oven

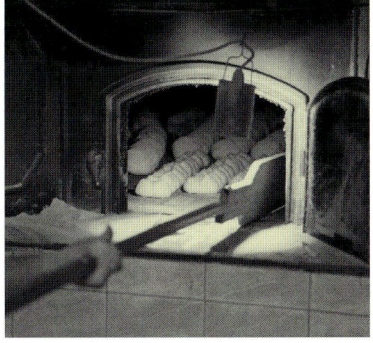

Step 6. Sorting out the bread in the oven

Step 7. The bread is ready

Baker's peels hanging on the wall

The Maltese language is full of bread related idioms – Charles Cassar, Ġużè Cassar-Pullicino, Giovanni Bonello and others have listed many of these – *Malta qatt ma rrifjutat qamħ* (Malta never refused wheat – meaning presents are welcome), *ħobżu maħbuż* (his bread is baked – meaning a well-off person) – *x'ħobż jiekol dan?* (What sort of bread does he eat – meaning what type of person is he?)

Maltese bread is delicious and it is still eaten every day by most people although not in the same quantities as it was in the past when it was the main feature of most meals. People ate bread with a few dried tomatoes, olives, onions, cheese or anchovies with a drizzle of oil at lunchtime and with a bowl of *Minestra* (soup) in the evening. This was such an ingrained routine that a particular word was coined to describe the foods that accompanied bread – *kumpanaġġ*. This word is derived from the Sicilian *cumpanaggiu* through the Latin *companaticum* which means the same thing. Interestingly enough the word *ġewweż* is a specific verb used to describe the way the strongly flavoured foods that accompanied bread were eaten; a very small piece of cheese, anchovy, onion or similar was eaten to flavour the bread that was the focal part of the meal.

Modern life and consumerism has changed everything. Our beloved *ħobża* is fast disappearing and a sad impostor sits on the shelves of most supermarkets, masquerading as Maltese bread – this odd copy has a thin crust, the centre has hardly any holes at all and the characteristic springy texture is gone. There must be a concerted effort to save the Maltese loaf. Some kind of recognition must be given to our national loaf; imitations of the authentic loaf not made following the traditional system should be classified as such, while the genuine loaf must be established as a protected food, as much as a real wine or extra virgin olive oil. If this is not done soon, the taste of a real loaf of Maltese bread will be nothing but a delicious memory.

It is very difficult to make real Maltese bread – let alone in a small domestic gas mark or electric oven; so it is best to buy it from a real baker. The recipes that follow make good, ordinary home- made bread that is fun to make and delicious to eat – nothing like real Maltese bread, but good enough.

SOME BREAD RECIPES

A BASIC BREAD RECIPE

1 rounded tbs dried yeast or
1 x 11g sachet instant yeast
A lump of dough from a
previous baking (if available)
Approx. 500ml tepid water
1 tsp honey or sugar
1 tsp sea salt
750g Strong white bread flour
Olive oil

Pour the tepid water into a large bowl, sprinkle over the dried yeast, (add the lump of dough at this point if you're using it) and stir in the honey or sugar. Leave it for 2 or 3 minutes while you sieve 150g of the flour. Once the yeast has just started to rise to the surface of the water, stir in the sieved flour, cover the bowl and leave it in a warm spot for ½ an hour. Check the flour and yeast mixture; it should have risen noticeably. Skip this stage if using instant yeast.

Then sieve the rest of the flour onto the kitchen table or work surface and make a deep well in the centre of it, pour in the yeast mixture or instant yeast and tepid water and start to stir it into the flour until you have pliable dough. Knead for at least 10 minutes until it is smooth and silky. Roll the well-kneaded dough in some olive oil and put it in a bowl, cover the bowl and leave it in a warm place for about an hour to an hour and a half or until the dough has doubled in bulk.

Punch down the dough and then knead it until it is smooth and pliable again. If the dough feels sticky add a little more flour as you knead.

Shape the dough into little rolls, brush the tops with olive oil and sprinkle the rolls with sesame seeds. Put onto a well oiled baking tray, cover the rolls and leave them to rise again for about ¾ of an hour to an hour or till they have doubled in size.

Pre heat the oven to gas mark 8/220ºC. Bake the rolls for approximately 15 minutes for smaller rolls and 20 minutes for larger ones. To test whether they are cooked through, take one out of the oven and tap the base; it should sound hollow. When they are ready remove them from the oven and cool the rolls on a wire rack.

QUICK SOUR DOUGH

Souring dough is an interesting experiment. The bread baked from such dough has more flavour and texture than other home-made bread and keeps fresher for longer. There are different ways of doing this. In humid and warm weather simply mix some flour and warm water and fresh grape or apple juice to make sloppy dough – equal amounts of flour and warm water and juice – and leave it on a warm window sill to absorb the natural yeasts in the air. It will begin to ferment and the longer you leave it the sourer it becomes, but it may be used after three or four days. Simply incorporate it into your dough with the yeast and water in the basic bread recipe above.

Sweet breads are delicious at breakfast or for a snack; try the following combinations.
Use the basic bread recipe and knead in some of these:
- raisins and spices into the dough
- chopped dried figs and grated orange peel
- chocolate chunks or dates and walnuts.

or

Roll out the dough, sprinkle with chopped dried fruit or chocolate, sugar and spices and roll it up. Then either bake it as swirl bread or cut it into 7.5 cm chunks and arrange them cut side up in a well greased or lined baking tin, leaving them to prove in that way before baking them as usual.

or

A savoury version of this swirl bread is delicious with a soup for supper; try the following combinations:
- fried spinach, olives and onions;
- grated zucchini and mozzarella,
- shredded *ġbejniet moxxi* (semi-dry sheep cheese) and chopped fried artichokes.

Fig and orange rolls

CINNAMON SCROLLS

1 x sachet of instant yeast
Approx. 500ml of tepid water + the juice of 2 oranges
1 tsp of salt
2 tbs olive oil
The grated rind of 2 oranges
5 tbs soft brown sugar
750g of strong white flour
Ground cinnamon
Marmalade

Make the dough using the method given in the basic bread recipe, adding the grated rind to the flour and the orange juice to the water. Leave it to prove for an hour or until it has doubled in size, then very carefully stretch it out into an oblong shape until it is about a centimetre thick, then dust the surface generously with ground cinnamon, the grated orange rind and a soft brown sugar. Roll it up again, starting from both ends and rolling towards the middle, until the two rolled sides meet at the centre. Turn it on its side, so that the rolls sit on each other, and cut slices across the width. Put them carefully on a well oiled baking-tray, and leave them to rise again for at least 30 minutes. Then bake at the hottest temperature setting for around 15 minutes or until they are golden-brown. In the meantime heat about 5 tablespoons of the marmalade with water, sieve out the pieces of rind and use it to brush over the scrolls as soon as they come out of the oven. They are best served warm, but are just as good at room temperature.

FOCACCIA

1 tbs Instant yeast or one sachet x 11g of Instant yeast
350ml tepid water
1 tbs sugar
1 tsp sea salt
500g strong white flour
5 tbs olive oil for the dough plus extra for finishing off

Sieve the flour into a big bowl or onto a work surface, stir in the instant yeast, the sugar, the salt and olive oil. Make a well in the centre and pour in the tepid water stirring all the time until the mixture binds together, then begin to knead it into dough. The dough should be neither too hard and dry nor too wet and sticky. It is better to start off with slightly sticky dough, as it is far easier to add flour to sticky dough than it is to add water to hard, dry dough.

Knead the dough for a minimum of 10 minutes when it should feel silky and pliable. Shape it into a ball and leave it to prove for an hour to an hour and a half or until it has doubled in size. Once the dough has risen the first time all you have to do is very carefully stretch it out as thinly as you wish and put it carefully on a baking tray well dusted with semolina. Leave it to prove for half an hour then press your fingertips all over the dough, making little indentations all over the surface, drizzle it with olive oil, coarse salt and sage or basil leaves, then bake it at the hottest your oven will allow for at least 12 – 15 minutes. The thicker the foccacia, the longer it will take to cook. A quick drizzle all over the bread with olive oil will add to the flavour tremendously. It is delicious with any meal or cut into wedges and served with dips and pre-lunch drinks.

Focaccia variations
- Add chopped olives and rosemary to the dough,
- Add chopped, rinsed dried tomatoes, chopped chilli, fennel seeds and rosemary to the dough,
- Knead in some chopped sage or basil leaves.

Try some of these toppings on the foccacia dough to make unusual pizzas:
- Grated raw potato, lots of sliced and fried onions, anchovy fillets and marjoram and rosemary sprigs to taste.
- Thinly sliced and blanched courgettes, herbs and crumbled ricotta drizzled with olive oil.
- Try chunks of *ġbejniet moxxi* (semi-dried sheep cheese); rosemary and blanched garlic cloves drizzled with olive oil and chilli peppers.
- Try slicing some grilled and skinned peppers and mixing them with roasted onions cut into chunks, olives, capers, herbs and olive oil.
- Simply top the pizza with cherry tomatoes, small mozzarella balls and basil leaves before cooking, and then scatter the pizza with rocket leaves and Parma Ham before serving.
- Top it with pesto, ricotta and mozzarella, some thin asparagus and olive oil, bake, then scatter with parmesan shavings and rocket when it comes out of the oven.

GALLETTI

Galletti are the Maltese answer to the ubiquitous cracker. They are delicious with any type of dip, pate, salad or cheese board; add them to the bread basket or pack them in a picnic basket or lunch box. They are the perfect snack; try them with all sorts of different toppings or simply enjoy them as they are.

People usually buy them, as they are easily available in different sizes and shapes in all grocery shops and bakeries in Malta. In fact few cooks bother to make them but they are surprisingly easy to make and the taste of homemade galletti is so much better than commercial ones that it's worth making them.

200g plain flour
150g semolina plus a little
extra for kneading
3 or 4 tbs olive oil
A pinch of salt
I sachet instant yeast
Approx. 200 ml warm water
1 tsp sugar (omit if necessary)

Sieve the flour into a large bowl, add the salt and the oil, mix them well and rub the oil in to the flour, then stir in the semolina and instant yeast. Make a well in the flour mixture and add the water, stirring as you pour it into the flour to make dough. Knead the dough well until it is smooth and pliable. Cut it in half to make two manageable portions, put one to one side and roll the other out very thinly and cut rounds into the dough using a cutter of your choice. Traditional galletti come in large rounds but any shape will do; smaller rounds are more practical, while fun shapes like hearts or flowers are more original. Prick each one right through the centre of the biscuit with the prongs of a fork, put them on a baking tray that is dusted with semolina and bake at gas mark 6/200ºC until lightly coloured, about 15 minutes. Use the other half of the dough in the same way. If the dough has started to rise at all just knead it until it is soft and pliable again. If you think you might take rather long to make the first lot of galletti refrigerate it and it will rise much more slowly, if at all.

When the galletti are ready, cool them on a wire rack and store them in an airtight container to keep them fresh.

N.B. A little butter can replace the olive oil if preferred, but olive oil makes better, lighter galletti.

GRISSINI

1 x 11g sachet of instant yeast
400g strong flour
100g semolina
350ml tepid water
1 tbs sea-salt
3 tbs olive oil + extra
1 tsp honey or sugar

Put all the dry ingredients into a big bowl or heap them on the kitchen-counter, and make a well in the centre. Stir the tepid water, honey and oil together in a jug and pour this mixture slowly and carefully into the well in the flour, stirring slowly until you have dough. Knead it well for at least 10 minutes. When it is smooth and elastic, drizzle it with olive oil and put it in a bowl, cover it and leave in a warm and draught-free place until it has doubled in size. Turn the dough out onto the kitchen-counter and sprinkle it thoroughly with semolina. Punch it down. Knead it until it is elastic. Then pinch off golf-ball-sized pieces and roll them out into sticks. Dust them with a little semolina and lay them on a baking-tray lined with non-stick baking-paper. Bake them at gas mark 7/220ºC for around 10 minutes, or until they are golden-brown and crisp. For extra crispness put them back into the oven turned down to gas mark 2 ½/160ºC for about 10-15 minutes. Leave them to cool on a wire rack and store them in an airtight container to keep them fresh

CIACCINO

Ciaccino is a very flat version of focaccia, typical of central Italy, usually served with a glass of rose` wine as an aperitif, with dips or with some Parma ham and salad. It is quicker to make than usual bread as it only needs to rise once.

500g plain flour
1 sachet instant yeast
½ tbs salt
4 tbs olive oil
2 heaped tbs chopped fresh rosemary
Approx. 350ml warm water

Heap the flour up on a work surface and make a well in it. Stir in the yeast, salt, 1 tablespoon chopped rosemary and olive oil. Then add enough warm water to make dough and knead well until it is very smooth and elastic – about 10 minutes.

Rub it all over with a little oil and allow it to rise until doubled in size. Then cut it into about 6 pieces, roll out till paper thin, sprinkle with the rest of the rosemary and bake on well greased oven trays at 220ºC / gas mark 7 for about 10 -15 minutes until golden and crunchy.

Break into largish pieces and serve.

POPPY SEED LOAF

A batch of dough made with the basic bread recipe
250g Good Earth poppy seeds
four tbs of salt
a 23cm-diameter cake tin

Prepare the basic bread recipe to the stage where the dough is well risen. Then generously grease the cake tin and dust it with poppy seeds so that it is well coated in them. Knock back the dough, knead it again till it is elastic and shape it into 6 or 7 equal sized balls. Dissolve the salt in 500ml of warm water, then dunk the balls of dough into this and roll each one in more poppy seeds to coat them generously. Arrange them in the prepared cake tin to make a 'flower' shape, leaving enough space between each ball to join up as they rise. Leave the filled cake tin to stand for 30 to 40 minutes or until the dough-balls have doubled in size then dust the tops with the last of the poppy seeds and bake for about 35-45 minutes or until the bread is golden. To test whether the loaf is cooked through, take it out of the cake tin and tap the base; it should sound hollow. Eat this with salad and cheese, pulling it apart rather than cutting it up, separating the "petals" into individual rolls.

APRICOT AND SAFFRON BREAD

1 tbs Instant yeast or one sachet of Instant yeast
350ml tepid water
1 generous pinch of saffron threads
1tsp sea salt
1 or 2tbs olive oil
500 g strong white flour
200g Good Earth dried apricots
Zest of an orange
100g sugar
Poppy seeds

Mix the saffron into the warm water and allow it to infuse. Sieve the flour into a big bowl, stir in the instant yeast, the salt and olive oil. Pour the tepid saffron water slowly into the flour stirring all the time until the mixture binds together, then knead the dough for at least ten minutes. The dough should be neither too hard and dry nor too wet and sticky. It is better to start off with slightly sticky dough, as it is far easier to add flour to sticky dough than it is to add water to hard, dry dough

After a minimum of 10 minutes the dough should feel silky and pliable. Shape it into a ball and leave it to prove for an hour or until it has doubled in size. Chop up the apricots and put them on the kitchen counter, with the sugar and the orange zest. Knock back the dough and knead in the apricot mix. It may seem the dough will never absorb the apricots, sugar and orange but keep kneading and it will be absorbed. If the dough seems too wet, add a little flour and carry on kneading till the dough is smooth and pliable.

TO MAKE A SPIRAL: *When the dough is smooth, roll it into a long snake and wind it into a spiral. Put it on to a greased or lined baking tray and leave to rise again till it doubles in size – about ¾ of an hour or more. Then just before baking mix some castor sugar and water together and glaze the top of the dough – gently – and sprinkle on lots of sesame seeds, then bake at gas mark 7/210ºC for approximately 30 minutes or until browned and sounds hollow when tapped on the bottom.*

TO MAKE A PLAIT: *When the dough is smooth, roll it into a long, thin 'snake', cut it into three equal lengths and plait them together. Put the plait onto a greased or lined baking tray and leave it to rise until it doubles in size, which should take about 45 minutes. Bake the loaf at gas mark 6½ / 205ºC for around 35 – 40 minutes or until it is brown and sounds hollow when tapped on the bottom. Leave it to settle for at least 30 minutes before slicing it. While it cools, melt four tablespoonfuls of apricot jam along with a tablespoonful of water, in a pot over a high heat, until it bubbles briefly. Brush this heated jam over the loaf and sprinkle it with poppy seeds*

CINNAMON SWIRL BREAD

This is a delicious version of cinnamon toast that is perfect served at breakfast time – especially with a little honey.

600g strong plain white
flour + a little extra
1 tbs sugar
½ a tbs salt
4 tbs ground cinnamon
1 tbs sugar
1 sachet instant yeast
Approx. 500ml tepid water
A little olive oil

Mound the flour up on a kitchen counter or in a bowl and make a hollow in it. Rub in 2 tablespoons olive oil, then stir in the salt, sugar and instant yeast, add the tepid water slowly and stir gently to make damp dough. Knead vigorously for 10 minutes on the kitchen counter, stretching and folding the dough as you go until the dough is smooth and elastic. Then divide the dough in half; roll one half into a neat round, brush it lightly all over with some olive oil and leave to one side, then knead the cinnamon and sugar into the other half of the dough till it is an even brown colour, roll it into a neat round and brush it lightly with oil. Then leave the dough to rise in a warm but not hot place till approximately doubled in size.

Then gently flatten the plain ball of dough and spread it out to make an oblong shape; next do the same thing to the cinnamon round of dough and then pick up the cinnamon sheet of dough and lay it on top of the plain sheet of dough and roll it up tightly like a Swiss roll. Put it into a 30cm long loaf tin and leave to rise for about 45 – 50 minutes then bake it in the oven preheated to gas mark 7 /210ºC for 20 minutes then for another 20 minutes at gas mark 5/190ºC or till the loaf sounds hollow when tapped on the bottom.

BEAUTIFUL BRIOCHE

True brioche takes quite long to make but it is worth the effort as there is nothing as good as a well made brioche for breakfast. This dough must be made in a strong, free standing food processor as the dough should be nice and sticky which always makes it so tricky to knead properly.

100ml tepid milk (approximately)
1 x 11g sachet instant yeast
500g flour
A generous pinch salt
4 large eggs
225g butter
50g castor sugar

First mix 75g of the flour with the instant yeast in the bowl of the processor, add the tepid milk and stir till smooth. Leave it to prove for 10 minutes, then add the rest of the flour and start to mix the dough using the dough hook attachment. Add the eggs one at a time to make sticky dough. You may need to add a little more tepid milk or another egg if your eggs are small. Leave this to mix for about 10 minutes.

In the meantime beat the butter with the salt and sugar till smooth. Then, once the 10 minutes are up, carry on mixing the dough, adding the butter into the dough piece by piece until all the butter has been absorbed. Leave it to mix for another 5 or 6 minutes or until the dough is very soft, smooth and silky and comes away from the sides of the bowl easily if stickily.

Cover the bowl with stretch & seal and leave it to rise for about 2 hours or until it doubles in size.

Then flip it over three or four times, cover it again and put the bowl in the fridge for at least 4 hours but not more than 12 hours.

Then use the dough to make either of the following (or both – in which case make two lots of the basic dough)

LARGE BRIOCHE ROUND

Cut the dough into two pieces – one about one third of the whole and the other should be about two thirds of the whole. Then flour your hands and shape the larger piece into a ring and put it in the bottom of a well buttered non-stick brioche mould. Then, roll the smaller piece into a round and put it in the centre of the ring shaped piece of dough. Brush the top of this whole thing with an egg beaten with a little water and leave to rise for about an hour and a half.

Then preheat the oven to gas mark 6/ 200ºC and cook the brioche for 15 minutes, then turn it down to gas mark 3/165ºC and bake for another 30 – 35 minutes. Remove and cool for half and hour or so and serve dusted with finely chopped tangerine peel and icing sugar.

Cut the dough made above in two equal halves, push one end into the bottom of a well greased large loaf tin and make a hollow along the length by pressing down gently with your fingers. Sprinkle the hollow generously with coarsely chopped chocolate, cover with the other half of the dough, brush with egg and milk and carry on as above.

BRIDGE ROLLS

These lovely soft rolls are made from enriched bread dough similar to brioche dough – but much quicker and easier to make. There are many versions of bridge roll dough – in some recipes the butter is rubbed into the flour instead of being melted into the milk, and in others there is less or more butter added to the mix or fewer eggs – but this is the version that I find makes the best rolls.

250m milk
75g butter
750g white flour
½ a tsp salt
1 x 11g sachet instant yeast
1 tbs castor sugar
4 medium eggs
1 extra egg mixed with a sprinkling of salt, one of sugar and a tablespoon of water

Heap up the flour, salt, sugar and yeast together on the kitchen work top or in a large bowl and make a hollow in the top. Gently heat the milk in a saucepan with the butter. When the butter has melted, set this aside and cool slightly. Then beat the eggs into the milk and butter and check that the liquid is tepid. Stir the mix into the flour and other dry ingredients a little at a time to make dough. Then knead the dough for at least 10 minutes or until the dough feels elastic. Then oil a clean, large bowl with a little olive oil, coat the dough in a little more oil and put it in the bowl. Cover it and leave it to rise for about an hour or until it has doubled in size. (This depends on how cold or warm the weather is). Then take the dough out of the bowl and cut it into about 35 equal pieces. Then roll them into fat finger shapes and arrange them well spaced out on greased baking trays. (Or simply line with non-stick paper) Brush the rolls with the beaten egg mixture, and leave the rolls to rise for about 30 minutes or till well risen and approximately double in size.

Brush them with the egg mixture again and bake the rolls in the oven preheated to gas mark 7/200ºC. for 15-20 minutes or till golden and crisp, turning the oven down to gas mark5/190ºC for the last 5 minutes of cooking. (The smaller they are the faster they will cook)

Fill the Bridge Rolls with all or a selection of the following fillings:
(a) Stir some grainy mustard into some mascarpone cheese, and then add chopped gammon. Spread the filling in the rolls and top with some rocket leaves.
(b) Skin, deseed and chop up some ripe tomatoes and drain them with a little salt in a sieve. Then add some chopped hard boiled eggs, mint leaves and mustard powder.
(c) Grate some Parmesan cheese, mixed salad leaves, grilled minced bacon and toss it all with a little balsamic vinegar and olive oil.

BEER IN MALTA

When the tragic 1919 Sette Giugno bread riots broke out and swept through Valletta, it wasn't enough. There was a widespread belief amongst the populace that grain importers and flour millers were making excessive profits over the price of bread. The enraged rioters went on to burn down many of the flourmills[1], the Farrugia family flourmills at Hamrun among them, setting off a chain of reactions that was to result in the production of excellent beer.

The sons of Luigi Farrugia decided against rebuilding their milling business and instead started to manufacture oxygen and carbonic acid as L. Farrugia and Sons Ltd. This enterprise was doing very well when the question of what to do with the excess production of carbon dioxide arose; the idea of producing carbonated drinks and beer seemed like a natural progression and in December 1926 Mr Lewis Farrugia applied for permission to install a brewery at Strada Pastificio (today Farsons Street) Hamrun.

Malta never changes and there existed an exhausting tangle of monopolies, applications for licences and existing permits; the Lion brewery, for example, hung onto their English Ale monopoly while another company was all set to start to produce German style beers. However, Mr Lewis Farrugia carried on undaunted and the new brewery was completed by the end of 1927 and the first Farsons (a contraction of Farrugia and sons) beer was sold during the feast of St George at Qormi on 19th April 1928 and was a great success. The company never looked back and still produces great beer.

---

1   Unlike most other mills, St George's Flour Mills (the largest milling setup in Malta) was not ransacked but saved by the workers.

BEER BREADS

Yeast is one of the main ingredients in both beer and bread making, so it seems only natural to add beer to bread dough for a further boost. Different beers have a different effect on the flavour and appearance of the bread. Try the following two recipes.

LITTLE LAGER ROLLS

These light and crisp little rolls have just enough lager flavour to make them really savoury. They are perfect with meals, especially salads, or fill them with a coarse textured green olive paste and lettuce, or ham, mustard and rocket for picnics or school.

500g "00" flour
11g or one sachet instant yeast
1 heaped tsp salt
1 flat tsp sugar
Approx. 350ml Cisk Lager
Approx. ½ a bag Good Earth whole sesame seeds

Warm the beer over a low heat till it is tepid. Heap up the flour on a work surface or in a large bowl and make a deep well in it. Stir in the yeast, salt and sugar and add the tepid Cisk lager a little at a time, stirring to make dough. Then knead the dough for about 10 minutes or till the dough is smooth, pliable and silky. Put the dough to one side and leave to rise for about an hour or till doubled in size, then cut into walnut sized pieces, roll them into smooth balls, dunk them into some Cisk lager and dip the tops into sesame seeds. Put them onto a non-stick paper lined or well greased baking tray and leave to rise again for at least half an hour or till doubled. Then bake at gas mark 8/230ºC for about 15 minutes or till golden and crisp.

ALE AND FRUIT LOAF

This bread recipe is flexible; make as detailed below to serve with both savoury and sweet foods or add 100g – 150g sugar during the second stage of the recipe to turn it into a sweet loaf to be served lightly buttered at teatime.

500g "00" flour
11g or one sachet instant yeast
1 heaped tsp salt
1 flat tsp sugar
Approx. 350ml Blue Label Ale
100g Good Earth sultanas
50g Good Earth walnuts,
roughly chopped
4 or 5 tbs good Apricot jam

Warm the Blue Label Ale over a low heat till it is tepid. Heap up the flour on a work surface or in a large bowl and make a deep well in it. Stir in the yeast, salt and sugar and add the tepid Blue Label Ale a little at a time, stirring to make dough. Then knead the dough for about 10 minutes or till the dough is smooth, pliable and silky. Put the dough to one side and leave it to rise for about an hour or till doubled in size. Once the dough has risen well, knock it back and knead again, adding the sultanas and walnuts to the dough as you knead it. Once the fruit and nuts are well incorporated and the dough soft and silky again, cut it into 8 equal sized pieces and roll each into a ball. Arrange them in a ring shape on a well greased baking tray and leave to rise again for about half an hour in a warm, draught free place or until doubled in size. Preheat the oven to gas mark 8/ 230ºC and when the oven is hot and the dough well risen bake for about 20 – 25 minutes or until the bread is golden and sounds hollow when the base is tapped. Glaze the loaf while it is still hot with some apricot jam warmed up with a little water and sieved for a shiny, slightly sticky loaf. Cool the loaf on a wire rack and serve.

OLIVES AND OIL
Iż-żebbuġ u ż-żejt

The diffusion of Mediterranean identity, both physical and cultural, is defined and confined by olives trees; their silvery green leaves colour the scrubby landscape, the fruit flavours the food and is pressed into the oil that fuels the Mediterranean world. "The whole Mediterranean – the sculptures, the palms, the gold beads, the bearded heroes, the wine, the ideas, the ships, the moonlight, the winged gorgons, the bronze men, the philosophers – all of it seem to rise in the sour, pungent taste of those black olives between the teeth. A taste older than meat, older than wine. A taste as old as cold water.[1]" Perhaps "the temples" should have been added to the list, because here in Malta our most ancient monuments are the oldest free-standing temples in the world – older even than the pyramids – and it is amid the very oldest of these that the first traces of the story of olives in Malta appear.

A distinct layer of charcoal discovered during excavations at Skorba, one of the most interesting Neolithic sites in Malta that was occupied throughout Prehistory, revealed the carbonised remains of several tree species, one of which was Olea Europaea (Olive). What makes this find even more interesting is that the tests carried out at the Royal Botanical Kew Gardens by Dr C. R. Metcalf reveal that although "it is quite impossible to distinguish wild from cultivated material of this kind from microscopical characters … the samples came from the destruction level of the temple, and must represent the timberwork of its roof. The implication is that they were from well-grown olive trees, not from wild scrub olive."[2] This exciting evidence implies early olive cultivation – but, whether the trees were grown for the fruit or whether Neolithic farmers had discovered the means of extracting oil from the fruit will possibly forever remain shrouded in mystery. The only certainty is that olive trees were present on Malta from the earliest of times.

Probably, olives were cultivated originally in the Fertile Crescent – the birthplace of agriculture – and spread west from there, through the Phoenicians, Greeks and Romans. The first clear-cut evidence of olive oil

1 Lawrence Durrell, *Prospero's Cell*
2 D. H. Trump, *Skorba, excavation carried out on behalf of the National Museum of Malta 1961–1963*

production in Malta dates back to the Roman period and is found in the archaeological remains of Roman villas all over Malta. "The frequency of these complexes implies that the cultivation of the olive tree was well diffused on the islands, certainly much more than it is today, and it should not be too difficult to envisage large silvery–green patches of olive groves marking the Maltese landscape in Roman times" [3].

A perfect example of a Roman villa in Malta is San Pawl Milqi; one of the more extensively excavated Roman villas in Malta, where archaeologists have established that it was in use until the end of the Byzantine Period. The original Roman villa, built over the remains of an earlier Punic farmhouse, was developed during the Republican era. It was a rich villa; the walls were skilfully "constructed of large square stones and bricks"[4] by a master mason, the walls were plastered and decorated in green and white in parts, red and yellow in others and although the floors were not mosaiced, they were polished and strong. The villa was a perfect example of a comfortable Roman villa, a country house and centre for olive oil production, ideally situated on the slope of hills overlooking what was Benwarrad Harbour. Thus fulfilling criteria set out by Cato the Elder in his farmer's notebook called De Agri Cultura, "If possible, it should lie at the foot of a mountain and face south; the situation should be healthful, there should be a good supply of labourers, it should be well watered, and near it there should be a flourishing town, or the sea, or a navigable stream, or a good and much travelled road."

San Pawl Milqi chapel in Burmarrad, with the remains of an old Roman olive press in front of it.

Cato also provides lots of valuable advice for Roman olive farmers;
- Let the olives be pressed immediately, to prevent the oil from spoiling. Remember that high winds come every year and are apt to beat off the olives; if you gather them at once and the presses are ready, there will be no loss on account of the storm, and the oil will be greener and better.

---

3   Anthony Bonanno, *Distribution of Villas and some of the Maltese Economy in the Roman Period.*
4   T.H. Ashby, *Roman Malta*

OLIVE PASTE

This is made by stoning olives – either green or black and then blending them with herbs and other flavourings. I like to add crushed garlic, parsley and olive oil to the basic recipe then flavour the paste with different herbs and spices depending on the colour of the olives and what the paste is going to be used for.

Grated lemon zest and juice match well with green olives, as do the fresher flavours of mint, chives and fresh fennel fronds.

Grated orange zest, crushed fennel and coriander seeds, chopped chilli and finely chopped fresh rosemary go very well with black olives.

A filleted anchovy or two, mashed and stirred into the olive paste adds great flavour.

Olive paste is wonderful served with bread or galletti. It also makes a delicious relish served with some grilled fish or stirred into a bowl of hot pasta.

- If the olives remain too long on the ground or the floor they will spoil, and the oil will be rancid. Any sort of olive will produce good and greener oil if it is pressed betimes.
- For an olive farm of 120 iugera there should be two pressing equipments, if the trees are vigorous, thickly planted, and well cultivated. The mills should be stout and of different sizes, so that if the stones become worn you may change them.

Several trapetum were discovered during excavations at San Pawl Milqi. These are huge stone mills where the olives were crushed to an oily pulp, which in turn was put into a press where great pressure was brought down to extract the oil that flowed out and was caught in a tank where it was allowed to settle; the *amurca* (dark, bitter water) and other impurities sank to the bottom and the oil rose to the surface. The oil was then skimmed off into another, similar container and again allowed to settle; the process was repeated until all impurities had been separated. The pure oil was kept in jars which were glazed on the inside with wax or gum to prevent absorption; the covers were carefully secured and the jars stored away in vaults

The Ancient Romans made extensive use of olive oil; it went into almost every aspect of their lives. The different grades of olive oil were used for different purposes; the finest oil was used in cooking, in religious ceremonies and for medical purposes, and mediocre oil went into soaps while lowest grade oil was used for fuel and lighting purposes, especially in lamps.

Olives were served at all Roman meals; at breakfast, called *jentaculum*, olives were often eaten with bread and cheese or chopped up to make a topping called *epityra*, described in Cato's de Agri Cultura, made from stoned olives which are chopped and marinated in oil, vinegar, coriander, cumin, fennel and mint.

Although eating habits changed throughout the hundreds of years of Roman Civilisation, the popularity of olives was constant and olives were eaten at most meals. Both Pliny and Martial mention olives in their description of meals served at their houses: "If after all this, Bacchus stimulates your appetite as he usually does, noble olives will come to your aid, and roasted chick peas and hot lupins." wrote Martial, in a letter encouraging a friend of his to come to dine at his house; while Pliny mentioned olives in a teasing letter he wrote to scold a friend who did not come to his dinner party, "Look here, you accepted my invitation to dinner and then did not show up. You will be assessed for the costs, to the last penny, and they are not small. You will have to foot the bill for all these preparations: lettuce, one head per head; snails, three apiece; eggs, two each; pasta; all the above served with mulsum and snow-yes, you will pay the tab for the snow too, in fact especially for the snow, because it died on the dish as a result of your negligence; then olives, boiled beets, gourds, onions, and one thousand other items no less elegantly prepared…"

At the grandest, most ostentatious of all Roman banquets – the satirical Banquet of Trimalchio – olives appeared at table, "Among the objects placed before us was a young ass made of Corinthian bronze and fitted with a sort of pack saddle which contained on one side pale-green olives and on the other side dark ones"[5]. Olives were there at all of the Romans meals or, as Martial so succinctly put it, "These olives which have reached you, withdrawn from the oil presses of Picenum, begin and also end our repasts"[6].

People living in Roman Malta must have eaten the same food and processed olives in the same way as people did throughout the Roman Empire. Till today we make a dish of fresh olives called *żebbuġ misħuq* or cracked olives using a method very similar to the one described by Cato the Elder in De Agri Cultura that dates back to 160 BC.

TO SEASON GREEN OLIVES

Bruise the olives before they become black and throw them into water. Change the water often, and when they are well soaked press out and throw into vinegar; add oil, and a half pound of salt to the modius of olives. Make a dressing of fennel and mastic steeped in vinegar, using a separate vessel. If you wish to mix them together they must be served at once. Press them out into an earthenware vessel and take them out with dry hands when you wish to serve them."

MALTESE CRACKED OLIVES

To prepare olives in this way take some freshly picked olives – green olives are usually used – but pinkish purple olives are fine as are black ones- then wash and crack each olive by hitting each one just hard enough with a mallet to expose the stone slightly. Then the olives must be soaked for 3 or 4 days in lightly salted fresh water (stir a heaped tablespoon of sea salt into every 4 litres of water), which must be changed every day. Then taste the olives, they should be strong tasting but not overwhelmingly bitter. When the olives taste right, drain them, pat them dry and put them in a bowl; pour over enough olive oil to cover, then add chopped garlic, parsley, merqtux (Maltese marjoram) or oregano and a little salt and pepper. Put them in the fridge and leave them to marinate for a couple of days. This special dish is a celebration of the flavour of olives, to be enjoyed while olives are fresh and being harvested, as crushed olives only keep for a week or at most two, after which they begin to soften.

These fresh olives are worth trying with different dressings:
- Crushed black olives are very good marinated in a dressing made with some finely chopped fresh rosemary, crushed garlic, finely grated orange zest, crushed wild fennel seeds and enough olive oil to cover the olives.
- A different dressing for crushed green olives is made with chopped dried tomatoes, capers, crushed garlic and chopped fresh herbs like mint, parsley and oregano. Then add enough olive oil to cover the olives.
- Alternatively mix the cracked olives with some wild greens; stir in some chopped wild rocket and mustard leaves, some chopped wild fennel fronds, some chopped parsley, capers and garlic and olive oil.

5   Petronius Arbiter, *Trimalchio's Dinner*
6   Epigram XXXVI, *"A Jar of Olives"* Book XIII

The story of olive trees, their fruit and oil in Malta slipped into obscurity in tandem with the Roman Empire's slow slide into the darkness of the Middle Ages. Confusion reigned and the destruction wrought on the Islands and their population meant that villages and surrounding farmlands were abandoned. When the Arabs conquered Malta in 870 AD "they demolished its fortress, and they looted and desecrated whatever they could not carry… after that, the island of Malta remained an uninhabited ruin".[7]

This seems to have set the pattern for things to come because, what with pirate attacks and rapacious feudal lords, the ravaged population had little time or strength to do anything but struggle for survival. Most of the population moved into the centre of the islands, as far away as possible from the coast to avoid being killed or captured by Moorish pirates and taken into slavery. By this time cotton had been introduced as a successful cash crop, to the detriment of the slow maturing olive tree, and the money made from cotton exports was used to import vital grain and other food supplies "The Catalans were importing raw and spun Maltese cotton, either directly from Malta or from Sicily, at least from 1404 onwards; they carried cloth, oil, sardines and dried fruits to Malta in exchange."[8] Cotton growing was more practical than olive oil; it was planted and harvested, leaving nothing behind in the empty fields, unlike olive trees which were permanent and needed care and protection.

At the beginning of the 17th century Girolamo Manduca, a Maltese Jesuit, wrote about "a Muslim attack of about 1470 when Malta was sacked by 18,000 Moors who burnt all the casali and "all the olives" on the island. The old people had a tradition – Contano i Vecchioni per tradizioni – that Mdina was saved by the miraculous appearance of St Paul and St Agatha and many other saints, after the women inside the city had made cheese from their own milk within the space of three days and had bombarded the Moors with it in order to convince them that the defenders were well supplied; thereafter the Maltese vowed to make an annual procession to Żejtun on the day of St Gregory."[9] This story is an extreme example of hyperbole and is the stuff myths are made of, but it has its roots firmly in fact – in 1429 a large Hasfid fleet ravaged Malta for three days, almost capturing Mdina and carting off 3,000 inhabitants as slaves. During the raid the economy was wrecked and agriculture was damaged to such a degree that years of sterility followed.

Pirate attacks were not completely run by the Moors and many Maltese men joined pirate ships that operated in the Eastern Mediterranean to make some money, further depleting the manpower available in Malta for working the fields or defending the villages. Malta's most famous pirate Michele de Malta was at the height of his powers around the 1460's making piracy an ever more attractive option for beleaguered young men to the extent that "in 1440 foreign vessels were forbidden to recruit at Malta"[10] in an attempt to try and stem the flow.

7   Joseph M. Brincat, *Malta 870-1054 Al-Himyari's Account and its Linguistic Implications*
8   Anthony T. Luttrell, *Approaches to Medieval Malta*
9   Anthony T. Luttrell, *Girolamo Manduca and Gian Francesco Abela – Tradition and invention in Maltese Historiography.*
10   Anthony T. Luttrell, *Approaches to Medieval Malta*

"During the fifteenth century the frequency of droughts appears to have increased"[11] making rural life and agricultural activity much harder, and by the middle of the fifteenth century the records of the University indicate that Malta was a horribly poor and insecure place to live in, "one entry referring to Malta as a "rock in the middle of the sea far from help and comfort.""[12]

Attacks on Malta carried on, such as in 1526 when the Moors raided Mosta giving rise to the tragic legend of The Bride of Mosta which tells the tale of the cruel Moors who took almost 400 prisoners, including a bride, together with the guests all dressed up for the wedding. Another attack occurred when the Knights of St John were already here in Malta; in 1551 the Turks, led by the infamous corsair Dragut, assaulted Malta and burned and plundered their way round the countryside, they threatened and almost took Mdina and then left, stopping off at Gozo to pillage, loot and take almost the whole of the Gozitan population – some 5000 people – prisoner.

By the time the Knights of St John of Jerusalem came to take possession of Malta in 1530, the land that had been fertile enough before 870 AD that "it was visited by ship builders, because the wood in it is of the strongest kind"[13] was reduced to an arid rock where trees were limited to the few valleys and "a few olive groves (the remnants of a widespread oil-producing industry in earlier Roman times), some vineyards and fig trees".[14]

The worst was still to come – the Great Siege in 1565 when Malta was hit by the full force of the Ottoman Empire. Though Malta and the Knights just about survived, the war had a detrimental effect on the few trees still growing on the barren rock that was Malta of the time. Trees were cut down to fire the furnaces needed to forge weapons for the Knights of St John and Maltese militia and both armies cleared away trees that may have been utilized as cover and used the wood as fuel. The Turkish army raided farms all over Malta, confiscated their crops and animals and often burnt or destroyed the farmstead, devastating the rural economy and making life after the Great Siege very hard for the islanders. Bosio, chronicler of the Knights of St John, recorded the amusing story of fifty Turkish soldiers who planned an olive picking sortie during the Great Siege. They were foiled when a Neapolitan, who had escaped imprisonment in the Turkish camp, sought refuge in Mdina and told his rescuers about the olive harvest that was to take place in Lija Valley on the 28th August. The Maltese Militia men attacked and broke it up, leaving the Turks olive-less and one soldier less. He was killed in the scuffle, as was his Maltese captor; the same arrow killed them both.[15]

Amazingly enough the smoldering, devastated ruin that was Malta after the Great Siege was repaired and rose, under the Knights, to a period of peace and prosperity. The knights planted many areas of Malta with trees, the best known is Buskett, and they built palaces and planted gardens all over the island, setting an example followed by many families. However they

Sam Cremona

11   Brian Blouet, *The Story of Malta*
12   Brian Blouet, *The Story of Malta*
13   Joseph M. Brincat, *Malta 870-1054 Al-Himyari's Account and its Linguistic Implications*
14   Stephen C. Spiteri, *the Great Siege*
15   Victor J. Galea, *Qwiel u Qaddisin*

Ancient olive trees in Bidnija

favoured orange trees over olive trees and the olive groves of antiquity were never replaced and olive pressing on a large, national scale never restarted. There may have been some sort of olive pressing somewhere, but on such a minor scale that it has gone completely unnoticed. Imported oil was used; the Knights of St John dressed their salads with French olive oil – except on fasting days when common oil had to be used instead.

The fruit however carried on being collected and preserved and was one of the main sources of food. One of the earliest written references to olives in the Maltese diet comes from 1610, "The soyle produceth no graine but barley. Bread made of it and olives is the villagers ordinary diet: and with the straw they sustaine their cattell. Commin seed, Anis seed and hony they have here in abundance, whereof they make merchandize."[16] Many other travellers made the same observation throughout the centuries and this holds true till today. Olives go into fish, vegetables, pies, sauces and they are served as appetisers, added to sandwiches and put on pizza. Olives are stirred into pasta and kneaded into pasta or bread dough, they make a savoury addition to all sorts of biscuits and crackers. The possibilities are endless and the results delicious.

However, freshly picked olives are far too bitter to eat immediately and must first be cured in any number of ways: and the fresher and better quality the olives to be cured are, the finer the end result will be.

16   George Sandys, *A Relation of a Journey begun in Anno Domine 1610,* 2nd Edition 1621

CURING OLIVES

There many different ways to cure olives, but all methods aim to convert the bitter fruit into a delicious tasting nugget. One of the best ways to cure large green olives is in a simple brine solution. This method produces the most traditional type of olive; full of flavour, firm and perfect both with drinks and in cooking.

Wash some freshly picked olives thoroughly and go over them carefully, picking out any bad or wormy olives. Soak the olives for 4 or 5 days in fresh water, which must be changed every day.

Then make a simple brine solution by mixing sea salt and water. The best way to do this is to add 100g coarse sea salt to every one litre of water and stir till dissolved. A more popular but far less accurate method is to float an egg in the brine – when the egg floats the brine is right – unfortunately this is not very precise as the staler an egg the quicker it will float.

Put the olives into the brine and add lots of bay and olive leaves. Some lemon wedges, split chillies, branches of wild fennel, perhaps some myrtle, add excellent flavour; avoid garlic at this stage as the keeping qualities of garlic are limited. It is best to add fresh garlic to the olives just before serving or marinating them. Once the olives are submerged in the brine, top it all with a layer of bay leaves to help

keep the olives in perfect condition. Leave the olives in the brine solution for about four months then remove them, rinse the olives and taste them. If they are too salty soak them in clear, fresh water for a couple of days, changing it every day, otherwise just rinse them and store the olives in a lighter brine solution or oil before using in cooking or as appetisers.

SALT CURED BLACK OLIVES

This is the most delicious way to cure black olives. The result is the best kind of olive; slightly chewy and strongly flavoured olives that are ready to eat in about four to five weeks.

You will need lots of sea salt, freshly picked ripe, black olives and a strong basket. Check the olives, discarding any wormy or bad ones. Then cover the bottom of the basket with the coarse sea salt and follow this with a layer of black olives about one or two is full. Top with a final layer of salt, cover the basket with a cloth or net and set it over some kind of a container, so that the bitter juices extracted by the salt can flow out of the basket to be caught in the container. Empty the container of the bitter juices every now and again or it might attract little fruit flies. Check the olives at regular intervals and top up the salt if necessary, for about two weeks. Taste the olives after this time and if they are soft, chewy and taste right then rinse away all the salt, dry them well and put them in sterile jars and cover them with oil until needed. Otherwise, carry on with the salting process until they taste just right and then they can be rinsed, dried and stored in oil.

The story of olives in Malta reached an all time low during the British period. Under appreciated as a food or oil, the olive tree was largely ignored throughout the 170 years of British rule as the focus was on the cotton industry which provided employment for many people in rural areas. Olives were still grown and harvested to be eaten and there may have been some olive pressing, but again on such a small scale that it went unrecorded and little changed until recent years.

SHORTCRUST PASTRY

Short crust pastry is very easy to make with olive oil rather than the usual butter or other hard fat. It may be used for tarts and pies of any sort in the same way as the more traditional short crust pastry

200g plain flour
75ml olive oil
1 egg beaten with 5 tbs water
A pinch of salt

Sieve the flour into a mixing bowl, stir in the olive oil and then "rub in" the oil, much as you would butter. Then make a hollow in the top and add the egg and water mixture and stir until dough is formed. Flatten this slightly with your knuckles, then fold it in half and flatten it again, do this three or four times until the dough is fairly smooth but do not overwork it as this makes it tough and difficult to use. Leave the dough to rest for fifteen minutes to relax and make it easier to roll out. Then roll it out and use it to line a flan dish, and then fill it with anything you like.

Lemon flavoured, sweetened ricotta is a delicious filling; or try jam and roughly chopped walnuts topped with another layer of pastry for tea or with morning coffee; or fresh fruit sprinkled with sugar, or bake it blind, brush the base with melted chocolate and fill with sweetened mascarpone and berries and so on.

LIGHT LEMON TART

300g plain flour
25g icing sugar
100ml olive oil
1 egg + enough white
wine to make 100ml
4 eggs
250g castor sugar
100g ground almonds
Juice and zest of 3 lemons
150g Greek yoghurt
2 tbs olive oil
2 tbs semolina

Sieve the flour and icing sugar into a bowl, rub in the olive oil. Then beat the egg and wine together and stir into the flour to make dough. If the dough is a little dry add a little more wine. Then flatten the dough out and fold it in half and repeat to form firm dough. Put it to one side while you prepare the filling.

Whisk the eggs and sugar together till creamy and the sugar is dissolved. Then whisk in the ground almonds, juice and zest of the lemons, the olive oil and semolina till smooth. Then fold in the yoghurt carefully, making sure all is well incorporated.

Then roll out the pastry and use it to line a 24cm flan dish. Pour in the filling and carefully put it in the oven preheated to gas mark 2/150ºC and bake for 40 minutes or till firm and golden.

Just before serving sprinkle with castor sugar and caramelise with a blowtorch and sprinkle with julienned lemon zest. If a blow torch is difficult dust with icing sugar and put under a hot grill, but take care the pastry does not burn. You could always simply sieve over some icing sugar and serve it like that.

OLIVES IN PASTRY

These are perfect to nibble with drinks; they are savoury, crunchy and small. Success depends very much on the quality of the olives used; when our own, home cured olives finish I buy "Malta sun-ripe" Maltese olives.

200g plain flour
100g butter
A pinch of salt
1 jar Sun-ripe olives or 250g olives
1 egg beaten with 1 tbs water
Sesame seeds

Rub the butter into the flour until evenly distributed. Add the salt and then stir in enough cold water to make dough. You may need a little more water or flour if the dough is too dry or wet. Knead the dough lightly by folding it and pressing it down a couple of times, then shape it into a ball and set it aside. Allow it to rest for about 20 minutes. In the meantime, stone the olives and stuff with a few herbs. Pre-heat the oven to gas mark 5/190ºC then roll out the pastry and cut it into squares large enough to wrap in the olives. Pour some sesame seeds into a bowl, prepare the egg wash by beating the water and eggs together in a bowl and grease the baking tray. Cover the olives in the pastry squares and press the edges to seal, and give each one a quick roll between the palms of your hands to make little ovals. Then dip each one in the egg and water wash, roll them in the sesame seeds and put on a greased baking tray. Bake in the preheated oven for approx 20 minutes or until golden. These are best served warm, but are good at room temperature. Add these delicious olive rolls to a plate of fish instead of potatoes. Make them taste different by adding herbs to the olives. ,If making large quantities for a big party simply cut the olives in half as smaller nibbles at parties are more manageable.

FRIED AND CRUSHED OLIVES WITH ROSEMARY AND GARLIC

This savoury dish may be made with either very ripe, freshly picked black olives or any good quality cured olives. If the cured olives are very salty, wash them well, crack them and soak them in fresh water for a couple of hours to get rid of the excess salt. Then remove the stones, chop them up very roughly and fry them in lots of olive oil, garlic, a couple of anchovies and rosemary till soft and lightly browned. Serve this warm or at room temperature on small pieces of toasted ftira, dusted with finely chopped parsley. Proceed in exactly the same way if you are using very ripe, freshly picked wholly black olives.

An old olive tree trunk

In the last decade or so Maltese olive trees, Maltese olive oil and olives have undergone a huge revival spearheaded by my husband Sam Cremona, who in 1998 bought an olive press to be able to make oil for the family. However people started to bring him their own olives to press for them and the whole thing took off from there, giving rise to a whole new sector in agriculture in Malta. This has grown and there are now several presses in Malta and Maltese olive oil is a much sought after, delicious condiment that is very much in demand all over our islands.

A honey comb (Photo by Rebecca Cremona)

MALTESE HONEY
Għasel Malti

Maltese honey first hit the headlines when Caius Verres, the kleptomaniac Roman praetor who governed Malta between 73 and 71 BC, stood trial before the Roman Senate. Cicero accused Verres of many crimes including the theft of 400 jars of honey 'for which the Maltese islands have always been renowned'. The word spread and throughout the centuries almost all visitors to the Maltese islands sought out Maltese honey and remarked on the excellence of its flavour and consistency, comparing it favourably with Greek and Sicilian honey.

Honey was the only form of sweetening available before the Arabs brought sugarcane to the Mediterranean and it went into many ancient Roman desserts and cakes as well as savoury dishes. Try some of the following for fun:

APICIUS' STUFFED DATES

Curiously enough Ancient Romans stuffed stoned dates with finely chopped walnuts, rolled them in salt and fried them in honey to caramelise them. They were served either on an oiled dish or a dish covered with oiled bay leaves to prevent the caramelised dates sticking to the plate.

CATO'S GLOBI

These are delicious with coffee; of course the Ancient Romans would have served them with wine as coffee was still unknown in those days. Do not make globi using packaged, long life ricotta as it is too soft and watery for this recipe; the best sort to use is local, freshly made ricotta.

200g Maltese ricotta
50g semolina
1 small egg
Honey
Poppy seeds
Oil for frying

Beat the ricotta with the semolina and egg. Then heat up about 5cm of oil and when it is hot enough to brown a piece of bread in about 1 minute, drop spoonfuls of the dough into the boiling oil a few at a time and cook till golden – flip over if necessary. Then lift them out with a slotted spoon, drain them on kitchen paper, dip them in honey and roll them in poppy seeds.

TYROPATINUM

(Apicius' egg and honey custard)

This recipe is quite clearly the ancestor of Crème Caramel. Apicius suggests in his usual vague way that you take as much milk you think you need for the pan you have chosen, then sweeten the milk with honey and add 5 eggs for every hemina (approx. 500ml) of milk. Dissolve everything well and strain into an earthenware pot. Then cook over a slow flame; when it has set, sprinkle with pepper and serve.

500ml milk
5 egg yolks
1 heaped tsp cornflour
Genuine Maltese honey to taste (lots)
Freshly ground black pepper
Preheat the oven to gas mark 3½ / 175°C

Butter 6 ramekin dishes and put them in a roasting dish. Warm the milk and dissolve the honey in it (at least 5tbs), in the meantime, beat the egg yolks with the cornflour. Pour over the hot milk, whisking as you do. Pour the mixture into the buttered ramekins, pour very hot but not boiling water into the roasting dish to come ¾ of the way up the ramekins and put it into the oven for about ¾ of an hour to an hour or till they are firm – to check this pierce carefully with a skewer and it should come out clean. Chill for a couple of hours and then unmould them carefully and serve sprinkled with freshly ground black pepper.

N.B. a quick grating of lemon peel stirred in with the honey improves the taste tremendously but has no root in true ancient Roman cuisine

Al Himyari's short description of the 870 AD Arab attack on Malta indicates that Malta's honey bees were still as prolific as ever; he wrote that as a result of the attack Malta "remained an uninhabited ruin, it was visited ... by those who collect honey, because that is the most common thing there". This glorious abundance of honey carried on through the centuries; Quintin, writing one of the first detailed descriptions of Malta in 1536, praises Maltese flowers, especially roses and goes on to say that "honey becomes excellent, both for this reason and also because the bees produce it from thyme, violets and other flowers and store it in their common hives. Thus it may be conjectured how the island obtained its name, definitely revealing the glory of its honey by its own name." In fact, the name Malta is a corruption of Melita, derived from the Greek meli, melitos meaning honey. Many other travellers extolled Maltese honey in the same way, while others added more detail, G.F. Angus for example, who recorded all sorts of interesting details during his visit in 1811, noted that "The honey is highly esteemed; that made by the bees of Mellieha is reckoned the best; its price is 8d per pound."

Bees are seasonal workers and Maltese bees are busy throughout the year as there are flowers for each season. Autumn produces carob catkins which are particularly sweet and give honey chocolaty overtones; these are followed by all the winter yellow and white wild-flowers and thistles, followed by rusty pink Mediterranean heath and bright blue borage. Most fruit trees blossom in spring and the air is filled with the most beautiful, delicate flowers and scents. Any one that has had the good fortune to visit an orange grove in full bloom for example will understand why bees buzz from blossom to blossom with such drunken delight. The honey from these blossoms is particularly delicate and an appetising pale golden colour; perfect with anything, especially sipped straight from a freshly cut and dripping honeycomb. Throughout spring and early summer, bees will have all sorts of garden flowers and herbs, red sulla or clover to work on and last and best of all is wild thyme which bees use to make the most fragrant honey of all.

COLLECTING THE HONEY

The day traditionally set aside for collecting honey is the feast of St Anne on the 26th of July which comes just after the wild thyme season when bees have been at their busiest. To do a potentially painful job like this a farmer has to take certain precautions and protective clothing is all that is needed. Prior to the modern boiler-suit, farmers wore a *mustaċija* or muslin veil over their head and tied up any openings or gaps in his clothing that bees might fly into.

A large prickly pear leaf was the ideal holder for the lump of dried mule dung which, when set alight, produced just the right kind of smoke to drive away the bees – a proper metal smoker is used nowadays. The honey was then pressed out of the combs by hand onto a piece of muslin draped over the mouth of a *ġarra* or terracotta jar, then the waxy comb was dropped onto the muslin and pressed hard to wring out as much of the honey as possible.

The crushed comb was then left on the muslin so that every last drop of honey dripped into the garra overnight. A simple honeycomb spinner has replaced this; a more efficient method that simply spins the honey out of the combs, leaving the waxy structure intact to be returned to the bees for refilling.

Prior to this innovation, in order to extract as much of the honey as possible, the crushed waxy combs were melted down with a little water over a low flame and this was then poured into a cloth bag and wrung out. The liquid wax and water squeezed out of the cloth bag went into a *żinġla* or flat bottomed basin; this separated as it cooled, forming a plug of wax on the surface and a dark syrupy liquid beneath. The residue left inside the cloth bag was placed near the hive for the bees to collect and reuse.

The best part, the delicious honey that Malta was so famous for was stored in terracotta jars *(ġarra)* – today glass jars of all shapes and sizes are used.

The virgin wax, the part that floated in the *żingla* was often given to the church for candles; otherwise it was used as furniture polish or to soften calloused skin.

The water that collected beneath the wax on the surface in the *żingla* was called *l-qastanija.* This was very sweet syrup and kept for Christmas when it was used to make *qaghaq tal-ghasel*, a traditional ring shaped, honey filled pastry.

Step 1. Smoking out the bees

Step 2. Taking the combs out of the hive

Step 3. Cutting the honey out of the cones

Step 4. Spinning the honey

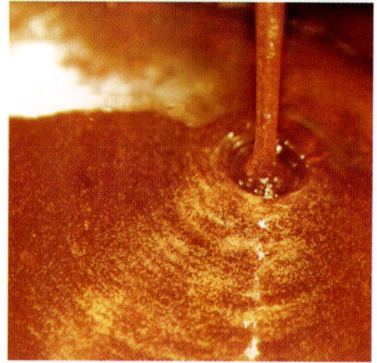

Step 5. Collecting the honey out of the spinner

Step 6. Combs are emptied ready for the next harvest

(Photos by Rebecca Cremona)

APIARY OR MIĠBĦA

Very old apiaries (*miġbħa/mġieba*) were frequent features of the rural landscape; most have been destroyed to make way for modern, concrete life but a few remain. Some are of ancient vintage; in Mellieha there is a large bee hive complex that probably dates back to the Roman period[1] built into the cliffs near Ras il-Pelligrin and another similar one that was built under the Knights in Xemxija[2] and are testament to the big business honey production was in those days.

Many farmers built smaller versions of these bee hive complexes for their own use; these were little low rooms, purpose built to shelter the bees and their hives; the walls were thick and the roof topped with *deffun* (traditional roofing material) which made them very strong and at the same time kept a steady temperature within the *miġbħa*. One low doorway faced south for warmth and light; vital for bees during the winter months as extreme cold kills bees. The bees entered the *miġbħa* through small round holes in the walls close to the roof to find their clay hives lying horizontally on shelves inside the room. Clay beehives kept outside were placed in a south facing location in a shallow hollow in the ground near a warm stone wall for protection against the cold north wind.

In fact, writing in 1804, Boisgelin mentioned the horizontal hives used in Malta and said that "A great many bees are kept in some parts of the island; the hives are horizontal in the Eastern style, and are much more easy of access than those of another form. The Maltese honey is very sweet, and has a most delicious flavour..."[3] Nowadays farmers use wooden boxes that are purpose made for bee keeping. The whole process is easier, the bees produce more honey in this way and they are less likely to pick up parasites that are to blame for so many of the diseases bees are susceptible to.

Miġbħa in Xemxija (Photo by Joe P. Borg)

1   Din L-Art Ħelwa, *Walks Red Tower/Foresta 2000*
2   Joseph Borg, *A Woodland Walk from Xemxija to L-Imbordin*
3   Louis de Boiseglin, *Ancient and Modern Malta*

COOKING WITH HONEY

Such an abundance of honey should have produced a proliferation of local dishes and there are a quite a few sweet dishes that involve honey. Many of the more traditional recipes include honey as this was the principal sweetener available to cooks before the Moors brought sugar cane and sugar to Europe. Most notable among these recipes are *qagħaq tal-għasel, żeppoli, xkunvat* and *kwareżimal.*

KWAREŻIMAL

The ingredients for these Lenten biscuits adhere strictly to the old fasting rules that governed eating habits through the forty days of Lent. Though these rules no longer apply, the biscuits certainly do and people need little prompting to eat Kwarezimal throughout the quaresima (forty days) of Lent.

Sicilians call their version of Kwaresimal "Quaresimali", but the only similarity lies in the name – the Sicilian version is similar to Tuscan cantucci and contain egg whites.

100g blanched almonds
100g plain flour
125g castor sugar
Dash brandy or orange flower
Grated rind of 1 orange,
tangerine and lemon
1 tbs cocoa
Honey and nibbed or roughly chopped
toasted almonds to decorate

Toast the almonds briefly and grind them up fairly roughly so that they are mealy rather than powdery. Put them into a large bowl and add the rest of the ingredients, stir them together and add enough water to make stiff dough. Kwaresimal are traditionally rather large, approx. 15cm long x 5cm wide. I prefer smaller ones and usually make them half the size, but as thick at 2cm.

Place them on well greased baking sheets and bake at gas mark 5 /190ºC for 20 minutes. They should be crisp on the edges but still soft when they are ready. Take them out of the oven and spread with honey and chopped almonds.

ŻEPPOLI

The charm and fascination of food runs far deeper than the first bite; it is intriguing and unravels connections between people, cultures and their shared histories. Every year on the 19th March the feast of St Joseph is celebrated in Malta and with particular verve in Rabat. Religious ceremony vies with the traditional and must haves include the renowned *żeppoli* without which *il-Festa ta San Ġużepp* would be very flat.

But are they *żeppoli* or *sfineċ*? In Sicily they are called *sfinci di san Giuseppe* and made in almost exactly the same way as ours are – except that the filling is far plainer and comprises sweetened ricotta sometimes garnished with a sliver of candied orange peel. Further North in Naples they go by the soubriquet *zeppole* and a candied cherry replaces the sliver of candied orange peel. In Malta these delicious pastries are sometimes named *sfineċ ta San Ġużepp* rather than *żeppoli*, but this probably refers to the generic term as there are *sfineċ tal-inċova, tal-bakkaljaw, tal-makku* and so on. The word *sfineċ* is derived from the Arabic *isfanj* which is a kind of deep fried sweet yeasted pastry, dusted in sugar or soaked in syrup. *Żeppoli* refers more specifically to the fried pastries associated with *San Ġużepp*.

So when you make some *żeppoli* or *sfineċ ta San Ġużepp* on the 19th March think of all those people in Sicily, Naples and North Africa possibly doing the same thing – just as they did all those years ago when the *isfang* first moved north and became *sfineċ, sfinċi, żeppoli, zeppole* and so on.

The filling for żeppoli

ŻEPPOLI/ SFINEĊ TA SAN ĠUŻEPP

The recipe for the dough is a basic choux paste recipe that is deep fried and filled with the traditional sweetened ricotta blend of chopped toasted almonds, chipped chocolate and finely chopped candied peel then drizzled with Maltese honey and chopped roasted almonds. These are sometimes filled with sweet custard or more simply fried and rolled in cinnamon flavoured sugar.

125g plain flour- sieved twice
1tbs castor sugar
250ml water
100g butter
Grated rind of a lemon and an orange
2 large or 3 small eggs

Bring the water to the boil and add the butter. Once this has melted, pour in the flour and sugar and beat until it comes away from the sides of the pan. Cool slightly and beat in the eggs and grated peel a little at a time until the mixture is smooth and shiny. It is probably best to use an electric beater for this as it is an exhausting job.

In the meantime prepare the filling by mixing together till smooth 300g ricotta with 100g of each of the following: chopped black chocolate, chopped candied peel and chopped roasted blanched almonds with 75g castor sugar.

Roast and chop an additional 100g of blanched almonds and put them to one side and have ready some good, preferably Maltese honey.

Once everything is ready, heat some sunflower or similar oil in a deep saucepan and drop in heaped teaspoons of the choux paste into the boiling oil. Remove to drain on kitchen roll once they are puffed and golden. Slit and fill with the mixture, drizzle with the honey, sprinkle with the nuts and serve.

N.B. They may be baked instead at gas mark 6/200ºC for about 15-20 minutes or till puffed and golden. Remove to a cooling rack, cut a slit in the sides to release the steam and finish off in the same way as above.

The noted writer and folklorist Ġużè Cassar Pullicino wrote about other less well known Maltese sweets made with honey in his excellent article *Antichi Cibi* of which the following are a selection:

Ruġġata was an orange drink made from juice of the *melarangia*[1] orange mixed with sugar and water or *ruġġata* could refer to a sort of sweet made from boiling oranges with honey and sugar – possibly candied peel or jam made with a mix of honey and sugar. *Ruġġata* refers also to a cold almond drink.

Ħelwa, Ġużè Cassar Pullicino quotes from Vassalli and says that helwa was a sort of *lasagne di miele* made first by boiling down some honey to reduce and condense it, then beating it till it turned white and elastic. Then it was cooled and allowed to harden into what today we would probably call qubbajt (nougat/torrone).

Cubbiata from the Sicilian cubbaitu meaning a type of caramel made from citron peel, sugar and honey. This obviously was another early form of *qubbajt*.

Komnata was similar to the drink known today as Punch. It was mentioned by Can. Agius de Soldanis and was made of hot wine mixed with honey, spices, cinnamon and cloves and given to mothers who had just given birth.

Qastanija is another of the sweets cooked with honey mentioned by Ġużè Cassar Pullicino and he quotes Vassalli who wrote that "this is a filling made of honey and fine flour mixed with spices and cooked, then cooled and used to fill Christmas rings. Joseph Aquilina added that the word is derived from the Italian *castagna* meaning chestnut and refers to the colour of the filling. All this is very interesting as older country people today remember their mothers making the filling for *qagħaq tal-għasel* with a by-product of the waxy honeycombs. This is a chestnut coloured, sweet syrup produced when the combs are melted down for their wax after the honey has been extracted. They called both this syrup and the filling *il-qastanija*. This was probably used to replace the more expensive pure honey. Townspeople who had little access to the real *qastanija* substituted it with black treacle or molasses – a similar coloured substance, but they had to add sugar as treacle isn't as sweet.

---

1   The Accademia Della Crusca translates this as "Frutta di color rancio" and "rancio" as the colour of saffron, between yellow and red.

The following are a more modern collection of honey inspired recipes – pure Maltese honey was used to cook all these recipes.

HONEY DRESSED SWEET RAVIOLI

300g plain flour
100g cold butter
Water

Rub the butter into the flour till it resembles rough breadcrumbs, and then stir in enough water to make dough. Knead very briefly just enough to form it into a ball and put to one side for 20 minutes. In the meantime make the filling as follows:
200g Maltese ricotta
Approx. 2 tbs icing sugar
A little grated black chocolate
Honey to serve

Stir the ricotta, icing sugar and chocolate together till well mixed. If the ricotta is too dry add a tiny dash of cream or milk.

Then, roll out the pastry thinly and cut out rounds of dough. Put a teaspoonful of filling on each round, moisten the edges with water, fold over and seal by pressing firmly with the tines of a fork or your fingertips.

Heat 5cm of oil and fry the ravioli till golden. Drain on kitchen roll, drizzle generously with honey and serve.

GBEJNA OR FETA IN FILO WITH HONEY

This makes an unusual start to a meal – it is quick to prepare and the combination of salty cheese with sticky sweet pastry is delicious served on a bed of peppery leaves. If you find feta too salty, soak it in water for a while – remember to pat it dry very well before wrapping it in the pastry to ensure the pastry will be nice and crisp.

6 gbejniet moxxi (half dry) or
6 slices feta cheese lcm thick
6 sprigs fresh thyme
Freshly ground black pepper
12 sheets filo
Olive oil
6 big tbs honey
Rocket and salad leaves to serve

Dressing
1 tbs grainy mustartd
1 tbs honey
5 tbs olive oil

Rinse the slices of feta cheese or gbejniet moxxi and pat them dry. Then lay each sheet of filo down flat, brush lightly with oil and fold in half lengthways and brush lightly with oil again. Place the cheese neatly on the short end, top with thyme and black pepper and fold in the edges and roll up to make neat parcels. Brush again lightly with oil and bake in the oven pre-heated to gas mark 6 for 15 minutes or till golden.

Take them out of the oven and immediately spread them with the honey. Serve them hot and crunchy with the rocket and salad leaves mixed with the olive oil dressing.

To make the dressing simply whisk all the ingredients together and pour over the rocket and salad leaves.

N.B. If the ġbejniet are too large simply cut them in half.

SAFFRON PANNA COTTA WITH HONEY *Serves 6*

This delicate and beautifully coloured dessert is lovely and fresh on a hot summer's night and only takes a moment to prepare. The amount of gelatine is calculated to survive the heat of summer – should you prefer a slightly softer panna cotta simply break one of the gelatine leaves in half and remove one half leaf from the total amount.

550ml fresh cream
8g or four leaves of gelatine
1 tbs icing sugar
Good pinch saffron threads
4 tbs honey

Put the gelatine in cold water to soften for about 10 minutes. In the meantime, bring the cream to the boil and simmer gently for a minute or two, then add the sugar and saffron threads and allow it to infuse for a couple of minutes. Take the softened gelatine out of the water, give it a quick squeeze and add it to the hot cream. Stir it until it has dissolved and then add the honey and stir again to dissolve. Pour this into six oiled ramekins or little cups and chill them in the refrigerator overnight.

To Serve
6 tbs honey
6 tbs toasted flaked almonds

Run a round ended knife around the edges of the panna cotta, and then dip the bottom of the ramekins briefly in hot water. This should make it easier to turn them out. Then turn them out onto a plate, drizzle with honey and sprinkle with flaked almonds and serve.

NUT BRITTLE

This resembles the qubbajt sold at villages feasts throughout the summer except that it is much thinner and so easier on the teeth. Traditional qubbajt is made with sesame seeds, but it is fun to make with other sorts of nuts for a change as they do the south of in Italy and Sicily. I have used tangerine peel as I love the flavour of tangerine and I preserve lots of it in winter by storing it under sugar or in the freezer. If you do not have any tangerine available use lemon peel instead.

100g Good Earth flaked almonds or sesame seeds or chopped pistachios or chopped hazelnuts
100g granulated sugar
1 tbs water
50g good Maltese honey
Slivers of tangerine peel or lemon peel (optional)
1 lemon, halved
2 big pieces non-stick grease proof paper

Run one sheet of non-stick grease proof paper under the tap, squeeze it out and flatten it out on a heat proof kitchen counter. Lightly oil one side of the other sheet and have it ready, along with the lemon halves, an oiled knife and a rolling pin. Then, put the sugar, honey and water in a medium sized thick bottomed saucepan and heat over a medium flame until dissolved. Then turn up the heat to boil the sugar and honey and add your choice of nuts and peel and stir. It may look as though there are too many nuts, but they will soon boil into place. Leave the mix to boil stirring occasionally until it is a dark golden colour – it will takes approximately 5 – 8 minutes. Then pour it out onto the prepared paper, flatten out using the lemon halves, then cover with the oiled paper (oiled side down) and roll out it out with a rolling pin to the required thickness, remove the paper and press down with the blade of the oiled knife to mark out squares or strips so that it will be easy to cut up the nut brittle when it is set.

Once it is set and cold, break or cut it into pieces along the prepared lines, wrap the pieces of nut brittle in clean greaseproof paper and store in it an airtight container.

Makes about 6 8cm x 2cm strips or approximately 24 squares

SAINT MARTIN
Il-festa ta' San Martin

It is a commonly recognised fact that any saint blessed enough to be associated with food traditions will have a far more popular following than many other saints. A good example of this is Saint Martin of Tours; he shared his cloak with a beggar on a freezing morning, he brought people back to life, healed others and performed many other exemplary actions that are somehow eclipsed by his association with wine, nuts, cakes and special breads.

This more terrestrial connection has its roots in a period of abstinence that started on the day after St Martin's feast celebrated on 11th November. This Medieval practice, in preparation for Christmas, lasted 40 days, and was, therefore, called *Quadragesima Sancti Martini*, which means in Latin "the forty days of St Martin." Naturally this gave rise to great feasting in anticipation of the fast and our modern traditions are the remnants of this banqueting.

Many countries all over Europe celebrate the feast of St Martin, but he is especially popular in Malta and Sicily where he features in popular traditions. *A san Martino ogni mosto è vino* is the Sicilian version of *F'San Martin jifthu l-inbid u t-tin* meaning that that year's wine should be ready to drink, the barrels/kegs are cracked open and the wine drunk with a generous helping of dried figs in Malta while in Sicily anise biscuits or sweet fritters are served with the new wine.

The dried figs referred to in the proverb are actually *tin taċ-ċappa* or a sort of dried fig cake flavoured with fennel seeds, anisette and bay leaves usually made by pressing dried figs together with fennel seeds, anisette and bay leaves. This is usually made in August when figs are in season and the sun is hot enough to dry the figs.

Make some fritters to celebrate San Martin and wine, along with *tin taċ-ċappa* and some *krustini* to dip into the wine.

Left: San Martin chapel, San Martin
Above: Statue of St Martin (Photos by Joe P. Borg)

FIG CAKE OR TIN TAĊ-ĊAPPA

First dry some figs; to do this, split some mature figs in half and lay them out on trays, put them out on a sun-flooded roof or terrace, cover them with netting and leave them there to dry until they are leathery. Take them in at night to avoid the night dew. The dry figs can be stored in airtight tins, but once the figs are dry, people sometimes preserve them in the form of *tin taċ-ċappa* a much tastier version of dried figs. These are prepared as follows: Once the figs are well dried, warm them through in the oven to sterilise and make them more pliable. Then, in a greaseproof paper lined container, lay dry bay leaves in the bottom of the container, top them with the warmed figs (cut side up), some flaked toasted almonds, a handful of raisins soaked overnight in Anisette, a sprinkling of fennel seeds; a generous sprinkling of Anisette liqueur and some crumbled bay leaves. Continue in this way until the container is full, then put down a last layer of figs, (cut side down this time) finish it off with a final layer of bay leaves and cover the whole lot with greaseproof paper and weigh down the figs evenly and very well for at least two weeks. This block of dried figs is ready to eat in time for the feast of San Martin on the 10th of November and is delicious served in thinly cut slices.

KRUSTINI

The fennel seeds used in the recipe below add tremendous flavour to these delicious biscuits; the best sort of fennel seeds are those that grow wild all over the Maltese countryside. Fennel plants flower throughout summer, then dry out and form umbrels full of seeds. These are best collected before the first autumn rains and should be stored in airtight jars.

400g flour
150ml olive oil
150g castor sugar
100g blanched almonds
– roughly chopped
50g shelled pistachio nuts
– roughly chopped
Grated rind of 1 lemon and orange
1 tbs finely chopped
candied peel or marmalade
1 egg
1 tbs fennel seeds
1 tbs lemon or orange juice
1 tbs anisette liqueur

Preheat the oven to gas mark 4/180ºC. Sieve the flour into a big bowl and add the oil and rub it in, much as you would a solid fat like butter. Then stir in the sugar, nuts, grated rind, candied peel or marmalade and the fennel seeds.

Then mix in the egg, juice and liqueur and stir to make dough. If the dough is too dry and won't hold together add a little more liquid in the form of water, more juice or liqueur until the dough holds together easily.

Shape the dough into a ball, divide it into 4 equally sized pieces and shape them into long rolls. Place them on a greased baking sheet and with a sharp knife slice up each log, then press the slices lightly together again and neaten the logs. Put the baking sheet in the preheated oven and bake for about 25 minutes.

Remove from the oven and cool for a couple of minutes, then slice carefully along the marks made before baking. Lay the slices on the baking sheets and bake again until golden and crisp, approximately another 15 minutes.

Remove them from the oven and cool completely before storing in an airtight tin.

64

SAN MARTIN'S FRITTERS

SICILIAN STYLE

1kg potatoes boiled and well mashed
500g plain flour
2 eggs
1 sachet instant yeast
100g sugar
1 grated lemon zest
1 pinch ground cinnamon

Make smooth, soft dough with all the ingredients with a little tepid water and leave it to rest and rise for an hour. Then drop little balls in boiling oil and fry till golden and puffed, then drain on kitchen roll, drizzle with honey and serve.

Fritters and St Martin feature in a Maltese proverb; *F'San Martin il-mara taqli ftira u raġel jiżra' l-imtira* is one that simply reminds everyone that while a farmer takes advantage of the dry weather typical of St Martin's summer to sow newly cut farrows, his wife quickly fries up a piece of bread dough as a delicious snack for him to give him the energy to keep going. This could be stuffed with fresh sheep's cheese or some fried onions and tomatoes (*it-toqlija*) or quite simply sugared and eaten with a cup of coffee.

SWEET SAN MARTIN FRITTERS

MALTESE STYLE

300g piece uncooked bread dough
A little sugar to serve
Corn oil to deep fry

Break the dough into golf ball sized bits, flatten well – make a hole in some if wished and deep fry in hot oil till golden. Serve warm, sprinkled with sugar.

SAVOURY SAN MARTIN FRITTERS

300g piece uncooked bread dough
50g stoned green olives, chopped up
2 onions, peeled and finely chopped
½ a tbs tomato paste (Kunserva)
1 tbs Maltese marjoram (merqtux)
Olive oil
1 pinch sugar
1 pinch salt

Fry the chopped onion in a little olive oil till soft, then stir in the marjoram, kunserva, sugar and salt and cook for a moment longer, then add the olives. Break the dough into golf ball sized bits, flatten then put a little of the savoury mix on each one and fold over to cover the mix and press closed to seal. Then deep fry in hot oil till golden and serve them immediately for the best results.

Alternatively replace the onion and olive mix with a piece of Ġbejna moxxa (semi-dry Maltese sheep cheese)

These traditions are fading into memory as modern life takes over traditional activities; but one tradition that is as popular as ever is *il-borża ta' San Martin*. This is a cloth bag filled with seasonal goodies given to children of all ages, it is usually filled with nuts, dried and fresh fruit, marzipan fruits and a sweet bread roll called, unsurprisingly, *ħbejża ta' San Martin*. There is a little ditty that illustrates this

"Ġewż, lewż, qastan u tin!
Kemm inħobbu 'l San Martin!"
Or
Walnuts, Almonds, Chestnuts and figs, I love St Martin very much.

The nuts were usually unshelled and were used to play games until they were cracked open and eaten – perhaps on the way to the Festa at Baħrija where St Martin is patron saint. An unusual part of the festivities to celebrate St Martin's feast in Baħrija is a popular turkey fair where turkeys, geese and capons are raffled and the lucky winners usually take the bird home to fatten up for Christmas lunch.

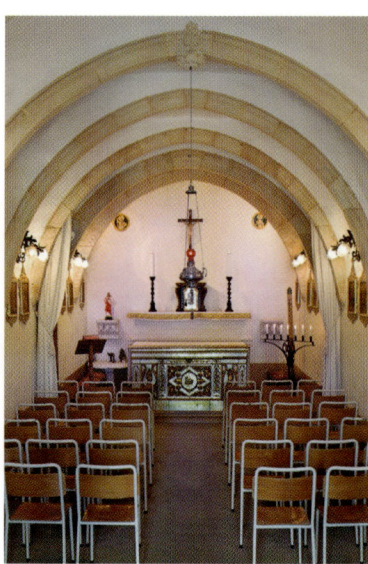

Left: "stony uphill stretch" leading to St Martin's chapel, above: interior of San Martin chapel, San Martin (Photos by Joe P. Borg)

Back in the 1920s the Feast of St Martin was celebrated with great verve by the little farming community around San Martin near Mgarr. Eric Brockman describes an idyllic weekend he spent at San Martin in 1926 to celebrate the eponymous saint's day. Such a way of life is long gone but we are left with a beautiful sketch of rural life where everyone is contented and everything is green and perfect. Mass was celebrated in the morning at the chapel on top of San Martin hill and afterwards, nuts and nougat were given out to all by Sir Hannibal Scicluna. Then everyone enjoyed a picnic lunch on San Martin hill, "Some lit fires and warmed cans of thick minestra, others had stews and ravjuli; but most were content with round loaves, anchovies, olives, tomatoes and oil."[1]

---

1   Eric Brockman, *Last Bastion*

ĦBEJŻA TA' SAN MARTIN

These are very soft, sweet rolls glazed and sprinkled with sesame seeds and sometimes there is a liquorice sweet stuck in the middle of the bun.

500g plain flour
1 sachet instant yeast
100g sugar
100g butter
Grated zest of 1 lemon and a tangerine
Approx. 250ml – 300ml tepid milk

Rub the butter into the flour, add the sugar, zest or vanilla and stir. Then add enough tepid milk to make rough dough and knead for about 10 minutes or until the dough is smooth and elastic. Leave it to rise for about an hour or until it has doubles in size, then knock it back by kneading it gently for a minute or two until the dough is elastic again. Shape into small rolls and place on a well greased or lined baking dish, leaving a good space in between each as they will rise and grow. Cover with a cloth and leave the rolls to rise for about an hour or until doubled in size.

To finish the rolls
50g sugar
75ml water
Sesame seeds

In the meantime preheat the oven to gas mark 6/200ºC and prepare a glaze by boiling down the sugar and water till syrupy. Once the buns are risen brush them gently with the glaze and sprinkle with the sesame seeds and bake them in the preheated oven for about 20 minutes or till golden and crisp. Remove and cool.

Optional – stick a pink liquorice sweet into the top of the buns.
Makes 12 -15 depending on size.

MINESTRA

Tura Schembri of Wardija described to me how she would have to be back home from the fields at about four o'clock every afternoon, to begin cooking minestra for the evening meal. She would use brushwood she had collected on her walk back home, or take firewood out of the storeroom and light the *kenur*, (a small stone stove). Lighting the *kenur* was a skill in itself, calling for just the right amount of wood. Once the flames had settled, she would put on a clay pot, called a *pagna*, filled with peeled, chopped vegetables and cold water, then leave it to boil. She would add *kunserva* for colour and flavour, and finally a little salt to taste. Sometimes she would make pasta to add to the mix. The soup would be served with some bread and oil, and perhaps olives. In the coldest months, the proportion of dried legumes, potatoes and pasta was increased, to make the minestra richer in protein and carbohydrates, and a better source of energy. This was the way minestra was made in rural areas in the 1920's.

2 or 3 tbs of olive oil
1 large onion
A handful of peeled garlic cloves (optional)
At least 3 stalks Maltese celery *(Karfus)*, leaves and all
2 ripe tomatoes, peeled and seeded
3 large carrots
1k pumpkin
3 large or 6 small *qaraghbali* or tender zucchini
½ a *qara' twil* (long marrow)
Some peas or French beans
½ a small cabbage
½ a small cauliflower
3 medium potatoes
Chicken or vegetable stock (or water and a cube)
Salt and pepper
1 or 2 tbs *Kunserva* especially if the tomatoes are the winter variety

To start off the minestra, chop the onion and celery very finely and stew them gently with the garlic cloves in the olive oil. In the meantime dice the peeled and seeded tomatoes, add them to the onions and allow them to cook gently while you wash, peel and chop the rest of the vegetables, adding them to the pot as you go. Add enough boiling water or stock to cover the vegetables comfortably, bring everything back to the boil, add salt and pepper, lower the heat and simmer for a minimum of one and a half hours.

FTIRA

Ftira is the round flat loaf best suited to stuffing up with goodies and eating at a picnic. Simply split the loaf horizontally, then dip the cut sides generously in olive oil, season it well, rub vigorously with the cut side of a ripe tomato and fill up with some of the following ingredients:

Some anchovies
Some boiled beans
Capers
Olives
Herbs like mint, basil, marjoram or parsley
Possibly some very finely
chopped raw onion

Then press down to compact the filling, cut into manageable wedges and serve.

Sir Hannibal Scicluna organised a "fair" near the little chapel on top of San Martin ridge. It was held in the afternoon and there were races of all sorts and prizes for the winners. Three legged races and sack races were run but the donkey races were the most popular. All the donkeys were groomed till they shone; donkey owners practically ran the race with their donkeys, urging them on at every corner, even giving them a good, encouraging shove forward at intervals and lifting them up whenever their little hooves skidded on the stony paths and they fell.

The prizes were banners or other things that were more practical like lengths of fabric and knives. Giuseppi Mangion *Il-Laġġa* of Wardija won a race at one of the San Martin Fairs and still had the prize banner when he described the races at the venerable age of 97[2] Memories of the festa are still clear in his mind and he remembers that particular year as he had been out hunting all morning at *Il-Miżieb*, the tree covered ridge slightly to the north of San Martin. After bagging a few turtledoves for his supper he decided to go to the San Martin festa and so returned home to Wardija to leave his gun and game bag there. He arrived at the festa just after lunch in time for the races and, being quick and light on his feet decided to take part. He was away, running along the narrow footpath, far ahead of the others, just about to overtake the leader, a certain Grezzju from Mellieha. Grezzju realised he was about to be overtaken and ran the rest of the race with his arms outstretched, blocking the path and making it impossible for Giuseppi Mangion, *Il-Laġġa* to overtake him and win the race although he could quite easily have done so. Bad luck one might have thought, but not at all as all Grezzju's first prize was a white belt, whereas Giuseppi was fortunate enough to win the Banner.

Eric Brockman described the 1926 races from a spectator's point of view; "the races, in the afternoon, run over a stony, uphill stretch of the chapel road, were some of the strangest I have ever seen. The division of the entrants into their proper classes, by ages, presented much difficulty. They counted their age by tens. One oldish man could get no nearer than "five tens since the year of the great storm". Luckily the family knew the tenants well enough to hazard fair guesses in every case. They removed their sandals and ran in bare feet."[3]

2   Interviewed by author 2002
3   Eric Brockman, *Last Bastion*

SUPPER

Eric Brockman spent some time in the kitchen watching the cheerful cooks preparing supper; they cooked on a *fuklar* or "tiled stone range over charcoal" that he likened to a range he'd seen in Pompeii. The girls kept it going by fanning the vents in the front of the *fuklar* and they were able to get close enough to work the range comfortably because there were "foot shaped hollows at the base of the tiled range."

'Few soups in the world are as good as Maltese soup. None is better. … The fish I would never have recognised as the despised Lampuka. Cooked as those laughing girls had cooked it, with a sauce in which I detected, amongst many unknown flavours, capers and thyme … there were cervelli in a rich jacket of beaten eggs, the tenderest of casseroled capons, endives, stuffed paprika – all richly flavoured and cooked with butter. There were pickled tomatoes, very hot, fresh white lettuces, tender young sweet turnips, eaten as we eat radishes and something that looked like celery but had a sharp, sweet taste. Among the cheeses were small, round goat cheeses, pickled and seasoned with black pepper, called *ġbejniet* …'[1]

---

1   *Ibid*

STUFFED PEPPERS

500g minced pork
1 large onion –
peeled and finely chopped
A knob of butter and a little olive oil
1 tbs chopped rosemary
1 egg
Salt and pepper
1 thick slice Maltese bread soaked in milk
6 medium peppers

Fry the chopped onion in the butter and oil till soft. In the meantime, mash the bread in a bowl, add the meat, rosemary and seasoning, pour on the onion and mix in very well, then add the egg and beat it all very well. Wash the peppers and split them down the middle and fill the halves with the meat mixture, sprinkle with wild fennel seed and roast at gas mark 4/180ºC for about 35 – 40 minutes or till golden and sizzling.

Alternatively fill the peppers with slices of mozzarella, anchovies, chopped tomatoes, basil leaves and freshly ground pepper and then cover the peppers with a mixture of dried breadcrumbs, garlic, chopped parsley and olive oil. Roast them at gas mark 4/180ºC for about 35 – 40 minutes or till golden and sizzling

LAMPUKI IN SALSA PICCANTE

Salsa Piccante
1 small onion
2 or 3 cloves of garlic
Olive oil
2 tbs capers – roughly chopped
4 tbs stoned Maltese olives
– roughly chopped
1 tbs sugar
2 tbs very good white wine vinegar
500g tomatoes; peeled, seeded
and finely chopped
2 tbs chopped mint and parsley

Peel and finely chop the garlic and onion and fry them gently in olive oil until soft and golden. Add the capers and olives and fry for a little longer before adding a tablespoon of sugar, stir then add the vinegar. Boil briefly to evaporate then add the tomatoes and simmer for about 5 minutes. Allow it to cool and add chopped mint and parsley.

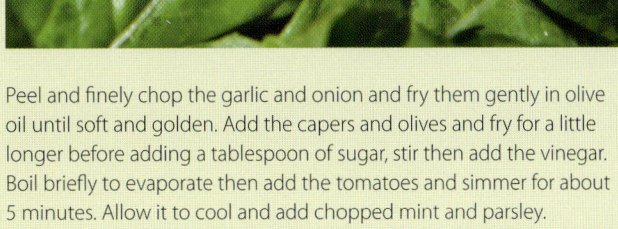

3 lampuki, filleted and skinned
Flour or semolina

Once the sauce is ready put it aside. Split the fillets down the middle and cut them in half across the middle and dip each one in the seasoned flour or semolina. Heat some olive oil in a large frying pan and fry the fillets till golden. Coat the fillets with the sauce and serve. The fish is also very good served at room temperature.

PUMPKIN SOUP

Pumpkins are at their best in autumn; the golden orange colour and flavour warm the cooler autumn evenings perfectly.

1 large onion
1 tsp sugar
1 kg orange pumpkin (*qara' ħamra*)
4 carrots
4 potatoes
500g pale yellow pumpkin (*Tork/bajda*)
4 stalks Maltese celery (*karfus*)
2 litres Vegetable stock or
water and a cube
Olive oil
Seasoning
1 heaped tsp freshly grated nutmeg

Peel and chop the onion finely and fry it in a little olive oil with the nutmeg and sugar till soft and golden. Peel both types of pumpkin, remove the seeds and cut them up, add to the onion in the pot and stir. Peel and cut up the rest of the vegetables and stir them in. Add the vegetable stock to cover, add a little water if necessary and season. Bring to the boil and simmer for about an hour or until all the vegetables are really soft. Blend until smooth or put through a vegetable mill (*pass puré*) and serve garnished as you like – perhaps with a swirl of plain yoghurt and finely chopped parsley or slivers of parmesan and black pepper or just simply a drizzle of excellent extra virgin olive oil

CHICKEN WITH SAFFRON

Saffron adds wonderful golden colour and flavour to this casseroled chicken that is perfect at this time of year. The 1850 edition of *'Il-Calendariu Tal-Bidwi'* mentions saffron in Malta in the section that lists the farmer's work for October. The calendar, published by the Società Economico-agraria, says that wild saffron *crocus longiflorus Raf* grew wild in areas like Buskett and Dingli and farmers in the surrounding area gathered the flowers to pick and dry the stigma to make saffron threads. These were used in cooking and for home made remedies. The author explains that this wild form of saffron is inferior to the cultivated *crocus sativus* and encourages the farmers to start to grow proper saffron by listing the expenses and probable sales of saffron with the conclusion that a rotolo and 6 ounces would earn Scudi 21.8.8.

2 chickens, cut up
2 medium onions – finely chopped
4 cloves garlic – crushed
Olive oil
1 large pinch saffron threads
– crushed lightly
2½ tsp ground ginger
1 flat tsp ground cinnamon
300ml white wine
300ml water or homemade chicken stock

Seasoning
2 tbs chopped parsley
The finely grated zest of 2 lemons
100g green olives – well rinsed
and soaked in water

Fry the onions and garlic in olive oil until soft and golden. Then add the saffron, ginger and cinnamon and stir in. Add the chickens and fry till well coated and just beginning to turn a pale golden colour. Take care the onions do not brown. Then pour in the wine and water or stock and bring it to the boil. Simmer very gently for about 1¼ hours or till the chickens are tender, turning the chickens every now and again. Then add the prepared lemon peel and olives and simmer for another 10 minutes before removing the chickens and serving them covered in the sauce and sprinkled with the chopped parsley.

N.B: If the sauce is too thin boil it for about 5 minutes to reduce and thicken it or stir in a teaspoonful of corn flour mixed with a 2 tablespoons cold water, and simmer till slightly thickened.

SPECIAL STUFFED CHICKEN

This recipe was inspired by Captain Harry Sullivan who is famous locally for his special roast chicken. He explained that his mother used to bone and stuff a chicken to extend it to feed her large growing family more efficiently; nowadays he prepares a chicken in this way for parties, family occasions and because it is so good. Another advantage of cooking a chicken like this is that the bones, which Captain Harry so expertly cuts out of the chicken, may be used to make broth served with some pastina or capelletti as a first course.

If you find it difficult to debone a chicken, Charles Butcher in Naxxar will bone the chicken without cutting through the skin, making it very easy to stuff and reshape – ask him to remove the leg bones too. If you use a frozen boneless chicken use about 8 large chicken wings and a gammon bone to make the stock instead of the bones from the chicken.

The cooking method is interesting as it is the only way that the bird will regain its natural shape. In the past, when few people had ovens at home the chicken would have been simmered in the stock until it was cooked completely and then browned in a little butter and olive oil in a pan before serving to make it look more appetising and taste better.

For the stock
Bones from the chicken and/or extra chicken wings and gammon bones
4 or 5 carrots
2 onions
A handful of fresh thyme leaves
4 stalks *karfus*/lovage
Seasoning

For the chicken
1 large chicken – boned
400g minced pork and veal
150g diced ham
1 very thick slice crust less Maltese bread soaked in milk
2 eggs
1 tbs fresh thyme leaves
1 tbs chopped fresh rosemary
1 small onion finely chopped
Seasoning
1 deboned quail
25g butter
75g minced chicken breast
1 tsp dried tarragon + extra
A little finely grated lemon zest
1 egg yolk

First make the stock. Put all the bones in a deep stock pot with the carrots, onions, thyme sprigs and karfus/lovage. Cover completely with water and bring it all to a rapid boil, season well and simmer for and hour or so before you start to stuff the chicken.

Put all the veal and pork, the ham, onion, rosemary, thyme, soaked bread and eggs in a bowl and mix well. In another bowl, mix together the minced chicken tarragon, lemon zest and egg yolk.

Then fry the deboned quail in hot butter with a pinch of salt and a little tarragon to brown it lightly – about a minute or two on each side. Take the quail out and pour the butter into the veal and pork mixture and mix it in.

Then, fill the quail with the minced chicken mixture and put it to one side (if there is any chicken mixture left over add it to the veal one). Put a layer of the veal and pork mixture in the bottom of the deboned chicken, lay the stuffed quail on top, cover with the rest of the veal and pork mixture,

making sure you push some of the stuffing into the legs and all the spaces inside the chicken. Close up all the gaps using toothpicks or needle and thread, and pat the chicken gently to make sure there are no big air bubbles or holes.

Then, using a sieve, remove the bones from the stock and put them to one side. Then lift up the flabby, shapeless stuffed chicken, and lower it carefully into the simmering stock and watch it firm up into a lovely round chicken again. Simmer for about 30 minutes while you preheat

the oven to Gas mark 4/180ºC. Then lift the chicken out of the stock very carefully and put it into an oven dish, drizzle with a little melted butter, salt and tarragon and pour some white wine and stock around it in the dish. Roast it for about an hour and a half till it is a deep golden brown – to check that it is cooked through, pierce it with a skewer, the juices should be clear – if pink roast for a little while longer.

The chicken is delicious both hot and cold, but slices better when it is cold or at room temperature.

ALMOND TART

This tart is surprisingly easy to make and is full of almonds – the *lewz* that are a part of the children's *Borża ta' San Martin*.

For the pastry
300g flour
50g icing sugar
150g butter

For the filling
250g castor sugar
250 g ground almonds
The zest of 2 lemons
3 eggs
100 ml cream, milk or plain yoghurt
1 large handful flaked almonds
5 tbs apricot jam or marmalade

First make the pastry. Put the flour and icing sugar into a bowl and rub in the butter. Add cold water and stir until dough is formed. Flatten this slightly with your knuckles, then fold it in half and flatten it again, do this three or four times until the dough is fairly smooth but do not overwork it as this makes it tough and difficult to use.

Leave the dough to rest for quarter of an hour as this helps it to relax and makes it easier to roll out.

In the meantime preheat the oven to gas mark 4/180ºC. Then mix all the filling ingredients till smooth and pour into the pastry lined flan dish and scatter with the flaked almonds. Cook the almond tart for about three quarters of an hour or till firm and golden. Glaze the tart as it comes out of the oven by brushing it with the sieved apricot jam or marmalade warmed with a little water. Serve warm or at room temperature.

TORTA TA' SAN MARTIN

This traditional cake is made from the same fruits and nuts typically given to children to celebrate St Martin's feast day. It is delicious served with a very cold Moscato wine.

250g blanched almonds
– roughly chopped
250g shelled walnuts – roughly chopped
150g pitted dates – roughly chopped
100g dried figs
100ml anisette
1 tbs honey
3 eggs – separated
50g butter – melted
6 tbs of flour
6 tbs of sugar + a little extra
Fennel seeds

Chop up the dried figs into rough segments and then soak them overnight in the anisette topped up with an equal amount of water and the honey.

The next day pre-heat the oven to Gas mark 4/180 C and then grease and base line a 20cm tin. Whisk up the egg-whites until they form soft peaks, and whisk in the sugar a little at a time until well mixed in, add the egg yolks, and whisk briefly, then the butter and finally fold in the flour, the chopped nuts, dates and the figs – including the soaking liquid. Pour the mixture into the tin, smooth the surface and scatter with the extra sugar and fennel seeds. Bake for 30 minutes or till golden and firm. Leave it in the tin for about ten minutes and then turn it out and serve with some good wine.

'Visiting ladies', Antoine Favray

Memories caught in paint

Paint is the medium artists have always used to capture moments in time, much as photographers use film or digital images today. Paintings that feature people celebrating Carnival, enjoying Mnarja, visiting each other or an old fashioned painted marmalade label all conjure up the sense of people enjoying themselves. The food memories evoked by these paintings are the subject of the chapters that make up this section.

'Carnival', Edward Caruana Dingli

CARNIVAL FOOD
Ikel tal-Karnival

The extravaganza of colour, noise and exuberance that is the three days of carnival thrive in an atmosphere of sheer indulgence. People focus on pleasure and this includes an abundance of all the favourite, rich foods forbidden during the forty days of lent that follow on the heels of Carnival fun. In fact the origin of the word Carnival comes from the Latin *carnem levare*, literally "to remove the meat".

Feasting before fasting is one of the more persistent themes of carnival which has taken place in Malta since the late middle ages. The most popular item on the carnival menu of the time was meat. This was because meat was forbidden food during lent and a treat at the best of times anyway in that deprived era; thus the demand for meat was great and various laws had to be passed to ensure people were not over-charged during carnival. In 1468, for example, a decree announced by the town-crier warned that during carnival-time the prices of meat were to remain as regulated by the standard official tariff.[1] People usually served meat with pasta – an early form of lasagne for example was a popular carnival meal at the time and found on the menu at the Santo Spirito hospital during Carnival time.[2] In fact lasagne is a traditional dish that is still very much part of Carnival in Naples and other parts of Italy that, like Malta, were part of the Kingdom of Two Sicilies.

1   Stanley Fiorini, 'Carnj per lu Carnivalj' in *Melita Historica*. 9 (1987)4(311-314)
2   *ibid*.

LASAGNE

In Medieval Latin *Lagana* meant a thin crepe or sheet of dough. This form of lagana resembled our modern *lasagne* but it was usually boiled till very soft or simply fried. A medieval recipe for lasagne that resembles our modern day version is found in *Liber de Coquina* (book of cooking) written in the mid-14th century by an anonymous Neapolitan. In this the cook is directed to boil the sheets of lasagne and then layer them up in a dish with ground spices and cheese.

While here in Malta, as long ago as 1519, lasagne was on the menu for carnival at Santo Spirito hospital in Rabat when the patients were served *lasagnj*, cheese, veal and wine. The document does not specify how the *lasagnj* were cooked, but it may have been somewhat similar to the Neapolitan version above, as the cheese and meat on the carnival menu seem to have been served separately to the *lasagnj*. [1]

Sometimes the Lasagne, meat and cheese were simply stirred together as they still do in Modica, Sicily

This early versions of lasagne was just the beginning of lasagne as we know it – there are now hundreds of different ways to cook lasagne apart from the best known *lasagne al forno* in which the lightly boiled lasagne are layered up with a rich ragù and white sauce before being baked. Alternatively the sheets of pasta may be filled with vegetables, fish, cheeses, even quite simply pesto and a little ricotta mixed with mozzarella. All are delicious and practical as they may be pre-prepared with great success. Nowadays commercially made pasta doesn't need to be par boiled prior to use which makes it even easier to make the usual baked lasagne – the trick is to use enough white sauce and to keep sauces on the liquid side rather than the dry side.

Carnival was a very popular festival at this time in Malta, so much so that it inspired people to adopt the word carnival as a Christian name! The Militia List of 1419-20, features the name Carnivali four times – three of the men were from Naxxar. The name Carnivali carried on being used for quite a few years and was still to be found on the Militia list as late as 1483 and 1546. [2]

Carnival continued to flourish under the rule of the knights and became so popular that when Pope Clement XIV died in September 1774 and the Bishop wanted to cancel Carnival, the then Bailiff de Rohan said, "One should not deprive the public of this fleeting recreation to which it looks forward so jealously and so avidly." [3]

1   *ibid*
2   *ibid*
3   Roderick Cavaliero, *The Last of the Crusaders*

PESTO LASAGNE

100g basil leaves
50g pine nuts
50g Parmesan cheese
4 cloves garlic
4 tbs olive oil
Approx. 12 sheets spinach lasagne
400g Maltese ricotta
250g mozzarella – cut up
2 tbs freshly grated Parmesan
Double quantity white
sauce (see page 89)
Pre heat the oven to gas mark 4/180ºC

First make the pesto by blending the basil, pine nuts, Parmesan, garlic and olive oil till smooth, adding a little water if necessary. Then grease an oblong ovenproof dish – approx. 30 x 22 x 5cm. Then make the white sauce as directed above, and pour one ladle of white sauce into the prepared dish before whisking the rest of it into the ricotta. Add the mozzarella and grated Parmesan to the ricotta and stir in well. Then start to make layers in the dish as follows; pasta – pesto – ricotta mix – pasta – pesto ricotta mix and so on till the dish is full and the ingredients used up. Then bake for 25 – 30 minutes till golden and bubbling on the surface.

Some Grand Masters introduced new ideas while allowing the older traditions to carry on. A food related carnival tradition called the Cockaigne, or *il-kukkanja* in Maltese, was introduced to Malta in 1721 by Grand Master Zondadari. Iit proved to be a very popular fixture that only came to an end when the knights left Malta. It took place on Palace Square on Carnival Monday and consisted of long beams fixed against the guardhouse that were covered in leafy branches and hung with quantities of food like baskets of fruit and eggs, great big hams, strings of plump sausages and fat, live animals, like chickens, pigs, hares and partridges. The whole food laden bower was surmounted by the figure of Fame holding the Grand Master's flag. Before the start of the game, a crowd of people gathered on the square and at a signal the participants rushed forward and climbed up, in a race to grab the food items hanging there and as soon as they had them in hand, they climbed down and were allowed to carry them off home. The contestant who reached the figure of fame and grabbed the flag first received a special largess from the Grand Master.

All dressed up for a Carnival ball in the 1920's

Another older carnival custom with a food connection is called il-*Qarċilla*.[1] This involved a prettily decorated pastry bride-doll and is played out by a man dressed up as a notary and his assistant. The carnivalesque Notary strolled down the main streets of Valletta followed by a retinue, one of which would be his assistant carrying a basket on his head containing a large pastry shaped like a bride. This attracted a crowd that followed the parade which then came to a halt; at which point the notary read out an entertaining burlesque of a marriage contract to the delight of the crowd who then fell on the pastry bride and ate it.

1   Ġ. Cassar-Pullicino, 'Antichi Cibi Maltesi' in *Melita Historica: Journal of the Malta Historical Society.* 3(1961)2(31-54)

This strange custom was described by Canon Agius de Soldanis in 1750 and translated by George Mifsud-Chircop as follows: "This game by country people takes place during Carnival, similar to that of the Gentiles .... A sweet pastry bride doll is made to the height of three or four palms, beautifully adorned with fine clothes. It is placed in a small basket and poised on the head of a masked man carrying a round cake (M. *kollura*) in his hand and accompanied by the rabble. Of these some play rustic instruments, others dance or sing; then, when they have gone round the village, they stop at street corners and it is customary for one of them to mimic the manners of a notary, reading in a public burlesque marriage contract set in Maltese rhyme, in favour of the pastry bride .... After much wandering, idle talk and nonsense characteristic of Carnival, the pastry bride is eaten and the Qarcilla comes to an end with the people getting drunk with wine."[2]

It is unclear exactly what the *kollura* or round cake that played a part in the qarcilla was; Agius' exact words were *una grande collura o cerchio di pasta pura.*[3] As the masked player carried the *kollura* in his hand, it must have been a fairly sturdy confection, yet tender enough to be called a cake. Perhaps it was made of the same ingredients as *qagħaq tal-għasel*, nowadays usually served at Christmas or *qagħaq tal-ġunġlien*.

QAGĦAQ TAL-GĦASEL

For the pastry
400g plain flour
50g butter
3 egg yolks
Anisette liqueur and/or water

Rub the butter into the pastry; add the egg yolks and anisette or water to make dough. Knead briefly and put aside for at least and hour.

For the filling
400g black treacle or golden syrup or a combination of the two
An equal volume of water
100g sugar
Grated rind of a tangerine, lemon and orange
4 tbs chopped walnuts (optional)
1 tbs chopped candied peel (optional)
1 tbs aniseeds
50g dark chocolate
75g marmalade
1 tbs mixed spice
175g semolina

Bring all the ingredients except for the semolina to the boil while stirring so that it doesn't stick and burn. Add the semolina very slowly, stirring all the time, once it has boiled, cook it for couple of minutes longer, stirring continuously. Once it has cooled, cover and refrigerate overnight.

The next day, cut the pastry into 8 pieces and roll each piece into rectangles. Scatter a working surface with semolina and roll spoonfuls of the filing – the "qastanija" – into snake shapes to fit the rectangles. If the filling is very sticky, just keep sprinkling the surface with semolina to reduce the stickiness.

Place a snake shape of filling onto each rectangle of pastry and roll it up, make a ring shape by pushing the two ends into each other and lay the ring on a baking tray well dusted with semolina, join side down. Cut little slashes gently into the pastry at intervals around the ring and open them up so that the filling shows through. Bake at gas mark 4/180ºC for about 15 minutes or until the pastry is barely touched with beige, as the dark brown of the filling peeping through the pale pastry is the traditional appearance of a well made Qagħaq tal-Għasel. They keep well in an air-tight tin.

2   George Mifsud-Chircop, *Past Carnival and New Year's Eve Drama in Malta*
3   A big ring or circle of pure pastry

QAGĦAQ TAL-ĠUNĠLIEN

These *qagħaq* are more like biscuits than the one made following the recipe above.

250g plain flour
1 tsp baking powder
100g castor sugar
100g butter
1 tsp crushed aniseeds
The grated rind and juice
of 1 small lemon
1 egg
Sesame seeds

Sieve the flour and baking powder into a big bowl, stir in the sugar and rub in the flour until the mixture resembles breadcrumbs. Stir in the peel and crushed seeds and make a well in the centre of the mixture. Then beat the egg and lemon juice together and stir it in a little at a time to make dough. Add a little water if the dough is too dry. Then knead it briefly and then break off ping pong ball sized balls of dough, roll them into thin fingers, bring the end together and seal to make rings. Put the sesame seeds into a large plate and press the rings of dough into them to coat them lightly. Cook them in the oven preheated to gas mark 5/190ºC for 15- 20 minutes or till golden. These biscuits keep well in an airtight tin.

NB: Some cooks like to lightly whisk an extra egg white and dip the uncooked dough rings into it before pressing them into the sesame seeds. It is easier for the seeds to stick to the rings in this way.

The wholly Roman Catholic Carnival festival survived the 160 years of Protestant British rule and today has evolved into a series of dances, float parades, costumes and masks. The food aspect of carnival is not as strong as it was as fasting is no longer obligatory; but as certain dishes are so delicious they remain embedded in traditional activities.

Perennial carnival favourites are usually overly sweet, rich and moreish. Pastel coloured, deliciously sweet and crunchy sugared almonds or *perlini* are typical and very much part of carnival; both for the pleasure that lies in eating them, as well as their potential for fun. Adrian Mercieca recalls perlini being made in "Strada Levante" in Valletta where a mechanical mixer that somewhat resembled a cement mixer turned and turned, rolling the almonds, sugar and food colouring around each other until the almonds were coated in the sugar. He remembers a bizarre carnival game that revellers particularly relished and which involved hundreds of the perlini everyone loved crunching; the participants dressed up as clowns, hired *karrozzini* (carriages) and went for a drive in them. Fooling around as only clowns can, they attracted the attention of the crowd which was rewarded with a hail of perlini. This mock battle was a strange old carnival tradition that could have been painful, so the clowns carried umbrellas to fend off the flying perlini and everyone had a good laugh. Herbert Ganado "enjoyed it best when merry makers in fancy dress walked past and pelted each other with sugared almonds. Couples in fancy dress rode in open acrriages, carried large boxes of sugared almonds and tossed handfuls to the hordes of children who milled around shouting, "Give us perlini! Throw us some perlini!"[1]

The splendid *Prinjulata* carnival cake full of butter, sugar, nuts and bright colours is the epitome of carnival food; it is rich and extravagant and includes all the goodies banned during lent. Perhaps less widespread but no less delicious are the deep fried pastry ribbons dripping in honey and bursts of colour in the form of hundreds and thousands called *Xkunvat* – my personal favourites – and very similar to the carnival fritters called *ciaccere, cenci, frappe, bugie* that are found all over Italy.

Great Aunt Josephine in Carnival Costume

1   Herbert Ganado/Michael Refalo, *My Century (Rajt Malta Tinbidel)*, Vol. 1

PRINJOLATA

This recipe for a prinjolata is fairly standard; of course there are other versions. Families treasure their own special prinjolata recipe, possibly handed down through carnival-loving generations, but variations are few and consist of little differences like layering up the sponge fingers instead of crushing them and stirring them in, or using only pine nuts in the "cake" instead of a mixture of almonds and pine nuts and other little changes. The recipe below makes a small prinjulata but as it is so stunningly rich a small piece goes a very long way.

The Cake
200g butter
250g icing sugar or castor sugar
The inside of 1 vanilla pod
or ½ a tsp essence
1 tbs milk
4 packets Pavesini or 30 sponge fingers
50g glace cherries, chopped – optional
75g pine nuts
75g flaked almonds

Italian Meringue
60g/2½oz sugar
5 tsp water
1 free-range egg white

Icing and Decoration
400g icing sugar
1 large egg white
Food colouring
100g black chocolate – melted
100g pine nuts – toasted

Make the cake: Beat the butter and icing sugar or sugar together till very white and fluffy. In the meantime, lightly roast the nuts and then chop them up roughly. Then crush the pavesini or sponge fingers with your fingers till they resemble very rough breadcrumbs. Then fold the Italian meringue (see below) into the butter cream followed by the nuts and biscuits, and form a sandcastle shape on a plate, cover with icing and decorate as directed below:

Make the Italian meringue: Put the sugar and water into a pan and dissolve over a low heat, then boil until the syrup reaches 110°C on a sugar thermometer. At this stage, put the egg whites in a bowl and whisk until firm peaks form. As soon as the sugar reaches 115C, remove the pan from the heat. Immediately resume whisking the egg whites and with the beater at its lowest speed, pour in the melted sugar, in a slow stream, until it is all absorbed. Then carry on beating until the meringue is tepid.

To Ice and decorate the cake: Put the egg whites into a bowl and whisk lightly just till it begins to foam a little, then start adding the icing sugar a little at a time, whisking well in between each addition until it thickens nicely. Then spread it carefully over the half ready prinjulata and decorate it by drizzling with colour, sticking the nuts all over the side and then dribble over melted chocolate.

NB: Some cooks stir chopped candied cherries into the cake mixture and stick some whole candied cherries onto the sides of the cake as part of the decoration.

XKUNVAT

These are very quick to make, the quantity below is enough for a plateful of xkunvat to serve about 6. The recipe doubles easily, but if you plan to cook enough for a big party, then make the pastry in two or three batches to ensure success and ease.

200g flour
25g butter
1 egg yolk
1 heaped tbs sugar
Anisette
Oil for deep frying
Honey or golden syrup
Coloured sugar or hundreds
and thousands

Rub the butter into the flour, stir in the egg yolk and enough Anisette to make dough, knead it briefly and allow it to rest for 20 minutes. Roll it out very thinly and cut it into strips with a pastry wheel. Roll up the strips and drop them into the boiling oil so that they'll take on the traditional twisted shape as they cook. Remove them once they are golden and drain them on paper to remove excess oil. Take care they do not burn. When they cool pile them up on a plate and drizzle over some honey or golden syrup and scatter with hundreds and thousands.

To convert these into Italian style fritters replace the anisette with grappa and cut them into squares or oblongs instead of strips. Then cut a slit down the length of each, gently pull one end through the slit and fry as above. Then drain them on kitchen paper and serve them dusted with icing sugar.

GIOVEDI GRASSO OR FAT THURSDAY LUNCH

The Carnival weekend commences with a big lunch on *Giovedi Grasso* or Fat Thursday, the Thursday that starts everything off. Herbert Ganado described the special family lunch served on "Fat Thurday" at his grandparent's house held to celebrate the first day of carnival. "He (his grandfather) adored Carnival and from *Jeudi Gras* onwards celebrated the occasion with a big lunch, told us funny stories, joked and made merry. He poured us a little wine in the beautiful, large, crystal glasses that Granny had for everyday use, and which she would quickly drown in water and say, "Careful, or the children will get drunk." *Jeudi Gras* lunch started off with baked macaroni and, as Grandfather caught sight of the glorious and triumphal entry of a dish of Maltese baked macaroni, he would smile broadly and stretch out his hand to get at one, two or even three crisply baked macaroni tips. ... Roast cockerel and a dish of baked potatoes followed, and of course the round of fried potatoes we loved so much. Finally to top the meal, *xkunvat* dripping in honey, a present from a Mellieha client that we enjoyed and ate with much licking of fingers. I adored those large round, fried potatoes and I have never tasted any as delicious since then." [1]

MQARRUN IL-FORN

The word *mqarrun* is a corruption of the Italian macaroni and refers to a specific sort of locally made pasta; an approximately 40 cm long tube of *pasta asciutta*. *Mqarrun* was commonly available until relatively recently and it was bought by weight from grocers, usually for the sole purpose of making *mqarrun il-forn* or *timpana*. Before cooking, the pasta tubes would be broken up into little pieces slightly longer than the penne we use nowadays – or as the author E.L.V. of *Ctieb Tal Chcina* (1908) recommends; "*ghalli ratal imkarrun imchisser ccheichen*". The manual also instructs cooks to send the prepared dish to the baker's oven and to see that it is baked for an hour. This is an indication that few households had ovens in 1908; an alternative method of cooking this dish would be to steam it in a well greased basin, it is then called *forma tal-mqarrun*.

Mqarrun was a Sunday or festive dish, served before the main course in the past when people were more active and ate much more. Nowadays it makes a meal in itself and is excellent in winter, followed by a fresh green salad and some fruit or a light dessert. *Mqarrun* is very practical; it may be prepared before hand and it freezes well.

Mqarrun is simple to prepare; a rich Bolognese sauce is stirred into some boiled pasta, grated cheese and eggs are stirred in along with a little milk and it is baked in the oven till firm and crisp on top.

Adrian Mercieca recalls that a Sunday Special version of *mqarrun* included cubes of fried *brunġiel* (aubergine), boiled eggs, poached brain and fried liver and was about 8-10 cm high and brought to table turned out onto a serving dish.

1   Herbert Ganado/Michael Refalo, *My Century (Rajt Malta Tinbidel)*, Vol. 1

The first step is to make some Bolognese sauce as follows. I have specified minced beef in the list of ingredients, but a mixture of pork and beef is popular as is the addition of a little bacon.

One finely chopped onion
2 or 3 crushed cloves of garlic (optional)
3 tbs olive oil
500g minced beef
2 bay leaves
One sprig finely chopped rosemary
100ml red wine
1½ kg ripe tomato, peeled, seeded and chopped or 750ml tomato sauce

First, prepare the sauce by frying the onion and garlic in the oil until softened and golden. Then stir in the minced meat and brown it, add the herbs and wine, and simmer until the wine is slightly reduced. Then add the tomatoes or sauce, bring it to the boil, turn it down and leave it to simmer very gently for about an hour. (This may be made up to a couple of days beforehand and refrigerated.

N.B. Use fresh tomatoes in summer; in winter use bottled ones as the taste of winter tomatoes is insipid and they contain little but water.

Once the sauce is ready preheat the oven to gas mark 5/190ºC

500g penne, penne rigati or tortiglinoi
150g grated Parmesan, Grana Padana or Kefalatori cheese
100ml milk
5 eggs
A little olive oil

Bring a large pot of water to a rolling boil, add a tablespoon sea salt and then the pasta. Boil until *al dente* then drain and put back into the pot. Add the Bolognese sauce, the milk cheese and eggs and stir well till everything is well amalgamated. Pour into an oiled oven proof dish and bake in the preheated oven for approximately 45 minutes or until firm and a dark golden colour.

In those days food was always taken to table on a serving dish. One elderly lady I spoke to remembered her mother firing a cook who sent food to table in a "cooking vessel". When asked to remember to turn the food out onto a serving dish next time, the cook exclaimed *U mhux xorta? (isn't it the same?)*; horrified, her mother felt the cook was "untrainable" and asked her to leave. In fact the *Ctieb Tal Chcina*, a cookery book published in 1908, so current at the time, gives instructions for this very thing; *Jech trida fil meida min ghair il forma (chif hu xierak) biex tinkalghalech, roxx il forma bis-smid uara li tcun dlicta bil butir. Biex tin-kalghalec bil heffa, dauuar sicchina bein il ghagin u il forma, akliba geuua id-dixx li ghandu jigi fil meida, tigha daktein fuk il kieh – arfa il forma bil mod u tcun lesta."[1]

ROAST CHICKEN, CAPON OR COCKREL

There is something special about roast chicken. It is one of the easiest and most successful things to cook and yet creates much more of a special meal feel than other chicken dishes; possibly because of the delicious smell of the roasting bird, the ceremonial carving and serving it at table, the fun of choosing the leg, breast or wing, arguing over who gets the oyster and extra bits of crunchy skin, disdaining the parson's nose and so on.

It is easy to add different flavours to roast chicken. In winter there is nothing nicer than wrapping the legs in slices of bacon or Parma ham and stuffing a few slices into the cavity along with lots of fried mushrooms, garlic and rosemary, in summer lots of chopped tarragon and 2 or 3 lemons squeezed over the chicken and stuffed into the cavity with more tarragon and lots of garlic make a chicken taste very summery, especially served with some *salsa verde*, while in autumn just rub a chicken with a mixture of honey and grainy mustard before roasting it or coat it in some Seville orange marmalade and it will be delicious.

A "French Roast" simply means roasting the bird breast side down for the first half of the cooking time, then turning it over for the second half; this is intended to ensure much juicier and more tender breast meat but the method tends to flatten the chicken a bit.

---

1   If you wish this to be on the table out of the cooking dish (as it should be); to turn it out easily dust it with semolina once you have buttered it. To turn it out quickly, run a knife in between the pastry and dish, turn it over onto the dish that is to be sent to table, and tap it twice on the bottom – lift the cooking dish carefully and it will be ready.

ROAST CHICKEN WITH BASIL AND ORANGE

This is a spring special that includes the last of winter Maltese oranges and early spring basil, perfect for Giovedi Grasso. Use the best chicken you can find; both free-range and corn-fed chickens are available at good butchers and they are better than the frozen variety.

1 chicken – about 1.75 or 2 kg
2 big or 3 small Maltese oranges – sliced up thinly
3 or 4 big handfuls fresh basil – very roughly chopped up
1 tbs dried tarragon
25g butter – melted
Salt
White wine
Chicken stock

Wash and pat the chicken dry. Then carefully loosen some of the breast skin around the breast meat near the wings and legs and slide in some orange slices and basil leaves. Then push the rest (except for about a tablespoon of chopped basil) into the cavity and put the bird into a roasting dish.

Stir the tablespoon of basil and tarragon into the melted butter and pour it carefully over the chicken. Scatter with salt, pour some white wine and chicken stock around the bird to about 2.5cm depth and roast in the oven preheated to gas mark 5/190ºC for about an hour, then turn the heat down to gas mark 3 ½ /175ºC and roast for another hour.

To Serve the Chicken
The chicken may be served immediately carved up and served with the juices from the roasting pan with some vegetables. However, it tastes so much better with a little gravy and it only takes a few minutes to make it.
Pan juices
About a glass of wine (add a tot of brandy on special occasions)
Seasoning
200ml Chicken stock
Corn flour or beurre manie
Cream or thick Greek style yoghurt (optional)

Using oven gloves, tilt the roasting pan very slowly to pour off any fat into a bowl – save this delicious dripping and use it on toast or to roast potatoes. Then put the roasting pan with juices on a medium heat and bring it to a simmer, stirring and scraping at any burnt bits, then add the wine (or brandy) and stir, then add the chicken stock and simmer for a minute or two. Taste and season well. Then either make the beurre manie by rubbing an equal amount of butter and flour together (you will need apprx. 25g of each) or mix 1 heaped teaspoon of corn flour with enough cold water to make a milky liquidy paste and stir either one of them into the pan juices. Once it has all dissolved, bring to a rolling boil till it thickens slightly, then add the cream or yoghurt and bring to boiling point and remove from heat. Pour into a bowl and serve with the chicken.

ROAST POTATOES

Maltese style roast potatoes are a mix of thickly sliced potatoes and onions baked in a hot oven with water, olive oil, salt, black pepper and some fennel seeds. These taste best when cooked in a baker's oven although they are very good cooked in a domestic oven.

CRISPS

Crisps or what Herbert Ganado called "the round of fried potatoes we loved so much" are always very popular so cook far more than you think you will need. They are very easy to make and taste far better than commercial ones. Once they are cooked, sprinkle them with whatever flavour you choose, try finely chopped sage, rosemary, black pepper, paprika, whatever appeals to you – do not forget a light sprinkling of salt. The crisps will be delicious and completely additive free.

To make them, simply peel some potatoes slice them very thinly, rinse them well and then dry them carefully. Deep fry the slices in hot oil, drain them on kitchen roll and sprinkle them with salt and any other flavours you like, see above.

GRILLED POTATOES

These potatoes are lovely with roast chicken – serve them as an alternative to the more usual roast potatoes.

8 medium potatoes
Olive oil, Herbs & Salt

Wash and scrub the potatoes and boil them till tender in salted water – approximately 40 minutes. In the meantime chop up the herbs and stir them into the olive oil. When the potatoes are ready, split them in half and lay them on a grill pan (lined with foil to avoid mess) and brush them with the herby olive oil and sprinkle lightly with salt. Put them under the grill turned up to high and grill till golden and crisp – this may take up to 15 minutes or more – the heat under grills varies tremendously. Then serve while hot with roast chicken, or anything else.

SWEET LASAGNE MILLE FOGLIE

To round off the meal either serve xkunvat (page 81) or serve this quick to make dessert inspired by the Medieval form of lasagne which were sometimes fried. Simply par boil some lasagne for a minute or two, drain them well and pat them dry. Then cut them across into four oblongs and fry them – either shallow or deep fried is fine (this is a very relaxed recipe) and drain them well on some kitchen paper.

N.B. They may be any size – simply trim or cut the sheets accordingly.
Then either:
Dust them generously with icing sugar and a pinch of cinnamon, heap them up on a plate and serve them.
Or:
Layer them up like a sweet lasagne, filling them with mascarpone flavoured generously with grated orange peel, cointreau, icing sugar and grated chocolate and serve the sweet lasagne mille foglie drizzled with melted chocolate and slices of fresh Maltese oranges

N.B. when oranges are not in season, flavour the mascarpone cream with grated lemon peel or cinnamon and replace the slices of fresh orange with strawberries or other seasonal fruit.

LENTEN FOOD

Lent, slinking in through the door after gaudy, frivolous Carnival and its delicious excesses, starts the quaresima with the sobering reminder of Ash Wednesday. However, a forehead dusted with grey ash from obligatory mass need not influence cooks to turn out dull, dry meals. Simply use seasonal and sanctioned ingredients with verve and Lent might become a forbidden pleasure.

A look through the Inquisitor's archives reveals that people have always found it very difficult to stick to the rigorous rules of denial when it comes to food and they fiddled around with the rules to try and find, or create, loopholes. In 1822 Gustav Parthey recorded a conversation with an old Maltese man at dinner who nostalgically recalled the clever cooks of the knights and how good they were at "disguising meat so that it could be served during lent. This they very often did with mixing it and covering it with fish. Besides fish, amphibians like frogs and turtles as well as all sorts of sea birds could be eaten during lent, because all these animals lived in the water."[1]

Many vegetables come into season or are at their best during Lent and although there are only two strict fasting days left – Ash Wednesday and Good Friday, religious strictures have coloured traditional recipes using these ingredients which most people still serve today. Broad beans, peas, artichokes, endive, spinach, cauliflower feature in many meals, as do ricotta, gbejniet, eggs and fish, and they all come together to form a spectrum of healthy and traditional Lenten meals.

ASH WEDNESDAY

On Ash Wednesday (the first day of lent) my mother used to serve a dish my father called XIHA for lunch; it is a satisfying and warming dish, especially on a cold day when there's been no nibbling in between meals.

---

1   Thomas Freller, *Malta and the Grand Tour*

XIĦA

500g penne
500g ricotta
150g grated parmesan
250g shelled peas
250g podded broad beans
5 eggs
30g butter
30g plain flour
½ a tsp grated nutmeg
300ml milk
Seasoning
1tbs finely chopped parsley

Boil the penne till *al dente* together with the peas and broad beans. Drain the pasta when it is ready. In the mean time make the white sauce: Melt the butter and flour together then bubble briefly. Remove from the heat and whisk in the milk using a hand held balloon whisk, return to the heat and stir with the whisk until it thickens. Remove from the heat and season the sauce with the nutmeg, parsley, salt and pepper. Beat the ricotta, eggs and grated cheese together, stir in the white sauce and add it to the boiled penne and vegetables. Pour it into a well greased oven dish and bake at gas mark 5/ 190ºC for about three quarters of an hour to an hour or till golden and firm to the touch. Serve hot with additional grated cheese.
(Enough for 6 people)

"SOPPA TAL-ARMLA" OR WIDOW'S SOUP

The vegetables used in this soup are all shades of green and white which gives it a characteristically pale appearance. It is so called because in the past the vegetables used were relatively inexpensive and the eggs and gbejniet added at the end were probably produced by widows themselves.

1 large or 2 onion, finely chopped
5 sticks of celery, roughly chopped
Olive oil
6 peeled and chopped potatoes
200g podded broad beans
200g shelled peas
200g cauliflower florets
The pale inner leaves of an endive
500g spinach leaves, washed and roughly chopped
2 litres water or vegetable stock
1 egg, 1 gbejna and approx. 50g ricotta per person

Fry the onion and celery gently in olive oil till golden and tender. Add the rest of the prepared vegetables and stir them around, allow them to cook briefly then and add the water or vegetable stock, season and simmer for about an hour. Once the soup is cooked remove it from the heat and add an *egg per person* into the soup and poach briefly. Serve and add a fresh *ġbejna* and a little ricotta to each bowl of soup.

98

A Maltese artichoke

ARTICHOKE HEARTS

Vegetable salads and stews are popular in Lent; they are both warming and a healthy alternative to protein rich meals.

Artichokes are a very popular vegetable at this time of year and always have been. So much so that Jean Quintin d'Autun remarked on it while he was here in 1536 and wrote," The people also feed on other thistles; not those which we, along with the Italians eat with so much relish (although they have a great abundance also of these) but these are much more sour." He meant the "wild artichoke" or *cynara cardunculus (qaqoċċ tax-xewk)* which grow on fierce looking bushes of spiny leaves and come into season late in spring, towards the end of the cultivated artichoke season.

They are edible; I have cooked and eaten them. They must be picked when young and tender using thick protective gloves. They can't really be eaten leaf-by-leaf as the cultivated artichoke is, but if you carefully cut away all the spikes and sharp leaves to make a wild artichoke heart, and then stew them gently in olive oil, garlic and herbs with a little water or white wine, then they are not sour and really very good. The Ancient Romans appreciated the taste of wild artichokes so much so that Pliny the Elder commented that "even the monstrosities of the earth are turned to purposes of gluttony" and adds sarcastically that by preserving them in vinegar and honey we need not let a day go by without having thistles on the table."

What is interesting to note is that by 1536, not all that long after the first proper artichokes the French and Italians ate "with so much relish" were cultivated, they were to be found growing in Malta in "a great abundance" and the Maltese word for artichoke is *qaqoċċ* – corresponding to *cacocciu* or *cacuocciula* in Sicilian dialect. These two facts indicate just how close Malta and Sicily were in the days before the Knights

Local artichokes are sown in August. The traditional method is unusual in that the farmer needs the previous year's plants rather than seeds. The old and shriveled artichoke roots, stored from the previous year's crop are cut up, soaked in water and then planted out. They must be irrigated regularly until autumn when the rains start to water the crop. Artichokes are harvested in December at the very earliest, but the plants continue to flourish and produce artichokes throughout spring.

Make the artichokes into hearts by cutting away the tough inedible outside leaves and stringy parts but leave a couple of centimetres of stalk on the artichoke and peel it to reveal the tender inner part. Then cut off the tops of the leaves that are left, and remove the choke with a strong teaspoon. Once the hearts are ready, rub them with the cut side of a lemon as quickly as possible and then put them in a bowl full of acidulated water (water, lemon and parsley stalks) to prevent them discolouring.

TO FREEZE: Blanch the prepared hearts in boiling water with a couple of lemons (used to make the hearts) for 5 minutes, then drop them in iced water, drain and open freeze them on trays. Once they are frozen solid, pack them into freezer bags or boxes and store them for up to nine months.

RAW ARTICHOKE HEART SALAD

Slice the hearts thinly from top to bottom and toss them in lemon juice to prevent discolouration. Then marinate them in olive oil beaten with lemon zest, finely chopped chilli pepper (seeds removed) and thyme leaves for at least half an hour, longer if possible. Then sprinkle them with a tiny amount of finely chopped parsley and serve on a bed of rocket and lettuce leaves. Top with parmesan shaving, a last drizzle of olive oil and a grinding of pepper and serve with toasted Maltese bread.

STUFFED ARTICHOKE HEART SALAD

8 fresh artichokes
3 or 4 lemons

Make the artichokes into hearts by cutting away the tough inedible outside leaves and stringy parts but leave a couple of centimetres of stalk on the artichoke and peel it to reveal the tender inner part. Then cut off the tops of the leaves that are left, and remove the choke with a strong teaspoon. Rub them well with the cut side of a lemon and put them in acidulated water (water and lemon) to prevent them discolouring.

The ingredients for the stuffing are:
8 thick slices Maltese bread, crumbled
1 very finely chopped onion
2 crushed cloves of garlic
2 tbs each mint and parsley
2 tbs chopped capers
2 tbs chopped olives
2 tbs olive oil

Make stuffing by mixing the ingredients together. Push it into the cavities of the raw hearts. Turn the hearts head down and put them into a saucepan, pour in about 4cm of water and cut up one of the squeezed out lemon halves and put the pieces around the artichokes. Pour a good bit of olive oil over everything add some salt and pepper, bring the whole lot to the boil, then lower the heat so that everything cooks at a very gentle simmer for at least 40 minutes. Pierce one carefully with a toothpick to check they are soft and cooked through.

Serve warm and cut in half with a rocket and lettuce salad and balsamic and olive oil dressing.

STUFFED ARTICHOKES

4 large artichokes

For the stuffing
A big chunk of fresh Maltese bread
1 tbs vinegar
Water
2 or 3 crushed garlic cloves
3 tbs chopped parsley
4 chopped anchovy fillets (optional)
1 tbs chopped capers
1 tbs chopped olives
4 tbs olive oil
Freshly ground pepper and salt

Cut the crust off the bread and put it in the vinegar and a little water for a few minutes then stir in the rest of the ingredients and put to one side while you wash the artichokes. Wash the artichokes well, trim away any smaller leaves and cut off the stalk, then holding the bottom firmly in your hand hit it against the sink or other firm surface and the leaves will open up slightly. Make a hollow in the centre, remove the choke with a long handled teaspoon, fill with the stuffing and then gently close the artichoke. Stand the stuffed artichokes in a saucepan, and fill with water till half way up the artichokes, drizzle with olive oil and salt and bring to the boil with a couple of lemon wedges and bay leaves till tender and a leaf comes away easily. The artichokes will take about an hour to cook till tender, but start checking after 45 minutes as they may fall apart if overcooked.

N.B. Some cooks prefer to push a little stuffing in between the leaves so that the diner will get a bit of stuffing on each bite. This makes a delicious alternative to the method above that takes a little patience but is worth the bother. Cook in the same way as the recipe above but for a slightly shorter time.

GOOD FRIDAY

KARAMELLI TAL-ḤARRUB

Karamelli tal-Ḥarrub are the only sweets people are traditionally allowed to eat on the feast of Our Lady of Sorrows and Good Friday. These are sold during processions or when people visit seven churches, either on Thursday evening or on Friday morning. One method of making these little sweets is to boil down some carob syrup till it reaches the hard crack stage and then pour the mixture onto an oiled surface and mark it into little squares. Allow it to cool before cutting it up into sweets and wrap each one in greaseproof paper.

A Sicilian version of *Caramelle di Carrube* calls for equal amounts of carob pods and honey to be boiled together until everything is caramelised. The mixture is then poured onto an oiled surface, marked into little squares and allowed to cool before being cut up into sweets.

To make the syrup Take a kilo of carob pods and roast them in a single layer on an oven tray at gas mark 5/190ºC for 10 minutes. Break them into small bits and soak them overnight in 2 litres of water. Boil the carob pods in their soaking water for five minutes then simmer them for half an hour. Strain the water into a clean saucepan, pressing down on the pods to extract the maximum flavour. Add a kilo of sugar, dissolve it over a low heat and once the sugar is completely dissolved, turn up the heat and boil it for at least half an hour or till it is as thick as you like. Add a dash of whisky (optional). Pour it into sterilised bottles and seal.

SNAILS FOR LUNCH

Most people in Malta like to eat ricotta ravioli with tomato sauce on Good Friday but a more unusual and popular traditional Good Friday meal is boiled snails. Some planning is required for this as you must first starve the snails for about a month. If cooking snails in Summer, cook them immediately since they will be starved anyway due to the arid Summer environment. Rinse them a couple of times in salted water. After this, boil them for 15 to 20 minutes before serving them with "arioli" made as follows:
Pound softened Maltese galletti with basil, mint, parsley, garlic, capers, olives and anchovy fillets and then dilute the mixture with oil and mix all the ingredients together, adding more olive oil if needed, then season and serve with the boiled snails.

HOT CROSS BUNS

Hot cross buns are an Easter tradition we have adopted from the British. They are traditionally served on Good Friday and make the perfect breakfast, especially if you eat at least two, as Good Friday is one of the few fasting days left on the Roman Catholic calendar. The first time I made hot cross buns (about thirty five years ago) they were like little bullets, but my family was game and bit into them anyway – a Lenten sacrifice? The hot cross buns have improved since then and work every time.

N.B. you will need a small piece of short crust pastry to make crosses on the little buns.

500g plain flour
A pinch of salt
2 tsp sugar
1 sachet instant yeast
3 tbs olive oil
Approx. 350ml warm water

Mound the dry ingredients on a wooden table, make a hollow in the middle and pour in the water. Start to mix it all together, adding flour into the water from the outside of the mound until you have pliable dough. Add more flour or water as necessary, but the dough should be slightly sticky as it will rise better.

Start to knead gently and once the dough is smooth add the following ingredients to the dough:
200g sultanas
100g brown sugar
2 or 3 tsp mixed spice
2 tbs candied peel
and carry on kneading for about 10 minutes.

Leave it to rise for about an hour and a half or until it has doubled in size. Then flatten it gently and cut it into pieces of equal sizes. This is up to the individual: some like them big; others small. Roll each one until smooth and round, place on an oiled baking tray.

Cut the short crust pastry into strips and lay them gently onto the buns. Leave them to rise for about ¾ of an hour, then put them into a hot oven, gas mark 8 /220ºC and bake for about 15 minutes. Test them to check they are cooked through by tapping the base of the buns. They should sound hollow.

While they are cooking, melt 25g sugar in 25ml boiling water and brush the hot cross buns with this as soon as you take them out of the oven and put them on a cooling rack.

FIGOLLI

These iced pastries, made in a variety of figurative shapes, are given as gifts on Easter Sunday. The word *figolla* **is a corruption of the Sicilian/ Italian** *figura* **or** *figurella* **(which means 'figure'), as the liquid consonants are frequently interchanged in Maltese. Figolli are made of pastry filled with an almond mixture. The whole is then iced to create a picture.**

To make the pastry, you will need
250g of castor sugar
750g of flour
350g of butter
The yolks of 4 eggs

Rub the butter into the flour and sugar, make a hollow in the centre and put the yolks into it. Mix until you have smooth dough, adding a dash of water or Martini Extra Dry if it is too dry. Put the dough to one side while you make the almond filling, for which you will need:
600g of almonds (finely ground)
600g of castor sugar
The grated rind of 2 lemons
4 egg-whites

Stir together the dry ingredients and then add the egg-whites. Carry on stirring until you have a fairly dry paste. Roll out the pastry and cut it using a commercial cutter in a traditional shape. You will need two pieces of the same shape for each figolla. Spread one piece fairly thickly with the almond paste, leaving a free space all round for sealing. Moisten this filling-free edge, place the identical piece on top, and seal all round by pressing with your fingers. Bake them at gas mark 5/190ºC for 30 minutes, or until they are golden-brown. Place them on a rack to cool. Ice and decorate them with little silver balls and a small chocolate egg pressed into the centre.

A coffee grinder

COFFEE AND REBELLION
Il-Kafé u r-Rewwixta

The original recipe for Maltese coffee lies in one of the very first books ever published on the subject of coffee. It was called *Virtu del Kafe* and was written by Domenico Magri in 1665. In fact Giovanni Bonello[1] records that Magri claims his expertise on the subject of coffee came from "diligent intercourse with 'those Turks, most skilful makers of this concoction.'

Magri discusses coffee both as a drink and health tonic. He wrote that among its many other virtues, it quells sexual desire, reduces stomach cramps associated with menstruation and soothes those who suffer from haemorrhoids. He recognised that coffee was a stimulant and advised students to drink it as well as those who feel sleepy after supper so that "the heaviness of sleep will disappear."

Naturally, one of the first books about coffee is bound to contain a recipe and Magri explains that the ground coffee should be boiled and then allowed to settle for as long as it takes to say the creed – *per lo spazio di un credo*. He further recommends that some cloves should be ground up and boiled with the coffee and that it should be sweetened with sugar.

MAKING MALTESE COFFEE

Magri's instructions written in 1665 describe the steps still followed to prepare traditional Maltese coffee today – it is very interesting as the method is very similar to Turkish coffee – a legacy from those first cups of coffee prepared by Turkish slaves and prisoners perhaps.

In the past, green coffee beans were first roasted as needed in an *inkaljatur*, a metal, cylinder shaped coffee roaster with a handle that sat on a stand that stood over a fire. The handle was rotated to turn the cylinder and the coffee beans inside it were slowly rolled around and roasted over

---

1   Giovanni Bonello, *Deceptions and Perceptions*, 2000, Patrimonju Publishing

106

the fire, filling the whole house with the most delicious smell of coffee. The beans were then ground up and boiled in a *stanjata* (a tin coffee pot- often enamelled) as follows: first fill the pot with water, bring it to the boil, remove from the heat and stir in ground coffee to taste. Then put it back on the fire and let it all come to the boil again – carefully watching the pot to see that it doesn't boil over which it tends to do very quickly. Then remove it from the heat and leave the coffee grounds to settle before serving the coffee. The coffee is usually flavoured with some cloves and aniseeds by grinding the spices along with the coffee beans.

The first recorded reference to coffee drinking in Malta is found in the Archives of the Inquisition in Malta. In 1633 a Muslim slave was taken before the Inquisitor Martino Alfieri for, among other things, frequenting a spice shop in Birgu where Muslims went to enjoy the drink popularly known as coffee. This was probably considered an offence because coffee was still frowned on by many priests as it was thought of as "Muslim wine" or "The devil's brew", although some years earlier the Pope's advisors had tried to force Pope Clement VIII to ban coffee as a "bitter invention of Satan". Luckily the wise Pope tasted coffee first, found it delicious and stumped the anti-coffee brigade by baptising it and declaring that as "This Satan's drink is so delicious…it would be a pity to let the infidels have exclusive use of it. We shall fool Satan by baptising it."

Papal approval or not, slaves carried on roasting and brewing coffee in the *Bagno degli Schiavi* or slaves prison in Valletta and this aromatic habit of theirs gave rise to a curious phenomenon; that of knights sneaking into the Slave Prison to partake of the Turkish slaves' exotic brew. This strange sight was remarked upon by Gustav Sommerfeldt in 1663 who wrote that Turkish prisoners earned "money by preparing coffee, a powder resembling snuff tobacco, with water and sugar." The knights and upper class Maltese liked the drink so much that they soon started roasting, grinding and brewing the beans at home as it was much easier than going to the prison. This gave rise to a demand for silver coffee pots which was quickly fulfilled by Maltese silversmiths and so the silver Maltese coffee pot was born which soon became what it was to remain, a much desired possession.

Banking on the popularity of this and other new beverages like chocolate, some enterprising people soon opened cafes in Valletta. One of the earliest indications of this commerce was in 1663 when Albert Jouvin de Rochetfort visited Malta and wrote that in Valletta there are "some Greeks who sell sorbet, coffee and chocolate which are sorts of liquors hot, or alternatively with ice".

CONSPIRACY

The most dramatic historical event with a coffee connection in Malta is linked to one of the few rebellions in our history; the Great Slaves Conspiracy of

The coffee shop owner stood before the Grand Master and 'declared every particular relative to the conspiracy'. From a set of original coloured illustrations at the Inquisitors Palace, Vittoriosa

1749. Joseph Cohen, a baptised Jew who owned a coffee shop in Valletta, overheard slaves plotting to kill the Grand Master and take over Valletta while sipping coffee in his cafe. Louis de Boisgelin describes the foiled coup perfectly, "These two men usually met in a coffee-house solely resorted to by the slaves. It was kept by a Jew, who had a wife and child; he himself was a new convert, and was not only acquainted with the conspiracy, but was to act a principal part upon the occasion.

"The negro and the Persian, in one of their meetings at this coffee-house, became heated by the fumes of tobacco, and the spirituous liquors which they had taken too freely: they began to dispute most violently, and in the heat of argument some imprudent expressions escaped them, which were overheard by the Jew's wife, and gave her the greatest uneasiness.

"From words the negro and Persian proceeded to blows; and the former was so carried away by passion, that he drew his stilletto, and attempted to stab his adversary, who however made his retreat unhurt. Terrified at the danger he had escaped, and reflecting upon the still greater which threatened him, the Persian did not lose a moment, but flew to the commander de Vignier, who was commandant of the Grand Master's guards, and throwing himself at his feet implored his protection, and declared all he knew of the conspiracy. His officer received him well, put a variety of questions to him, and, after listening attentively to his answers, dressed himself hastily and repaired to the grand-master, accompanied by the Persian.

"In the meantime the Jew reproached the negro in the bitterest terms for his violent conduct, which had exposed them all to the most imminent danger; but he received no other answer than threats and curses. The moment the negro quitted the coffee-house, the Jew's wife, terrified at all that had passed, entreated her husband to go without loss of time, and reveal the whole affair to the grand-master himself. He accordingly set out immediately for the palace, and appearing alone before Pinto, fell on his

knees, and declared every particular relative to the conspiracy. At the same moment arrived the commander de Vignier with the Persian, who, being confronted with the Jew, confirmed the truth of what he had advanced. The grand-master was convinced of the reality of the plot, and orders were given to apprehend the negro."

As a result some 150 slaves were arrested, the planned uprising failed and Mr Cohen was given the lease of his house and some 300 scudi as a reward. The moral of the tale; when gossiping over a quick coffee – whisper.

Patrick Brydone, a Scotsman who visited Malta in 1770, twenty one years later reported that, "This day (the 6th of June) is held as a thanksgiving for their deliverance from a terrible conspiracy that was formed about twenty-one years ago, by the Turkish slaves; at one stroke to put an end to the whole order of Malta. All the fountains of the place were to be poisoned; and every slave had taken a solemn oath to put his master to death.

"It was discovered by a Jew, who kept a coffee-house. He understood the Turkish language, and overheard some discourse that he thought suspicious. He went immediately and informed the grand master. The suspected persons were instantly seized and put to the torture, and soon confessed the whole plot. The executions were shocking. One hundred and twenty-five were put to death by various torments. Some were burned alive, some were broken on the wheel, and some were torn to pieces by the four galleys rowing different ways, and each bringing off its limb. Since that time, the slaves have been much more strictly watched, and have less liberty than formerly." [2]

Coffee carried on growing in popularity over the years and many coffee shops opened and according to Bertel Thorvaldsen, newly arrived in Malta in 1796, "the coffee houses in Valletta are easy to find" probably because, as George French Angus said, most of the cafes were situated along Valletta's Strada Reale. As tea drinking is practically synonymous with English culture, it would be quite logical to presume that coffee would soon be eclipsed by tea in fashionable circles when Malta became a British Protectorate at the start of the 19th century. However many English visitors to the Islands remarked on the popularity and quality of the coffee served in Malta. "The natives of this island are particularly fond of taking coffee" wrote William Birch in 1810 and went on to say that the busiest cafes were near the palace and that "the coffee, as prepared here is far superior in flavour to any I ever tasted in England ...it is uncommonly fine."

Coffee was served in homes all over the island, as well as in all the coffee houses in towns and the fabulous fragrance of fresh coffee seems to have been one of the scents most reminiscent of Malta to Princess Marie, daughter of the Duke of Edinburgh when she lived here for three years in the late 1880s, "...and a smell of coffee in the villages and also of a certain herb (or was it the fuel with which the peasants cooked their food?) were the characteristic Malta smells, to be met with all over the island. The women were fond of brewing their coffee in the middle of the street on small transportable stoves made of sandstone ...".[3]

Coffee is still one of the most popular drinks in Malta and the coffee–houses "near the palace" still flourish and serve excellent coffee, although they are more likely to be made in an espresso machine.

A delicious tradition popular in Malta is to stir a little anisette into a cup of strong coffee; this is especially good after a good supper except that the anisette is often replaced with orange flower water, *ilma zahar*, when the supper was too lavish and a little aid is needed to digest the meal. This is a fairly old tradition that was definitely in place in January 1797 when the Guardian of the Franciscan monastery, Joseph Antonius Grimaldi gave Peder Pavels a bottle of orange flower water with his coffee.[4]

2   Patrick Brydone, *A Tour Through Sicily and Malta: In a Series of Letters to William Beckford, Esq. of Somerly in Suffolk* (1st ed. 1773)
3   Ardern George Hulme-Beaman, *The Story of My Life*
4   Sven Sørensen + Joseph Schirò , ed., *Malta 1796-1797: Thorvaldsen's Visit*

Methods of preparing coffee include the traditional method listed and:

FILTER COFFEE AND PERCOLATORS

This is the simplest way to make coffee – simply spoon the right amount of ground coffee into a filter paper lined plastic cone, put it onto a mug or coffee pot and add water just off the boil. The water mixes with the coffee in the filter and drains away into the receptacle below, taking all the flavour but none of the gritty grounds with it. An electric percolator does this automatically and keeps any coffee left in the jug warm. However, coffee that is kept warm soon looses most of its flavour and is best drunk straight away.

This sort of coffee couldn't have been made before the development of filter paper which sieves out the ground coffee to make clear coffee. This happened in 1908 when Melitta Bentz, a housewife from Dresden was fed up of drinking gritty coffee. So she punctured the bottom of a brass pot, lined it with blotting paper taken from the notebook of her oldest son, added hot water and perfectly filtered coffee, without left over gritty grounds, dripped out of the bottom.

FRENCH PRESS OR CAFETIERE

French presses create a smooth coffee using a simple but effective process. A French press consists of a narrow, cylindrical glass jug with a plunger attached to a lid. The plunger consists of a strong metal or nylon mesh that acts as a filter as the plunger is pressed gently down through the jug full of coffee, trapping the coffee grinds at the bottom of the jug.

To make coffee in a cafetiere simply spoon in some ground coffee, pour over hot water just off the boil, stir it and then install the lid-plunger. After the coffee has brewed very briefly (about a minute or so) gently press down the plunger. A fine mesh screen forces the grounds to the bottom and traps them there. The coffee is now ready to enjoy.

NAPOLETANA

The Neapolitan flip coffee pot, or Napoletana, is a drip brew coffee maker for the stovetop. It consists of a bottom section which is filled with water, a filter section in the middle filled with finely ground coffee, and an upside-down pot placed on the top. When the water boils, the entire three-part coffee maker is turned over to let the water filter through the coffee grounds. Once the water has dripped through the grounds, the water-boiling and filter sections are removed, and the coffee is served from the remaining pot. If coarse grounds are used, the coffee is brewed quite mildly. Using a very dark, finely ground roast, in the "Neapolitan" style, this method makes good, fairly strong coffee.

MOKA EXPRESS

In 1933, Alfonso Bialetti invented the first Aluminium Stovetop espresso coffee maker. A Moka Pot is an Italian steam-based stovetop espresso maker that produces dark coffee that is almost as strong as that from a conventional espresso maker. It is an improved version of the Napoletano and like its

French Press or Cafetiere

Napoletana or Flip Coffee Pot

Moka Express

predecessor it breaks down into three parts; the bottom part is a little pot to be filled with water, the central section is a filter filled with ground coffee that sits in the middle and the top is a jug-shaped pot with a chimney in the middle. The separate parts are screwed together and put on the stove, the water brought to the boil so that the steam rushes through the filter full of coffee collecting all the flavour as it goes, then it shoots up through the chimney where it condenses down into the jug section. Once the moka express stops bubbling the coffee may be served.

ESPRESSO COFFEE

In 1933, Dr Ernest Illy invented the first automatic espresso machine. However, the modern-day espresso machine was created by Italian Achilles Gaggia in 1946. Gaggia invented a high pressure espresso machine by using a spring powered lever system. The first pump driven espresso machine was produced in 1960 by the Faema Company.

INSTANT COFFEE

In 1901, just-add-hot water "instant" coffee was invented by Japanese American chemist Satori Kato of Chicago. In 1906, English chemist George Constant Washington, invented the first mass-produced instant coffee. Washington was living in Guatemala and at the time when he observed dried coffee on his coffee carafe, after experimenting he created "Red E Coffee" – the brand name for his instant coffee first marketed in 1909. In 1938, Nescafe marketed freeze-dried coffee. This type of coffee is incredibly easy to make, simply add hot water and stir!

However coffee is made or whichever instant coffee is your favourite brand the taste comes from the coffee bean – and they come in two sorts; Coffea Arabica or Coffea robusta. Arabica beans make coffee that tastes much smoother and sweeter while robusta beans are rougher, more earthy and powerful in flavour. The taste is then brought out by careful roasting of the beans and the darker the roast the stronger the sweet chocolate and caramel notes in coffee are, as long as they are not burnt right out of the beans by overcooking, leaving a bitter, smokey flavour in their place. I prefer coffee made purely from Arabica beans but many experts recommend a blend of the two beans.

The best way to enjoy a really good coffee is to buy freshly roasted beans in a blend of your choice from one of the specialised coffee shops in Malta, store them in an airtight container in the fridge and grind them as required. If you prefer good quality ready ground coffee bought in vacuum packs, then the best way to keep the coffee fresh once the pack is open is to store it in an airtight container in the fridge and use it up quickly.

COFFEE GRANITA

A granita is not as smooth as a sorbet but should be flaky and light. The quickest and easiest way to make this is to brew some very strong, sweet coffee, allow it to cool down completely and then use it to fill ice-cube bags and freeze. Then, when coffee granita is required, simply put the ice cubes in a food processor and blitz till the ice is crushed. Put the crushed coffee granita into a shot glass and serve with a little whipped cream if liked and sprinkled with a pinch of grated chocolate.

Otherwise pour the strong hot coffee into a freezer proof container, add the sugar, and stir until the sugar dissolves. Cool to room temperature and then place the container in the freezer. After about 45 minutes an icy crust will begin to form around the edges and top of the container. Take it out of the freezer and use a fork it to break up the ice crystals as they form and stir gently, then return the granita to the freezer. Repeat this procedure about every thirty to forty-five minutes. The granita should be ready after four or five hours. Scrape the granita with a spoon or ice-cream scoop and serve with a little whipped ceam and grated chocolate or, far more simply, a sprig of fresh mint.

N.B. *Make the coffee much stronger and sweeter than usual – approximately 1 flat tablespoon sugar to every 100ml coffee – otherwise it will disappointingly bland.*

COFFEE ICE-CREAM

300ml milk
300ml cream
6 heaped tbs coffee beans
1 vanilla pod – split
6 egg yolks
150g castor sugar
1 heaped tsp corn flour
2 tbs whisky (optional)

Break up and lightly crush (but do not grind) the coffee beans in a pestle and mortar or in a food processor. Then put the cream, milk, the vanilla pod and crushed coffee beans in a pot and bring it to the boil, turn the heat down and simmer very gently for about 2 minutes – take care that it does not boil over and then leave it to infuse for 20 minutes.

Then, reheat the cream mixture and whisk up the egg yolks with the corn flour and sugar until thick. Then, strain the very hot, but not boiling, milk and cream into a jug and pour it slowly into the egg mixture, stirring fast all the while to stop the eggs curdling. Then pour the whole lot into a clean saucepan and cook on a low heat stirring the whole time until it is thick enough to coat the back of a spoon very well. Make sure that the mixture doesn't boil at all or it will curdle. Pour it into a bowl and allow it to cool down, then stir in the whisky (if using). Then either put it into an ice-cream machine and follow the manufacturer's instructions or put it into the freezer and as the ice-cream freezes, take it out of the freezer at regular intervals and whisk it to break up the ice crystals as they form. Keep whisking and freezing until you have a creamy mass. Serve the ice-cream in scoops with the following caramel flakes stuck in the top:

150g cup sugar
50ml water
2 tbs coffee beans, crushed in a pestle and mortar or chopped in a food processor till medium-fine

Put the sugar in a thick bottomed saucepan with the water and boil till it begins to caramelise, add the crushed beans and drop spoonfuls onto a large piece of lightly oiled greaseproof paper. Immediately cover it with another piece of lightly oiled grease proof paper and roll over with a rolling pin a couple of times to thin them out.

COFFEE WALNUT CAKE

This is an unbeatable combination of flavours that make a deliciously moist cake, perfect served at teatime.

250g butter
250g castor sugar
4 eggs
200g shelled walnuts
125g plain flour – sieved
2 tsp baking powder
2 tbs ground coffee
½ tsp ground cinnamon
1 tbs brandy (optional)

First grind 100g of the walnuts and roughly chop the rest and put them to one side. Then beat together the butter and sugar till white and creamy, then add the coffee and brandy (if using) and beat in. Next, add the eggs one at a time, beating very well after each till the whole mixture is fluffy. Then, using a big metal spoon gently fold in the walnuts, cinnamon, flour and baking powder. Spoon the batter into a well greased and base lined 23cm cake tin and bake for 45 minutes at gas mark 4/180ºC or until golden and firm. Cool and split in two horizontally. In the meantime make a mug of strong coffee, add 3 tablespoons of sugar and simmer to reduce by half and brush it all over the cake. Then make some butter cream as follows:

100g butter
200g icing sugar
4 tsp ground coffee – or more to taste
2 or 3 tbs brandy (optional)
Shelled walnuts

Beat the butter and icing sugar till light and fluffy, then beat in the ground coffee and brandy until smoothly incorporated, then spread it all over the cake and decorate with some walnuts.
Serves 12

COFFEE BISCUITS

175g of butter
75g of castor sugar
250g of plain flour
25g – 30g ground coffee
Coffee beans
A little melted chocolate

Beat the butter and sugar together until light and fluffy. Add the flour and coffee and beat until it all comes together in a ball of dough. Chill slightly, then roll out fairly thinly and cut out rounds using a 3cm diameter cutter. Arrange them all on a well greased baking tin and bake them at gas mark 4/180ºC for 15 to 20 minutes until they are lightly browned and firm. They will crisp up as they cool.

A delicious way to finish off these biscuits is to sandwich them with cinnamon and coffee flavoured butter cream made a follows:

50g butter
100g icing sugar
2 tsp ground coffee – or more to taste
1 generous pinch cinnamon
1 tsp cocoa (optional)

Beat the butter and icing sugar till light and fluffy, then beat in the rest of the ingredients until smoothly incorporated. Once the biscuits are completely cool, sandwich them together with the cream.
Makes approx 50 biscuits or 25 sandwiches

COFFEE CHOCOLATE MOUSSE CAKE

This delicious mousse cake is perfect to make in advance as it must be left to set for at least 8 hours. It keeps well covered in stretch & seal in the fridge for at least 3 days.

First prepare the tin as follows:
Prepare a sponge cake mixture using 6 eggs, 150g sugar and 150g flour. Bake it on two flat, well greased baking trays until firm and golden. Line a 20cm cake tin with cling film. Brush the sponges with Benedictine or brandy thinned down if you wish with a little weak coffee. Use the sponges to line the sides and base of the prepared tin. Put the extra pieces of sponge to one side to use to cover the top which will become the base once it is turned out.

Chocolate Mousse
150g black chocolate
25g butter
3 eggs – separated
25g castor sugar

Melt the chocolate bain-marie (in a glass bowl suspended over a pan of barely simmering water) then stir in the butter and when it is smooth, add the yolks and stir briefly. While the chocolate is melting whisk up the egg whites till firm, then add the sugar and whisk it in briefly. Once the chocolate mixture is ready, fold it into the whisked egg whites gently until everything is incorporated and smooth.

Coffee Mousse
3 eggs – separated
100ml cold espresso coffee
(use instant if nessecary)
2 level tsp powdered gelatine
75g soft brown sugar
2 tbs brandy or Benedictine
100ml fresh cream

Soak the gelatine in the cold coffee for 5 minutes; if using instant, make the coffee with hot water and allow it to cool before soaking the gelatine in it for five minutes, and then dissolve the gelatine in the coffee over a low heat. Set aside to cool. In the meantime whisk the egg yolks and sugar until very thick and pale in colour, then whisk in the coffee and liqueur and set aside. Whisk the egg whites and cream separately and fold both gently into the coffee mixture.

To finish
2 tubs mascarpone
50 – 100g icing sugar
A generous dash brandy or whisky
2 tsp ground coffee
½ a bar dark chocolate

Fill the centre of the sponge lined tin with the two mousse mixtures stir them very gently to swirl together. Then cover the top with the bits of left over sponge. Brush over with a little more brandy and cover with cling film and chill for at least 8 hours or overnight. Turn out the cake carefully, remove the cling film and cover the well chilled cake with the mascarpone whisked with the icing sugar, ground coffee and brandy or whisky to taste. Top with chocolate curls made by running a potato peeler down the sides of a bar of chocolate. *Serves 10*

ZUCCOTTO

There are quite a few reasons for the name and shape of this traditional Italian dessert that was fashionable a few years ago. One explanation claims the name is derived from the cake's resemblance to a little pumpkin – another that the cocoa and icing sugar decoration on top reminds Florentines of the dome of their cathedral or that the shape is reminiscent of a skull cap, thus its name. What ever the reason, it is a delicious dessert and deserves to regain its popularity. This cake may be filled with flavoured whipped cream or ricotta.

You will need to make a sponge cake first

3 large eggs
125g sugar
125g flour
1 flat tsp baking powder

Whisk the eggs until thick and foaming; add the sugar a little bit at a time until the mixture is thick enough to leave a really good trail that lasts. Fold in the flour mixed with the baking powder until well amalgamated and then pour into a well greased 23cm cake tin. Bake at Gas mark 5/190ºC for approx 25 minutes or until golden and firm to the touch, remove it from the oven and cool.

Make the filling

250ml mascarpone
250ml fresh cream
3 – 5 tbs rum, Benedictine or whisky
100g icing sugar
2 tbs freshly ground coffee
100g dark chocolate
1 leaf of gelatine

First melt the chocolate in a Bain Marie, and then soak the gelatine in some cold water till it softens and swells. Then heat the alcohol of choice with a tiny dash of water and dissolve the gelatine in it but make sure it does not boil and allow it to cool slightly. In

the meantime, whisk the fresh cream and put it to one side. Then whisk the mascarpone with the icing sugar and alcohol of choice with the gelatine. Fold the whipped cream into the mascarpone and once it is all well mixed divide it in half, stir the chocolate into one half and the coffee into the other.

To assemble the cake

Line a 1 litre pudding/mixing bowl with cling film. Cut the cake in half horizontally and put the bottom half aside. Then brush the cake generously with some more rum,

brandy, Benedictine or whatever is popular and press it gently down into the prepared bowl. If this seems tricky, cut it into wedges, then brush them with alcohol and fit the wedges into the bowl. Then spread the sides with the chocolate mixture, ensuring the sides are well covered. Then fill the hollow in the middle with the coffee flavoured cream. Brush the other half of the cake and use it to cover the top of the cream. Cover and refrigerate for at least 12 hours to set nicely. Turn out the cake and dust the top with cocoa and icing sugar.

COFFEE CHOCOLATE PUDDING

This really has to be made at least a day or two ahead of time for best effect.

200g of butter
200g of castor sugar
250g plain chocolate
5 eggs
Approx. 1 litre of strong black coffee
2 packets Marie biscuits

Cream the butter and sugar until they are light and creamy, beat in the cooled, melted chocolate and then, one at a time, the eggs. When this is ready make some very strong coffee and dip the Marie biscuits lightly into the coffee and start making alternate layers of coffee-moistened-biscuits with chocolate cream until you fill a pretty glass bowl. Refrigerate for at least a day or two.

TO MAKE 8 MINI VERSIONS OF THE ABOVE
Line 8 standard sized ramekins with cling film. Fill and chill as directed above. To serve turn them out onto individual plates, dust with icing sugar and encircle with a little whipped cream. Top with a chocolate mint leaf made by brushing the underside of a mint leaf with melted chocolate, leaving to harden and then peeling off the leaf.

ESPRESSO DESSERT

This is very quick to make and tastes wonderful. The flavours develop if it is allowed to sit in the fridge for a couple of hours, but works just as well if it is made and served within a very short time.

300g Maltese rikotta
1 tbs coffee, freshly ground to a fine powder
Icing sugar to taste
Brandy to taste
Wafers/biscotti/Pavesini etc

Beat he rikotta, coffee, icing sugar and brandy together till smooth. Chill well and serve shaped into quenelles (little ovals) with wafers on a pretty plate. Drizzle with a little honey.
Serves 6

COFFEE CHOCOLATE SEMI-FREDDO

3 eggs
120g sugar
100g black chocolate – melted
2 tsp espresso or very strong coffee
Good pinch cinnamon
300ml cream
Sponge finger biscuits – eg: Savoiardi or Pavesini biscuits

Whisk the yolks till thick, then add the sugar and cinnamon and carry on beating. Then add the melted chocolate and coffee and whisk.

Whisk the egg whites till very thick and fold into the chocolate mixture. Whisk the cream till thick and fold it in.

Line a fluted cake tin with cling film. Then cover the bottom and sides with Pavesini sponge fingers dipped in brandy. Fill this with the semifreddo mix and top with a layer of brandy dipped Pavesini sponge fingers. Freeze the semi-freddo till you need it – it keeps well in the freezer. When you need the semi-freddo, turn it out, peel off the cling film and leave the semi-freddo to soften slightly before serving – about ½ an hour –depends on how warm your kitchen is.

BEEF AL KAFE

Although many people may think this is very odd it is worth trying out as the taste of coffee fades out, blends with the beef and brings out the best caramelized, smoky flavours in the grilled meat. The coffee colours the outside of the beef black which contrasts appetisingly well with the pinky/red interior of the rare steak

1 kg 3cm middle cut of rump
4 tbs ground 100% Arabica coffee
2 or 3 sprigs rosemary – finely chopped
Course sea salt – crushed
Olive oil
Freshly ground black pepper
Fresh rocket salad

Rub the coffee all over both sides of the steak and leave in the fridge for about 2 hours. Then preheat a large griddle pan till it is really hot and grill the steak for about 3 minutes on each side. Remove from the pan and leave to settle for a couple of minutes on a wooden board. Then slice it up and serve scattered with the rosemary, salt, black pepper and olive oil on a bed of rocket.
Serves 4

PAPARDELLE WITH PORK RAGU

The mugful of coffee in this recipe, used much as you would stock gives the pork a deliciously gamey flavour. Try and use the best quality pappardelle you can find or make your own for a special treat.

500g chunk of pork neck
1 large onion very finely sliced up
2 tbs finely chopped rosemary
1 bay leaf
1 dash brandy
2 glasses good Maltese red wine
Olive oil
1 mugful good coffee
1 square dark chocolate
Approx. 10g porcini mushrooms soaked in water for an hour

Put the pork fatty side down in a thick bottomed saucepan and fry very gently in its own fat, turning over a couple of times until it is browned. Add the rosemary and onion and cook until the onion is a deep golden brown and very soft. Then add the wine and bay leaf and simmer for about 10 minutes. Then cut the meat in half horizontally, add the rest of the ingredients, cover the pot and simmer for about and hour and a half or until the meat can be shredded up easily. Then shred the meat using two forks, removing any remaining hard bits of fat and taste to check for seasoning.

Boil 500g papardelle till al dente, toss with the sauce and serve.
Serves 4

AFFOGATO

Affogato is a quick and easy typically Italian dessert for those of us in a rush. Simply put some scoops of top quality vanilla ice-cream in a glass and "drown" or pour some good, very strong coffee over it. Serve immediately with some amaretti biscuits. Flavour the coffee with a dash of your favourite liqueur to jazz it up a bit.

ICE-CREAM AND VISITING LADIES
Il-ġelat u n-nisa li jiġu jżuru

Don Ignazio Saverio Mifsud left Malta on 26th April 1746 aboard a *speronara* sailing to Rome, where he was to be ordained to the priesthood and graduate in jurisprudence. The voyage lasted eighteen days; a slow sea journey fraught with fears of pirate attacks and bouts of seasickness that he recorded in a diary. On the 27th April 1746 while ashore at Marsamemi, he wrote that they admired – *la Tartana della Neve* – the Ice Tartana or the special ice transport ship sailing by, packed to the brim with compacted ice as it ferried that precious commodity from Mount Etna to Malta.[1]

It seems the Knights of St John, who used ice in their famous hospitals, introduced this popular item to Malta. Snow and ice was imported from Sicily, without which, it would have been difficult to survive the heat comfortably and impossible to make ice-cream or chill a drink. Giovanni Bonello noted that as far back as 1697 a French publication stated that in Malta, "… an island on the 34th degree there is no lack of iced dishes and of snow, thanks to the efforts of a contractor who charges two sols six diniers per pound, on the understanding that he supplies snow all the year round. He brings it from the mountains of Sicily and pays a fine of nine ecus for every day he fails to deliver it."

Ice brought to Malta from the Order's ice caverns on the upper slopes of Mount Etna was stored at the Snow Depot in Valletta, just inside what is now called Victoria Gate. In 18th-century Malta, ice was shipped from Sicily continuously. *Tutti si refocellano col bere in neve, che portano da Catania di Sicilia; una gran barca sempre andando, altra venendo, e il consume e furioso.*[2] Jean Houel, the traveller and diarist, describes the snow and ice business on Mount Etna, it was sold to the whole of Sicily and Malta, and to 'a great part of Italy' – 'for even the peasants in these hot countries regale themselves with ices during the summer heats, and there is not entertainment given by

1   NLM Lib. Ms. 1 with thanks to Liam Gauci, *The Journey Of Don Ignazio Saverio Mifsud The Grand Tour Of A Maltese In 1746. All The Places He Touched Upon*
2   Victor Mallia Milanes, *Descrittione di Malta anno 1716,* Everybody refreshes themselves with iced drinks made with ice brought over from Catania in Sicily. The demand was so great that boats had to go to and fro constantly.

'Ladies', Antoine Favray

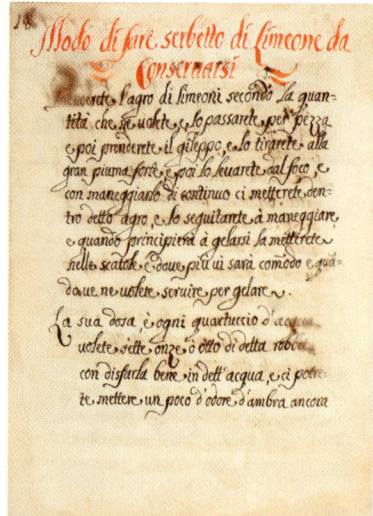

the nobility of which these do not always make a principal part: a famine of snow, they themselves say, would be more grievous than a famine of either corn or wine,' Houel describes the snow and ice business on Mount Etna in some detail: 'This grotto was rented, or sold, to the Order of Malta, which, finding neither ice nor snow on the barren rock on which it is situated' — that is, Malta – 'has rented on Etna several caverns, where people in their employ are careful to heap up and conserve the snow, which they send to Malta as it is needed. The grotto has therefore been arranged at the expense of the Order; stairways have been built; two wells have been carved, through which the snow is thrown down, and which serve to illuminate the grotto. On the ground above the grotto a large extension of land has been levelled, and surrounded by high walls, so that when the winds, which are very strong at this altitude, bring down the snow from the higher peaks into this enclosure, it is retained and piled up into a heap. It is then thrown down into the grotto through the wells, where it is compressed and can be conserved without melting in the summer heat. The thickness of the lava, which serves as a ceiling to the grotto, guarantees this. When the shipping season arrives, the snow is put into great sacks, which are forcibly filled; it is beaten down, and this compression gives it consistency and makes it very heavy. The men transport it out of the grotto, and load it on mules, which carry it to the shore where small boats are waiting. In these climates the lack of snow is feared as much as the lack of grain, wine or oil. I was in Syracuse in 1777, and no snow was to be had. It became known that a little ship passing by was loaded with snow. Without a moment's deliberation, everyone ran down and demanded that the ship be unloaded, and when the crew refused, the ship was attacked, and taken, and the Syracusans lost several men in the battle.'[3]

Apart from bringing icy relief to feverish foreheads at the Knights' hospital ice was sold to make ice-creams and chill drinks – for a *tari* per *Ratal* back in 1664. Ice-creams were in great demand from the start and in 1659 a certain individual called Federico sold ices or *agghiacciata* from a shop under the arches in Valletta and slaves were sent around village streets hawking ices.

Ice-creams were often made in the shape of fruits, flavoured with fruits or chocolate, cinnamon, coffee, pistachio and other flavours. A recipe book by Michele Mercieca written in 1748 preserved in the library at Valletta lists a variety of recipes, including one that perfectly describes how to shape and paint ices to look just like fruit. He recommends that you fill your fruit shaped moulds with orange flavoured water enriched with *conserva d'aranci* (marmalade) or candied peel and syrup. He adds that should oranges be unavailable, orange flower water is an acceptable substitute. Once this is done, place the moulds into the *bozzone* (buzzun, bezzun or ice pail) and freeze them till solid. Remove the orange ices from the moulds, wrap them in greaseproof paper and store them under snow until needed. To add a realistic tint to the fruits, he goes on to say, use saffron mixed with a little lemon juice and paint the ices with a brush to make them look more like real oranges.

---

3   Jean Houel, *Voyage Pittoresque en Sicile (1784)*

Ice-cream often rounded off special meals, such as served to Patrick Brydone and his companions in Sicily when they were on their way to Malta. The ice-cream must have been made following a recipe similar to the one above, because the fruit shaped ices were so well made that they completely fooled the ship's captain. Patrick Brydone describes his sea captain's first encounter with ice-cream; an event hilarious to the detached observer but ghastly to the unsuspecting diner, "The dessert consisted of a great variety of fruits, and still a greater of ices: these were so disguised in the shapes of peaches, figs, oranges, nuts, & etc. that a person unaccustomed to ices might very easily have been taken in, as-an honest sea-officer was lately at the house of a certain minister of your acquaintance, not less distinguished for the elegance of his table, than the exact formality and subordination to be observed at it. After the second course was removed, and the ices, in the shape of various fruits and sweetmeats, advanced by way of rear-guard; one of the servants carried the figure of a fine large peach to the captain, who, unacquainted with deceit of any kind, never doubted that it was a real one; and cutting it through the middle, in a moment had one large half of it in his mouth; at first he only looked grave and blew up his cheeks to give it more room; but the violence of the cold soon getting the better of his patience, he began to tumble it about from side to side in his mouth, his eyes rushing out of water, till at last, able to hold no longer, he spit it out upon his plate, exclaiming with a horrid oath," A painted snowball, by G—d!" and wiping away his tears with his napkin, he turned in a rage to the Italian servant that had helped him, with a" D--n your maccaroni eyes, you son of a -- what did you mean by that?" The fellow, who did not understand a word of it, could not forbear smiling, which still convinced the captain the more that it was a trick; and he was just going to throw the rest of the snowball in his face, but was prevented by one of the company; when recovering from his passion, and thinking the object unworthy of it. he only added in a softer tone," Very well neighbour, I only wish I had you on board ship for half an hour, you should have a dozen before you could say Jack Robinson, for all your painted cheeks." ; I ask pardon for this digression, but as it is a good laughable story, I know you will excuse it." Ice-cream was quite clearly one of the most fashionable desserts of the time.

Modo di Fare Aggiazzata di Limone[4]

Prendete l'aqua che ve bisogna e poi ci spremerete un limone per quartuccio. Se li limoni sono di grandezza douverosa e li tagliatere la scorza sottilmente e getarete nella detta aqua – ogni cosa cioe infusione e quando ci sara stato un buon pezzo levarete li mezzi limoni e passarete il resto per pagliazza e poi ci metterete sette onze e mezza di zuccaro per quartuccio e la gelarete.

---

4   Michele Mercieca, *Libro di Secreti per Fare Cose Dolci di Vari Modi*, 1748

Two modern versions of the recipe above are as follows:

PERFECT LEMON SORBET

This makes a very tangy sorbet that is absolutely delicious. To start off you will need two big glass bowls, put ½ a litre of water in one bowl along with the pith-less zest of 10 lemons (This is easy to do if you peel the lemons with a potato peeler). Put 350g castor sugar in the other bowl and add the juice of the 10 lemons and 200ml water and mix till the sugar dissolves. Leave the two bowls in the fridge overnight or for 8 hours. Strain the two mixtures into a freezer proof bowl stir and freeze the lemony mix. Take it out of the freezer every now and again to break up the ice crystals as they form, to make a smooth mixture. In the meantime whisk one egg white until stiff over a pan of simmering water, add 55g icing sugar and whisk it in then remove it from the heat and allow it to cool, and then whisk it into the half frozen sorbet. Allow the sorbet to freeze, whisking it every now and again until it is frozen through, but smooth, as a sorbet should be.

This keeps well in the freezer but it is best fresh. Allow it to soften slightly at room temperature before serving it, perhaps with some limoncello poured over it and a mint leaf or two on top for a really spectacular lemon taste.

QUICK AND EASY LEMON SORBET
200g castor sugar
300ml water
300ml strained lemon juice (about 6 large lemons)
Mint leaves and limoncello (optional)

Put the castor sugar and the water in a small saucepan and over a medium-low heat. Heat the pan gently, stirring, until the sugar has completely dissolved. Bring to the boil and boil steadily for 5 minutes (without stirring), or until the solution has attained the consistency of a thin syrup. Leave to cool, then stir in the lemon juice.

Pour the lemon mixture into an ice-cream maker and process following the manufacturer's instructions. Alternatively, if you don't have an ice-cream maker, pour the lemon mixture into a shallow container and freeze for an hour. Remove from the freezer and beat with an electric mixer until smooth, then return to the freezer. Repeat this procedure twice to produce a smooth, fine-textured sorbet, then leave to freeze until very firm. Serve in scoops and top with some mint leaves and limoncello. (optional)

Modo per fare aqua aggiazzata canella[5]
Prendete la canella second la quantita che volete fare, la pestarete bene e poi li gettarete sopra l'aqua che vi bisogna, e ce la lasciarete stare Quattro o cjinque ore infusion e se hao poco colore gli ene potete dare un poco con la pezza e poi la colarete e ci metterete (very unclear word) e le ripassata la gelarete. La sua dose, ogni quartuccio d'aqua vuole sette onze e mezza di zucchero.

---

5   Michele Mercieca, *Libro di Secreti per Fare Cose Dolci di Vari Modi*, 1748

Michele Mercieca's recipes are brought to dazzling life in one of the 8 dialogues recorded by Canon Agius De Soldanis in 1750. They are renowned principally for their linguistic value, but it is the vignettes of 18th century life preserved within the dialogues that make them unique. One of these highlights a visit between two refined ladies – *in-nisa puliti* – that took place in summer.[6] The humid heat was quite unbearable and the visitor, exhausted and overheated by her walk, dressed in her heavy ghonella, was welcomed indoors lamenting the appalling heat, *"... għaliex barra hemma l-għomma wisq. Emminni ma flaħtx nasal."* Her stifling ghonella was lifted off and her hostess invited her to sit down in an armchair, carefully chosen for her, as one of them was too high for her comfort. She sat next to her friend and the ladies started to chat, indulging in a good grumble about their servants. Then a tray of iced drinks was brought in; *"Ħu l-inġazzata u ixrobha"* the hostess encouraged her visitor to have a frozen drink which she gratefully accepted, choosing an almond flavoured one rather than a lemon one, thus bringing the recipes above to life perfectly.

The ladies carried on chatting while enjoying their frozen drinks; they discussed the latest rumours about a possibly imminent Turkish invasion, how women suffer during wars and then comforted each other with the thought that the newly built Fort Chambray was sure to offer some deterrent to the Terrible Turk.

The evening began to draw in and the visitor decided to leave as she had to accompany her husband on his evening walk, for she fears his roving eye and wants to keep it, and him, in check for as she says, *"Ma' dawn l-irġiel trid toqgħod magħhom bix-xemgħa tixgħel"*.

That ice, frozen drinks, granitas and ice-creams have always been popular is illustrated time and time again both in Michele Mercieca's book and documents, travelogues and diaries of the time that cite the importation of ice from Sicily.

"...cafes, which are open at a very early hour. Travellers passing only a short time in Malta will find these places extremely convenient, as they can drop in at any hour of the day and take coffee or ice, which latter article is consumed in Malta to a very great extent. It is obtained from Mount Etna in the form of snow, and boats are constantly arriving from Catania laden with this useful and cooling substance. In the cafes it is no uncommon thing to see them grinding up whole vats full of frozen snow, which, at first sight, appears very singular to a stranger in so warm a climate. Most of the cafes are situated in the Strada Reale, opposite the Library. I found the best attention at "Saits," and some of the prices are as follows:- Cup of coffee, 1 ½ d.; breakfast, 5d.; ice-cream, 2 ½ d.; lemonata ice, ½ d.; Rogiata ditto, l ½ d.; other ices, including chocolate, coffee, cherry, strawberry, and pine-apple, 2 ½ d. or 3d."[7]

6   Ġużè Cassar Pullicino, *Il-Kitba bil-Malti sa l-1870*
7   George French Angas Mark, *Malta and Sicily, in the autumn of 1811,* 1842

Nothing is more salutary during the sirocco than iced beverages; they revive the spirits, strengthen the body, and assist digestion. Snow is therefore considered at Malta as one of the first necessaries of life ; it is brought from Sicily and administered to the sick. Whenever there is a scarcity of this article, all that remains in the ice houses is entirely reserved for the use of the hospitals.'

Robert Montgomery Martin, *History of the colonies of the British Empire*, 1843

Ice-cream is now much more accessible than it was back then. Ice-cream vendors set up shop in vans and take their ice-creams directly to people. About 30 years ago an ice-cream van was part of the scenery during the summer term outside the school I went to, however, we were never allowed to buy an ice-cream because of a probably quite unfounded rumour that a girl once found a rusty nail in her ice-cream.

Vans visit beaches and summer festivals, other vendors sell their ice-creams from stalls on roadsides and ice-cream is no longer the treat it once was. Ice-cream parlours flourish in large towns like Sliema and Valletta where they are popular meeting places. Supermarkets sell commercial brands that are delicious and high on children's 'must have' lists for surviving the summer holidays in comfort.

Most people buy their ice-creams or use an electric ice-cream machine to make ice-cream. For those who don't own one of these gadgets, simply put the ingredients in a shallow freezer proof-bowl, put it in the freezer and take it out at intervals to whisk and stir it. This breaks up the ice crystals and makes a smooth, creamy ice-cream. Little changes after all, the *buzzun* is replaced by the freezer, but the principle remains the same.

SORBETS

Fruit sorbets are the most refreshing ice-creams to have in the summer and surprisingly simple to make.

STRAWBERRY SORBET

I kilo fresh, ripe strawberries
250g granulated sugar
500ml water
1 lemon

Wash and hull the strawberries then liquidise them till very smooth. Put the strawberry juice in a bowl and chill it. In the meantime make syrup by dissolving the sugar in the water over a low heat, then boil it for five minutes. Allow the syrup to cool.

Mix the syrup and strawberry juice together in a freezer proof bowl and put in the freezer. As the ice-cream freezes, take it out of the freezer at regular intervals and whisk it to break up the ice crystals as they form. Keep whisking and freezing until you have a creamy mass. Squeeze the lemon and add the juice to the sorbet at this point, then whisk it again a last time and freeze it. Allow it to soften slightly at room temperature before serving.

You may substitute liquidised peaches, kiwis, or other similar summer fruit for strawberries with equal success

CREAMY ICE-CREAM

The best and most successful method is to make a basic, rich egg custard with cream, flavour it as you wish and freeze and whisk it.

250ml milk
250ml cream
6 egg yolks
150g castor sugar
1 heaped tsp corn flour

Put the cream and milk in a pot and bring it to the boil while you whisk the egg yolks, corn flour and sugar until thick. Pour the very hot, but not boiling, milk and cream over the egg mixture, stirring fast all the while so that the eggs don't curdle. Put the whole lot into a clean saucepan and cook on a low heat until it is thick enough to coat the back of a spoon very well. Watch the mixture doesn't boil at all or it will curdle. At this point you may wish to add about 150g dark chocolate broken into squares to the hot custard and stir it in until it melts to make chocolate ice-cream or scrape the insides of two vanilla pods into the mixture to give it a vanilla flavour. Pour it into a bowl and allow it to cool down. Put it into the freezer and as the ice-cream freezes, take it out of the freezer at regular intervals and whisk it to break up the ice crystals as they form. Keep whisking and freezing until you have a creamy mass. You may wish to stir other flavours into the ice-cream at this point: pulverised roasted nuts are good, crushed amaretti biscuits soaked in amaretto liqueur with grated chocolate is really good, some puréed fruit is pretty stirred through for a ripple effect or more simply chopped fruit for a speckled effect – some praline makes a rich flavoured ice-cream. Try any one of these and success will be yours.

TANGEREMON SORBET

200ml of freshly squeezed lemon juice
200ml of freshly squeezed tangerine juice
300g of sugar,
300ml of water,
The peel of 1 Malta-grown
tangerine (chopped very finely)
Hollowed-out Malta-grown
tangerine halves

First freeze the hollowed out tangerine halves. Then dissolve the sugar in the water over a low flame, bring it to the boil and simmer it for five minutes. Add the chopped peel and turn off the heat as soon as you do so. Leave the sugar-water to cool, and then stir in all the juice. Pour it into an ice-cream machine and follow manufacturer's instructions or make it as follows: Put the mixture into a freezer-proof bowl and then into the freezer. Check progress, and when it starts to freeze, take it out, whisk it, and put it back in the freezer. Repeat the process until the sorbet is thick and smooth and then give it one final whirl in the liquidiser and return it to the freezer. Allow it to soften slightly before serving it, either in small glass bowls or in the tangerine halves

LEMON VERBENA SORBET

200g sugar
500ml water
2 large handfuls lemon verbena leaves
A few extra tender lemon verbena
leaves – finely chopped
2 egg whites
The juice of 1 lemon
Curls of lemon zest to decorate
Lemon verbena flowers or
tender leaves to decorate

First bring the water to the boil, add the lemon verbena leaves to the water and leave them to infuse for about 3 minutes. Strain the infusion into a saucepan and make it into syrup by dissolving the sugar in the infusion over a low heat, then boil it for five minutes. Allow the syrup to cool. Pour the cooled syrup into a freezer proof bowl and put in the freezer. As it freezes, take it out of the freezer at regular intervals and whisk it to break up the ice crystals as they form. Keep whisking and freezing until you have a creamy mass. Then whisk up the egg whites till they form peaks and fold into the sorbet with the chopped leaves and lemon juice, then whisk it again a last time and freeze it. Allow it to soften slightly at room temperature before serving.

To serve: serve small scoops of the sorbet in pretty glasses with some lemon verbena liqueur, decorated with a few extra leaves and flowers, curls of lemon zest and an almond biscuit.

N.B. If lemon verbena is difficult to come by simply substitute mint or thyme for the lemon verbena to make an equally delicious sorbet, and use other liqueurs such as Limoncello, Cointreau and so on.

MULBERRY (TUT) SORBET

1.2 kg of black mulberry tree fruit (tut)
400g of castor sugar
Water

Cook the mulberry fruit in a glassful of water for 15 minutes or until they are soft. Liquidise them still in the water, adding more water if the mixture is too thick. Leave it to cool, and then sieve it into a freezer-proof bowl, pressing down onto the sieve very hard to extract as much of the juice and pulp as possible, while leaving the seeds behind. Bring 400ml of water to the boil and dissolve the sugar in it. Pour this sugar-water mixture into the bowl with the mulberry puree. Put the bowl into the freezer, and remove it at regular intervals to whisk it, breaking up the ice crystals as they form. Repeat this process until you have a creamy mass. This keeps well in the freezer for a couple of months. Remove it from the freezer a few minutes before serving it, so that it thaws just a little.

PRICKLY PEAR SEMIFREDDO

2 eggs x 2 – separated
80g sugar x 2
The seeds from 1 vanilla pod/200ml
sieved prickly pear purée +extra
200ml cream x 2
A 4 egg sponge cake made the usual way
Alkermes or prickly pear liqueur

First line a 24cm round cake tin with cling film, slice the sponge and cover the bottom with a thin slice of sponge cake soaked in Alkermes or prickly pear liqueur, then do the same to the sides. Whisk one lot of yolks till thick, then add the sugar and carry on beating till really thick and fold in the vanilla. Whisk one lot of egg whites till thick and fold into the vanilla mixture. Whisk one lot of the cream and fold it in and pour it into the sponge lined cake tin and freeze it. Do exactly the same with the second lot of ingredients – replacing the vanilla seeds with the prickly pear purée.

Pour in the prickly pear semifreddo mix on top of the frozen vanilla semi freddo and top it with a last thin layer of alcohol soaked sponge. Freeze the semi-freddo till you need it – it keeps well in the freezer. When you need the semi-freddo, turn it out, peel off the cling film and leave the semi-freddo to soften slightly before serving – up to ½ an hour –depends on how warm your kitchen is and then, just before serving dust it with icing sugar and serve slices of the semi freddo with quartered prickly pears and a little of the extra prickly pear purée.

N.B. Make the prickly pear purée by peeling, blending and sieving prickly pears with a little lemon juice and icing sugar.

STRAWBERRY SEMI FREDDO

100g white chocolate – melted
4 eggs – separated
150g sugar
The seeds from 1 vanilla pod
250 g strawberries, washed and hulled
400ml cream
Pink sponge fingers or use
Savoiardi/boudoir biscuits
Cointreau

Line a 24cm round cake tin or a fluted mould with the sponge fingers lightly dipped in Cointreau and put to one side. Melt the chocolate in a Bain Marie (in a bowl suspended over a pan of barely simmering water), then cool slightly. Purée the strawberries till smooth with the icing sugar and a tot of Cointreau and put to one side. Whisk the egg yolks till thick, then add the sugar and carry on beating till really thick. Whisk in the cooled melted chocolate a little at a time, whisking all the while and then fold in the vanilla and a dash of Cointreau. Then, in separate bowls, whisk up the cream and whisk up the egg whites till both are thick. Next; first fold the cream into the egg yolk mixture and then fold in the egg whites and then, last of all swirl in the strawberry purée to make ripples of bright red strawberry through the creamy white mass; do not over mix it or you will lose the ripple effect. Then pour it into the sponge finger lined cake tin and freeze the semi-freddo till you need it – it keeps well in the freezer. When you need the semi-freddo, turn it out, peel off the cling film and leave the semi-freddo to soften slightly before serving, then decorate the top with strawberries and serve.

GRAND MARNIER SEMI-FREDDO

4 tbs diced sponge cake
6 tbs Grand Marnier
4 eggs separated
100g cater sugar
Grated rind and juice of an orange
300ml fresh cream
Chocolate shavings

Soak the diced sponge cake in the 3 tablespoons of the Grand Marnier and put to one side. Whisk the egg yolk with the sugar until very light and fluffy, add the orange juice, grated rind and the other three tablespoons Grand Marnier and whisk again. Then whisk up the egg whites and the cream separately and very gently fold them into the yolk mixture until smooth. Half fill 6 freezer proof cups or ramekins, scatter with the soaked diced sponge and cover with the rest of the mixture. Freeze for at least 4 hours and for up to a couple of weeks. To serve: Dip the ramekins in hot water for a minute or so and turn out onto a pretty serving plate, cover with some chocolate shavings and serve.

MEASUREMENTS IN ITALY

The word for a pound in Italian is "libbra." Unsurprisingly, weights and measures varied wildly everywhere throughout the peninsula before the introduction of the metric system:

1 Pound (Rome) 339g
1 Pound (Tuscany) 348g
1 Pound (Ferrara) 346g

Everywhere, though, pounds were divided into 16oz. People working from very old Italian recipes, unless they are sure of which pound is meant, tend to estimate 350g as a compromise.

Thus: oz: 1/12th pound (approximately 29g based on a 350g pound)
dragma ("dram", aka "ottavo"): 1/8th of an ounce (approximately 3.6g)
scrupolo: 1/3 of a dragma (approximately 1.2g)
grano (grain, aka "pizzico"): 1/24 of a dragma (approximately .05g)

Other old Italian measurements included:
boccale (bottle): about 1 litre
fiasco (flask): 2 "boccali" (2 litres)
mezzetta (halves, aka "foglietta"): 1/2 of a "boccale", about 1/2 litre
quartuccio (quarter): 1/4 of a "boccale", about 1/4 litre

BASIL AND CHAMPAGNE SORBET

This delicious sorbet takes a little more time than usual to make as the alcohol in the champagne makes it tricky to freeze. It is far easier to make in an ice-cream machine but can be done by hand; just keep in mind that it will take longer to freeze – almost twice as long. This sorbet is ideal to serve as a refreshing interval between courses during a long meal as well as a lovely dessert.

900ml water
900g sugar
1 bottle champagne or Spumante
Zest of 1 lemon
3 tbs very finely chopped fresh basil

Peel the zest off the lemon using a potato peeler. Then make the syrup; simply dissolve the sugar and lemon zest in the water over a low heat and boil it vigorously for 10 minutes. Cool the syrup, then strain it and chill the syrup well. Stir in the rest of the ingredients and pour it into the ice-cream maker and follow the instructions to make sorbet. Otherwise pour it into a shallow freezer proof bowl and freeze, taking out of the freezer at intervals to whisk as it freezes, making smooth and soft ice crystals rather than large, hard ones.

Serve the sorbet in old fashioned champagne glasses decorated with some curls of lemon zest.

A perfect orange blossom and a ripe orange

ORANGES
Laring

In *Malta of the Knights* (1926) Elizabeth Schermerhorn described the beautiful walled gardens at San Anton Palace, depicting a luxuriously scented scene, where one can just imagine that "cavaliers in velvet and satin and ruffles of lace took snuff and gossiped among these fragrant bowers"[1] and, one would think, picked and ate some of the oranges that were, in those days, considered exotic and very special fruit. "Those glistening groves of orange-trees whose fragrance is wafted through the grilled openings of the tunnel bear the famed luscious fruit which it was the Grand Master's pleasure to present to the Sovereigns of Europe, still reckoned the finest in the world. In the eighteenth century they contained seven hundred orange trees and one thousand lemon trees, and the terrace was "covered with strawberries producing three crops a year." The air is languid with the heavy perfume of strong scented flowers, and faint with orange blossoms and roses; and something of the pensive wistfulness of old Moorish gardens lingers about Paules' fair pleasance where, beneath the drooping fringes of glossy palms and sweet thickets of roses, other and yet other, gardens are half revealed between wreathed arches and vine-smothered walls; and the dark quiet vistas and in a crumbling fountain, or a softly dripping stone basin, or a round, quiet pool where swans "float double"."[2]

However, it is unlikely the cavaliers ate any of the oranges before the 18th century because the original oranges grown there would have been bitter Seville oranges (citrus bigaradia), first brought to Malta from India by the Arabs sometime in the 10th century. Oranges were grown for their rare beauty as well as to dry into aromatic pomanders studded with cloves and to extract perfume from the thick skin. The oranges were used to flavour ices and in confectionary; but most of all they were grown for the orange blossoms that scented the air in orange gardens all over Malta, and the flowers were used to make orange flower water and neroli essential oil used in perfumes like Hungary Water and eau de cologne.

---

1   Elizabeth Schermerhorn, *Malta of the knights*
2   *ibid*

MARMALADE

Oddly enough marmalade is generally thought to be a Scottish invention; a curious fact when oranges do not grow in the British Isles. The story goes that sometime in the 18th century James Keiller, a humble Dundee grocer, seized the moment when a Spanish ship took refuge from a winter storm in Dundee harbour; he thought he would make a killing on the fruit market and bought the entire ship's cargo of oranges very cheaply. To his horror, he found that they were Seville oranges and owing to their bitterness he was unable to sell them! His ingenious wife, Janet, in true Scottish style did not wish to waste the fruit, so used the oranges, instead of her normal quinces, to make some pots of preserves. They proved to be so popular that the Dundee public demanded more and from then on the Keillers maintained a regular order for Seville oranges and supplied first Dundee and then most of Scotland and England with orange marmalade. The name marmalade comes from the fact that in Portugal, where the modern use of the word originated, "marmelada" refers to a solid gel-like substance made of quinces – which is the fruit Mrs Keiller originally used to make her preserves.

The orange marmalade label on the left is by Edward Caruana Dingli and was commissioned by my great, great grandfather Achille Samut in 1933. The labels were used on jars of marmalade made with Maltese oranges for the Malta stand at the Great London Exhibition in the 1930's.

Jars of home made marmalade

FINE CUT SEVILLE ORANGE MARMELADE

There are many different recipes for marmalade; the one below makes very good marmalade. Grapefruits, tangerines or lemons may be used instead of the oranges in this recipe with great success – except that tangerines do not set as firmly as the other fruits.

10 fresh Seville oranges
2 litres of water (use bottled)
Sugar

Wash all the oranges, cut them in half and squeeze them. Then, using a teaspoon, scrape away most of the fibrous part of the pith and slice up the peel as thinly as possible. Put all the sliced fruit into a large non-reactive saucepan and add the juice and water. Put the pips and left over bits of squeezed out fruit and pith in a muslin bag and add them to the pot. Bring all the fruit, water and pips (in the bag) to the boil, cover the saucepan and turn it right down to a very low heat and simmer very gently for at least two hours. In the meantime, wash approximately twelve 300 g. jars well in hot soapy water, rinse them and put them on a roasting pan. Sterilise them by heating them at gas mark 3/160ºC in the oven for at least 20 minutes. Boil the lids for 10 minutes. Weigh the cooked fruit and water mixture and then add the same weight of sugar. Put it all into a big jam pan and dissolve the sugar over a low heat. The marmalade must not boil before all the sugar has melted otherwise it will crystallise during storage.

Once the sugar has melted bring the marmalade to a good rolling boil and boil till setting point is reached. Stir it every now and again with a wooden spoon to make sure the marmalade doesn't stick to the bottom of the jam pan and burn. To find out whether setting point has been reached put a spoonful of marmalade on a saucer, allow it to cool for about 15 seconds then push the back of a spoon through the little pool of marmalade. It should wrinkle up. If it doesn't then carry on boiling the marmalade until setting point is reached it always takes at least 20 – 25 minutes boiling time. Allow the marmalade to cool for a moment or two before potting otherwise the peel will float and spoil the appearance of the marmalade. Pour the hot marmalade into the hot jars using a jug and seal well. The marmalade keeps well, for at least two years.

DUNDEE MARMALADE

This method makes a thicker marmalade than the recipe above and the lovely sweet-tart flavour of the recipe is more pronounced. Stir a generous dash of good whisky into the marmalade just before potting it for a warming taste of Scotland.

Fresh Seville oranges
Water
Sugar

Wash the oranges well, then, boil the whole oranges in enough water to generously cover the oranges till they are tender – about an hour to an hour and a half. Then allow them to cool, and take them out of the water, RESERVING the boiling water to use at a later stage. Cut the boiled oranges in half and remove all the pips and put them in a little muslin bag. Chop or slice up the now pip-less fruit as thinly or thickly as you wish and mix into the reserved boiling water. Then weigh the pulped fruit and water, add an equal amount of sugar and proceed as in the recipe above.

JARS

In the days before new jam jars and new lids were so easily available cooks collected a variety of jars, washed them well and gave them a quick boil before filling them with marmalade or jam. When lids were unavailable they followed this method to seal the jars:

First they cut out neat rounds of greaseproof paper to fit very neatly on top of the marmalade and a whole set of rounds about 2½ cm larger than the diameter of the jar. Then when the marmalade (or jam) was in the hot jars, they would dip one of the smaller rounds of greaseproof paper in some Brandy or Whisky and lay it carefully directly on top of the marmalade, then dip one of the larger rounds of greaseproof paper in some beaten egg-white and stretch it over the top of the jar and hold it down till it stuck and was as tight as a drum. Most people decorated the jars with fabric and ribbons and stored the marmalade in the pantry.

The Seville orange, called *bakkaljaw*[3] in Maltese, was almost completely eclipsed by its sweeter, juicier cousin from China when Portuguese Grand Master Manoel de Vilhena and Pinto de Fonseca introduced some of the "red Portuguese" orange trees to Malta. This variety, called *citrus sinesi*, was discovered by Portuguese traders in China and taken back to Portugal and on to Malta. Once here, it really took root and became the back bone of a trade boom that lasted throughout the 18th century before it slowly waned, declined and petered out at the beginning of the 20th century.

Something special happens to orange trees in Malta; the fruit they produce is simply delicious and must be a result of the combination of the type of soil and climatic conditions. Even today, when oranges are available from all over the world at any time of year a locally grown Maltese orange is a treat for the senses. This has been the general consensus for hundreds of years, Patrick Brydone wrote, on the 5th of June 1770, that "The Maltese oranges certainly deserve the character they have of being the finest in the world. The season continues for upwards of seven months, from November till the middle of June; during which time, those beautiful trees are always covered with abundance of this delicious fruit. Many of them are of the red kind, much superior, in my opinion, to the others, which are rather too luscious. They are produced, I am told, from the common orange bud, engrafted on the pomegranate stock. The juice of this fruit is red as blood, and of a fine flavour. The greatest part of their crop is sent in presents to the different courts of Europe, and to the relations of the chevaliers. It was not without a good deal of difficulty that we procured a few chests for our friends at Naples." [4] As most people know, June is the very tail end of the orange season and the oranges still on the trees at that time of year are not the best at all, and yet they were still considered superior.

home made marmalade

---

3   Joseph Aquilina, *Maltese-English Dictionary* says *Bakkaljaw* is derived from the Spanish Bacala meaning salt cod – (perhaps a corruption of the latin *bigaradia*?),

4   Patrick Brydone, *A Tour Through Sicily and Malta: In a Series of Letters to William Beckford, Esq. of Somerly in Suffolk* (1st ed. 1773)

Such was the demand for Maltese oranges that "King Louis XV of France's daughters, Mesdames de France decided to rent a garden in Malta to have oranges every week. The princesses' private secretary was regularly giving orders to his most Christian Majesty's chargè d'affaires who had, among many other important activities, the essential task of sending oranges to the King's daughters."[5]

Maltese gardeners became expert orange growers and many orange gardens sprung up around Malta, Alain Blondy mentions that Abbè' Savoye' father "had a marked preference for the Garden of the Lions at Santa Venera ... (and) he praises the quality of the gardens in Spinola at St Julians and that of San Anton at Balzan as well as those of Siġġiewi, Attard and in the vicinity of Birkirkara. On the other hand, he did not want to have anything to do with those of Qormi"[6]. Gardeners in Malta took great care of their orange trees, "The gardens in Malta are generally ornamented with groves of orange and lemon trees; but these are not permitted to grow to any great height on account of the wind, which would blow off the fruit, and break the branches. The greatest attention is paid to the orange-trees, which are commonly watered twice a-day. Their tops are trimmed into a round form resembling an umbrella; and they grow on one single straight stem, as do likewise the lemon-trees, the branches of which are sometimes suffered to extend till they form a kind of bower. These trees are almost all raised in tubs, and placed in the most sheltered spots."[7]

The hundreds of dozens of oranges sent abroad are quite amazing and fascinated traders such as Mr Poussielgue who wrote in 1775," one fails to understand the infatuation for this fruit. The demand for it is rampant, thus, increasing the price by half its value. No ship leaves here without carrying a large quantity. Of all freights, it is the easiest to sell."[8]

The Maltese trade in oranges slowed down for various reasons but mostly because other countries like Sicily, Italy and Spain started to grow oranges in larger quantities and it was far easier to send the fruits overland then by sea, especially during the Napoleonic wars. Of course our own, special orange trees were sent abroad to many places like Sicily and Tunis where similar climatic conditions and huge tracts of land are obvious advantages and all that is left of the splendid era when Maltese oranges were in such demand is the name – the Maltese is still a much sought after variety – the only thing is that nowadays they are likely to have been grown in Sicily or Tunis.

5   Alain Blondy, 'A treasure of 18th Century Malta: The Maltese Orange' in *Treasures of Malta* Vol. X No. 1
6   *ibid*
7   Louis de Boisgelin, *Ancient and modern Malta,* Volume 1
8   Alain Blondy, *The Commerce of Oranges in the XVIII Century*

CANDIED PEEL

Approx. 2 kg thick skinned oranges or grapefruits
1 kg granulated sugar
2 tbs coarse sea salt
500ml water

First cut the fruit in half and squeeze it out and cut the squeezed out halves into half again to get regular sized ovals. Put the peel into a large saucepan and cover with water, bring to the boil and simmer for 10 minutes. Drain and discard the water. Cover the peel with fresh water, bring to the boil and simmer for 20 minutes, drain again. Put the peel into a large glass bowl and cover with fresh, cold water and leave for 24 hours.

The next day, put the sugar and water in a large saucepan, bring it to the boil and dissolve the sugar.

Add the peel, reduce the heat and simmer for two or three hours or until the peel is translucent and most of the syrup has been absorbed.

Remove the peel and dry on racks in a cool airy place for a couple of days. Then dust with castor sugar and store in an airtight container. Cut into strips and serve with coffee after dinner or use in cakes and biscuits.

ORANGES PRESERVED IN OLIVE OIL

Oranges preserved in olive oil are simple to make and very useful to have in the kitchen, especially when fresh oranges are out of season. They add a zesty tang to salads and marvellous flavour to roast chicken.

Wash and dry some fresh, Maltese oranges. Cut them into thin slices – about 5mm thick – then lay them in a colander and sprinkle them with coarse salt, make layers of salt and citrus if you need to. Allow them to drip for about 24 hours, then press the excess liquid out of the oranges with the back of a spoon and shake off the excess salt. Put them neatly into a STERILISED jar and cover them generously with olive oil. Make sure there are no air pockets where bacteria may form as they will spoil.

Uses
Marinate chicken breasts in the fruit and oil before barbequing or grilling, stuff a chicken with the orange slices and two handfuls basil leaves for great flavour. The orange slices are very good chopped up and scattered over an avocado pear salad with some parsley and black pepper. Serve this on a bed of rocket leaves and dress with olive oil and balsamic vinegar.

PICKLED ORANGES

141

These are perfect served with rich meats like pork, duck or goose and useful to have to hand to add to gravies or sauces. Make these with the first local oranges if you want to serve them with Christmas lunch as they need to mature for at least three weeks before using them. They keep well, at least two years – simply darkening in time.

6 large oranges
1 tsp salt
500g sugar
2 tbs golden syrup
175ml vinegar
125ml water
6 cardamom pods – split open
1 tbs black peppercorns
12 cloves
Small piece cinnamon stick

Put the oranges and salt in a large pot, cover with water and bring to the boil, then turn down the heat and simmer gently for half an hour or till the oranges are tender. Drain them and leave them to cool.

In the meantime, put the rest of the ingredients in a pot and bring them to the boil, stirring constantly. Turn down the heat and simmer gently for 10 minutes then set it aside to cool.

Slice up the boiled, cooled oranges and add them to the pan of cooled, flavoured pickling liquid. Bring it back to the boil, stirring every now and again, then turn down the heat and simmer gently for 15 minutes.

Remove from the heat and allow it to cool for 5 minutes; then ladle the oranges and their liquid into warm sterilised jars and seal. Store in a cool dark place for at least three weeks before using the pickle.

ORANGE MERINGUE TART

Pastry

Filling
The grated zest and juice of
4 fresh, local oranges
5 egg yolks
2 flat tbs corn flour
75g castor sugar
75g butter
50ml fresh cream (optional)

Mix the cornflour, sugar and orange zest in a medium saucepan. Then measure the orange juice; you should have about 350 ml – add a little water if you need to make up the amount. Then stir the juice gradually into the mixture in the pan and cook over a medium heat, stirring constantly, until thickened and smooth. Once the mixture bubbles, remove from the heat and beat in the butter until melted. Beat the egg yolks (save whites for meringue), stir into the pan and return to a medium heat. Keep stirring vigorously for a few minutes, until the mixture thickens and plops from the spoon. (It will bubble, but doesn't curdle.) Remove the pan from the heat and stir in the cream if using.

Topping
5 egg whites
250g sugar

Whisk the egg whites until thick, then add the sugar, a little at a time, whisking in between each addition until all the sugar is used up and the mixture thick and firm. To assemble the tart pour the filling into the baked pastry case, cover it with the meringue, put spoonfuls of meringue around the edge of the filling (if you start in the middle the meringue may sink), then spread so it just touches the pastry (this will anchor it and help stop it sliding). Pile the rest into the centre, spreading so it touches the surface of the hot filling (and starts to cook), then give it all a swirl. Return to the oven for 15 mins until the meringue is crisp and slightly coloured. Let the pie sit in the tin for 30 mins, then remove and leave for at least another 30-60 mins before slicing.

ORANGE CAKE

This cake is perfect for dessert, really easy to make and keeps very very well so it is ideal for those hostesses who like to prepare ahead when entertaining. Store the cake in a tin, or any other air-tight container, and it will keep for up to a week.

50g stale breadcrumbs
200g Castor sugar
100g ground almonds
1½ tsp baking powder
200ml sunflower oil
4 eggs
The zest of 3 oranges
The zest of ½ a lemon

Syrup

Juice of the oranges above
Juice of the lemon above
75g sugar
2 cloves
1 cinnamon stick
Greek yoghurt to serve – optional

Stir all the dry ingredients together in a large bowl. Then, in a separate bowl, whisk the oil, grated zest and eggs together and pour over the dry ingredients and beat them all together till smooth. Pour the mixture into a 23cm well greased and base lined tin. Then put it into a cold oven, turn it on to gas mark 4/180 C and bake it for 40 minutes or until it is firm and golden brown and a skewer poked into the middle comes out clean.

While it is baking make the syrup by gently simmering syrup ingredients for 5 minutes or till thickened. Then, when the cake is cooked, carefully remove it from the tin, pierce it all over with a toothpick or skewer and gently spoon over syrup until it is all soaked up. Decorate with the cinnamon stick. Serve it with a little well-strained yoghurt that is sprinkled with toasted flaked almonds and green pistachios and drizzled with honey.

To strain yogurt: put plain yoghurt into a sieve lined with coffee filter paper and leave it in the fridge for a couple of hours or overnight, until it is as thick as needed. You could use a clean pop sock instead.

The cake is slightly flat as I prefer a flat pudding cake; should you prefer a higher cake simply use a 20cm cake tin and cook for approximately 10 minutes longer.
Serves 10

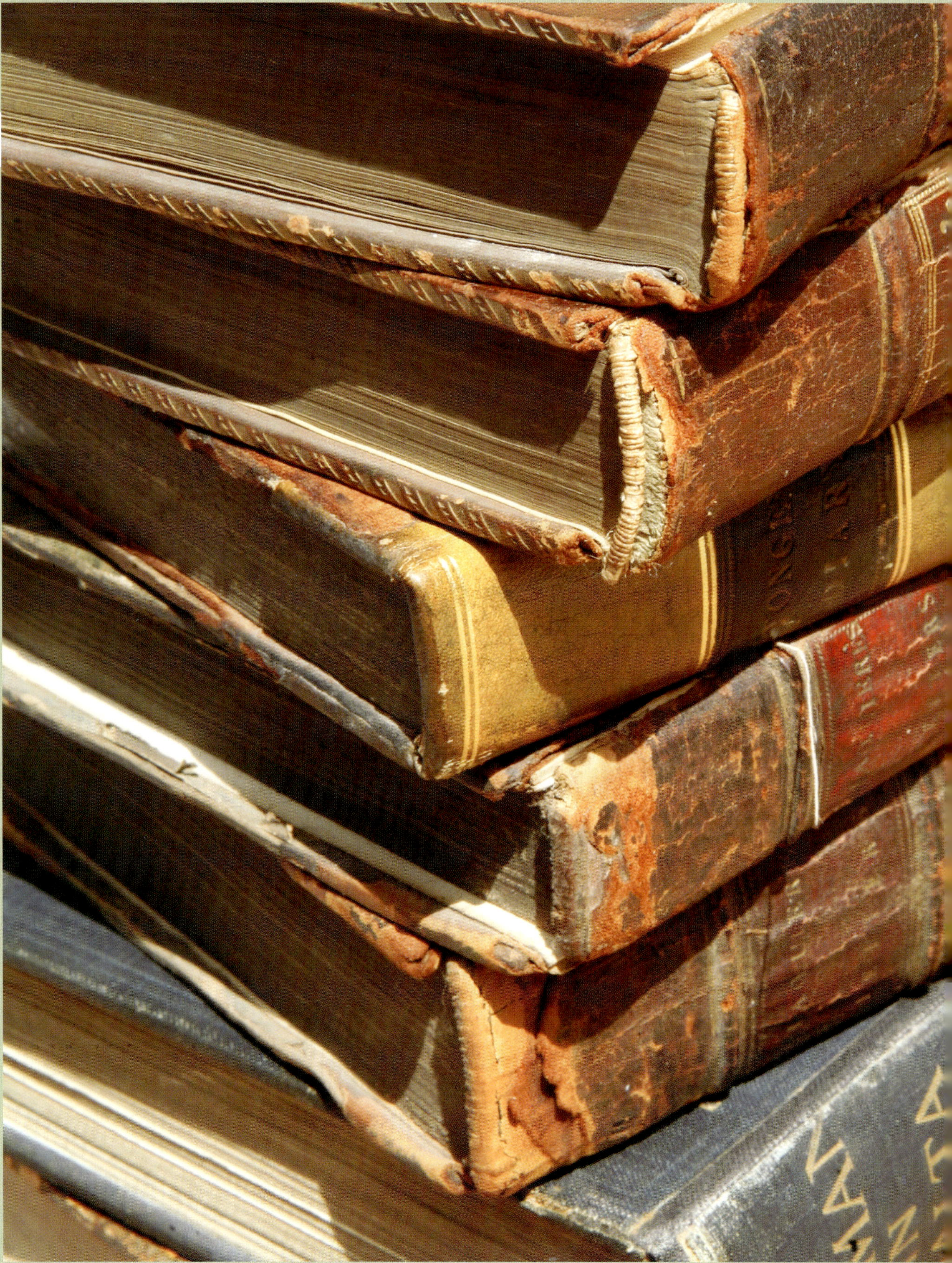

Memories
traced on paper

Old books and documents provided a fascinating source for the chapters that follow. References to food and eating habits in Malta are scattered throughout many antique travellers' diaries and a few of the hundreds of documents and manuscripts found in the National Library of Malta. Strung together they form a chain of memories that inspired the chapters found in this section.

servite in Carrozza à due Cavalli col seguito d'altre Sig.re di Cort
più prossime paventi in diversi calessi di Palazzo, e nel smont.
dalla Carrozza furono incontrate dal Cavallerizzo minore in m
canza del Maggiore nell'ingresso della scala principale, ed
accompagnate dal med.simo sin'al piano superiore della d.
scala, ivi furono incontrate dal Ricevitore, in mancanza del
Maestro di Casa, che l'introdusse sin'alla porta della Camera
dell'appartamento d'estate, ove si ritrovò S.A.S. M.e Priore
della Chiesa, il V.do Bali dell'Aquila Vicecancelliere, il
V.do Bali Senescalco ritrovandosi anche in anticamera tut
gl'Ufficiali di Palazzo e molti Cavaglieri per il corteggio d
S.A.S., ed altri Paventi e Nazionali invitati dal soprad. Barr
D'amico Inguanez, preventivamente commissionato dal Rice
tore giusta la mente di S.A.

IX. Entrate le Commadri col seguito delle sopradette Paventi n
la Camera, si trattennero per qualche tempo coll'A.S.S.; ed
in quest'intervallo nella d.ta Cappella si diè principio al suon
d'armoniose sinfonie, quale durò sin doppo la funzione d
Battesimo.

X. Doppo brieve conversazione N.e Priore della Chiesa si portò al
soprad.ta Cappella e vestito pontificalmente dalli due Assisten
che furono il M.ro di Cerimonie della Maggior Chiesa Cont
ed Altro parati con rocchetto, e mozzetta, si pose a sedere co
S. Assistenti ed i Cappellani di Palazzo, come di sopra si disse.

XI. Avvisata l'A.S.S. dal suo Cammariero Maggiore, ch'il tutto
era pronto, s'aprì la porta dell'appartamento che corrisp

A BAPTISM AT THE PALACE

28TH APRIL 1765

Magħmudija fil-Palazz

The entry that refers to the detailed description of the baptism of the infant son and heir of Baron Don Gio Francesco d'Amico Inguanez is found in the index of the third book in the National library Manuscript 1953. *"Funzione di Battesimo parta dall' Gran Priore della Chiesa Fr D Gio Domenico Mainardi nella Capella del Palazzo Magistrale al Bambino figlio del Barone D Gio. Francesco D'Amico Inguanez il di 28 Aprile 1765 (cap XXV pg: 96)"*

This prestigious event took place during the reign of one of the most regal of Grand Masters, the Portughese Fra Manoel Pinto y Fonceca after whom the infant was named Emmanuel. The meticulous report of the whole ceremony conveys the air of sumptuous ceremony and restrained excitement surrounding the event; the Prior was *"vestito pontificalmente"* and the altar and chapel were richly decorated. *"L'Altare s'adorno con quaranta candelieri d'argento e sue candele, e fiori, in mezzo al quale so colloco una nicchia d'ebano, parte incrostata di finissime pietre e bronzi dorati, in cui si rapprezenta in perfettissime figure di rame dorato S. Gio Battista in atto di Battezzare NJ*

In mezzo della cappella sopra tapeto che copriva tutt' il pavimonto si pose un tavolino coperto di damasco cremisitrinato d'oro con tavaglia di finissima seta e di sopra un bacile d' argento coll' aqua Battesimale in un cocchiaro d' argento ed un bacilotto con li vagri Ogli in cassetta d' argento

Left: NLM Lib. Ms. No. 1953 Archives of the Order of Malta (Photo by Joe P. Borg), Above: old christening cups from the early 20th Century

portati dalla Chiesa Parochiale della Vittoria dal Sagrestano di stessa Fr Vincenzo Gullo."[1]

So the stage was set and the players, so ably described by the author of the document, poised to bring the ceremony to life. He describes the carriages, some drawn by two horses, others by a single horse, that carried the family and their *pui prossime parenti* to the palace where they were met in the ground floor loggia, at the foot of the magnificent spiral Grand Staircase and accompanied upstairs to the Baptismal ceremony. The account of the ceremony is rather long drawn out, as I suppose was the Baptism, but then the writer carries on to say, *"Finita la sudetta funzione... furono serviti di copiosi rinfreschi, cioccolate, confitture e biscottini di diverse qualita, come anche nell' anticamera e sala ove si ritrovarano molti Cavalieri con i sopra ri nazionalita ad altri persone che concorsero per assisteva alla soproccennata funzione.*

Dopo i rinfreschi SAS regalò due grandi e bellissimi Bocchetti alle due Commadri e licenziatele, le accompagnò sin alle porta della gran sala, ed indi si ritirò al suo appartamento d'inverno, le Commadri e parenti furono accompagnate nell istessa maniera che furono ricevute e montate in carozza e calessi si ritornono alle loro abitazione."[2] The reader is left with the lingering scent of old fashioned pastries and the clatter of departing horses' hooves that still seem to echo through the beautifully hand written pages.

---

1 "The altar was laden with forty candles in silver candlesticks and quantities of flowers, in the middle of which was an ebony niche partially encrusted with precious stones and gilded bronze figurines of St John the Baptist baptising Jesus. In the centre of the chapel, on a carpet that covered the whole floor, was a table covered in damask embroidered in gold thread, covered in a very fine silk cloth and on top of that, a silver bowl, with baptismal water in a silver flask and the oils in a silver box brought from the parish church of (Our Lady) of Victories by the sacristan of that same church Fr Vincenzo Gullo."

2 Nicholas de Piro, *Occasions, Social Events and Occurrences in the Palace.* Archives of the Order of Malta National library of Malta no 1953. "When the ceremony was over... the guests were served with abundant refreshments including chocolate, sweets and a variety of biscuits. The same was served to the many Knights and guests who gathered in the next room to celebrate the baptism. After the reception, the SAS bestowed the two Godmothers and Godfathers with beautiful large Bocchetti and accompanied them to the door of the great hall before retiring to his Winter apartment. The guests were then accompanied in the same way that they were received, they got into their carriages and went back home."

PER FARE MARZAPANI RIPIENI[1]

Pestarete le vostre amandole cio` e fare la vostra pasta di marzapani e poi ne farete i parti d' uso di pasta e ci aggas marktarete la vostra marmelata e lo cporirete con altra parto e poi ne farete pezetti d'uso di marzapani e poi li cuocerete e saro perfettione.

STUFFED ALMOND BISCUITS

First make some amandole or marzipan as follows:

100g ground almonds
100g castor sugar
1 egg white
Grated zest of 1 lemon or 1tsp very finely chopped tangerine peel

Put all the ingredients into a bowl and mix them well together with a fork to make a firm but slightly sticky dough. If the dough is too dry add a tiny dash of brandy; if too wet add a little more ground almonds. If you double or triple or further multiply the quantities you will need to use less egg white, so add it carefully.

Then finish them off as follows:
Candied orange or grapefruit peel
Icing sugar

Chop up the candied peel. Then break off walnut sized pieces of marzipan and roll them into a ball. Make a little hollow in the top of each ball by pressing gently with your fingertip, fill it with chopped candied peel and draw the edges together over the filling and roll to seal and then coat them in icing sugar. Bake in the oven preheated to gas mark 6/200ºC for about 7 minutes or until a pale gold colour.
Makes 10

1   Michele Mercieca, *Libro di Secreti per Fare Cose Dolci di Varii Modi,* 1748

MODO DI FARE BISCOTTINI DI SAVOJA[1]

Prenderete dell'ove secondo la quantita che volete a li pesarete, e poi pesarete tanto zuccaro quanto pesaro l'ove e poi li sbatterete bene insieme e poi ci metterete tanto fior di farina, quanto pesa il zuccaro e amanaggiarete bene con una cocchiara e poi metterete detta pasta sopra alla carta della grandezza d'un pane e lo spolvizzarete con zuccaro asciutto e lo cuocerete e quando ha preso colore allora cavarete e lo distaccarete subito dalla carta con un coltello e ne farete le fette lunge e poi li rimetterete nella detta carta versate la detta pasta alla ruersa e le rimetterete nel forno un momento e poi le cavarete e sono a perfettione.

BISKUTTINI

3 eggs
175g castor sugar
1 tbs anise seeds – crushed
The grated zest of an orange and lemon
1 flat tsp baking powder
250g plain flour

Preheat the oven to gas mark 5/190ºC Then whisk up the eggs till fluffy, add the sugar a little at a time and carry on whisking till thick. Gently fold in the anise seeds, the baking powder and the flour till well incorporated. Line two baking trays with non-stick paper and, using a large tablespoon, form three equal log shapes of batter by laying down spoonfuls of the mixture next to each other and smoothing the edges. Then scatter with sugar and bake them for 25 minutes, and take them out of the oven, allow them to cool briefly and slice them up. Lay the slices out on baking trays lined with non-stick baking paper and bake them again to toast and crisp them up in the oven turned down to gas mark 2/150ºC for about 10 – 15 minutes. Do not be tempted to cook them too long as they crisp up on cooling. Store the biscuits in an air tight container. *Makes approximately 40*

---

1   Michele Mercieca, *Libro di Secreti per Fare Cose Dolci di Varii Modi*, 1748

HOT CHOCOLATE AND CHOCOLATE SORBET

The chocolate used in the 18th century was different to the type of chocolate available today; it was probably very like the type of chocolate still produced in Modica in Sicily where the original chocolate making technique from the 16th century has been maintained. One step of the traditional process requires working the cocoa beans with a stone rolling pin on a Mexican metate (a lava stone slab) over a fire. This process grinds the roasted cocoa beans over a fire that does not allow the cocoa mass to go over 40 degrees Celsius. This means that when sugar is added it is mixed in but does not melt, thus imparting the grainy texture this chocolate is famous for.

Chocolate was a very fashionable drink in 18th century Malta. So much so that when Venetian Giacomo Capello wrote his description of Malta in 1716 he reported that Grand Master Perellos was far too fond of women, even though in 1716 he was 80 years old. The Grand Master held daily audiences for the ladies of the town; he served them hot chocolate and sweet pastries, they chatted and flirted with him and gossiped about their errant husbands and he always took their side.[1]

Modica chocolate (above) and an old silver chocolate pot

HOT CHOCOLATE

1 litre full cream milk
250g dark chocolate
A little ground cinnamon
A little grated chocolate
200ml whipped cream

Pour the milk into a small saucepan, add the chocolate to the pan and melt slowly. Whisk till smooth and then pour into a thick wine glass and top with a spoon of whipped cream sprinkled with grated chocolate and cinnamon.
Enough for 5 people

---

1   Victor Mallia Milanes, *Descrittione di Malta Anno 1716*

MODO DI FARE CICOLATA GELATA IN CICHERE[1]

Farete cose misurate tante chiccare d'aqua second la quantita che volete e poi ci metterete due onzi di cicolata per chiccara. La cuocerete dove ve piace cotta che sara ferrete le vostre chiccare fredde e sbatterete bene la cicolata in qualche cosa di grandezza capace e con un schumatore verrete levando la spiuma, e la metterete in chiccare e piene che saranno metterete nella casetta in .... d gelare e che la casetta sia di rame e ben gelate che saranno le sevirete.

This chocolate sorbet recipe is my take on the old recipe above; it is milk and cream free and intensely flavoured. It is smoothest when made in an ice-cream machine but tastes very good when churned by hand.

350g sugar
750ml water
100g cocoa powder
75g best quality milk chocolate
50g best quality dark chocolate
50ml chocolate or coffee liqueur (optional)

Put all the ingredients except the liqueur into a saucepan and stir till the sugar is dissolved. Then simmer for 10 minutes until thick, smooth and creamy. Leave the mixture to cool and pour it in the ice-cream machine and proceed as directed OR pour it into a freezer proof bowl and put in the freezer. As it freezes, take it out of the freezer at regular intervals and whisk it to break up the ice crystals as they form. Keep whisking and freezing until you have a creamy mass. Serve with the liqueur poured over.

---

1   Michele Mercieca, *Libro di Secreti per Fare Cose Dolci di Varii Modi*, 1748

MODO PER ROSOLI DI CANNELLA[1]

Prenderete la cannella secondo la quantita dell' aquavita, e la pesterete non molto fina con qualche garofalo, e poi ci metterete infusione la detta aquavita e ce la lasciarete stare sei o sette ore e poi la colarete e ci metterete il gileppo a discrizione e poi la passarete per manica insino che vien chiara e se vi servite de zuccaro ogni quartuccio d aquavita vuole sette onze e mezza di zuccaro.

homemade liqueurs

CINNAMON LIQUEUR

This is amazingly good and extremely easy to make as there is no fiddling involved.
1 bottle Grappa
10 Good Earth cinnamon sticks
4 cloves
12 tbs sugar

Hit the cinnamon sticks lightly with a kitchen mallet – just enough to flatten and crack them. Then put all the ingredients in a large jar and stir. Close tightly and allow it to infuse for 2 weeks, shaking the jar gently every couple of days. Then strain into very clean bottles and mature for a month. Serve this liqueur as cold as possible.

NB: Use a little less or a little more sugar – the amount specified above is fairly flexible, it depends on how much of a sweet tooth you have.

1   Michele Mercieca, *Libro di Secreti per Fare Cose Dolci di Varii Modi,* 1748

IL-QUĊĊIJA

Similar food is served at a traditional Maltese first birthday party called *il-quċċija*. The main event at the gathering is a light hearted attempt to augur the baby's future in a most unusual way. A tray is laid out with a variety of objects that might have some kind of relevance to the child's future; for example, if the child is a boy the tray will be laid with more masculine items, a toy sword (army), a thermometer (medicine), a cross (the church), a pen or ink pot (law), while girls are offered more domesticated items, although the difference is less nowadays and girls are offered the same sort of things as boys. There are some things like an egg (plenty), a book (scholarship)and a coin(riches) that are present for both.

The tray is offered to the child and the first thing picked is supposed to predict the child's potential career. I grabbed a book and an egg at the same time; I suppose they didn't think of putting a wooden spoon on the tray!

This custom was noted by an anonymous visitor to Malta in 1792 and he described it as follows, "The only custom peculiar to Malta, and which is solely preserved in rich families, is that of the "Cuccika"; an assembly of relations and friends is so called, who meet together with the fathers and mothers of families on the first anniversary of the birth days of their children. When all the parties are collected in the great hall, which is always the part of the house the best ornamented, the child, if a boy, is presented with two baskets, the one containing corn and sweetmeats, and the other some trinkets, pieces of money, an inkstand, a sword, &c., the choice which he makes of these things decides the employment or character which it is supposed he will take upon him in life; if he chooses the inkstand, it is a sign that he is destined for commerce or the bar, if he prefers the sword, much is expected from his courage, &c ... If the infant is a female, necklaces, silks, ribbands, &c are subitituted for the sword, &c. &c." [1]

Once this simple ceremony is over, guests celebrate the child's apparent prosperous future with good food and drink as people have always done. Typical foods are delicate little sandwiches, sweet biscuits and cakes. A dish traditionally served at the *quċċija* is a plate of *Xkunvat* (little sweet pastry fritters) and there is nothing better than perfectly cooked *xkunvat*.

Curiously enough *quċċija* originally had a different meaning to the more familiar one. Ġużè Cassar Pullicino[2] quotes Canon Agius de Soldanis who wrote in 1750 that originally *il-quċċija* was linked to a time of mourning and sadness, when a dish of boiled wheat grains mixed with raisins, almonds and walnuts was blessed and served to the poor for the intercession of the soul of the deceased. This habit was so popular that some people even specified a sum of money for *il-quċċija* in their will.

---

1   *A Description of Malta with a Sketch of its History and Fortifications,* 1792,
    translated from the Italian in 1801 by an officer resident on the island
2   Ġ. Cassar-Pullicino, 'Antichi Cibi Maltesi' in *Melita Historica : Journal
    of the Malta Historical Society.* 3 (1961) 2 (31-54)

Unblessed boiled wheat started to be served at children's first birthdays and then, though the name stuck and became synonymous with a first birthday party, the dish of boiled wheat slipped off of the traditional menu to be replaced with wheat and nut biscuits. In nearby Sicily a dish of boiled wheat called *cuccia* is served on the feast of St Lucy. The boiled wheat is sweetened with condensed wine or sweetened ricotta and decorated with chocolate, candied peel and ground cinnamon.

Some traditional biscuits are usually served, and the following are good examples of what might be served.

BISKUTTINI TAR-RAĦAL
OR VILLAGE BISCUITS

3 eggs
200g sugar
200g flour
Grated rind of a lemon and an orange
3 tsp crushed aniseeds or caraway seeds

Preheat the oven to gas mark 8/230ºC until you put the biscuits in, at which point the oven must be turned down to 190ºC/gas mark 4. Separate the eggs and beat the whites until stiff. Add the sugar a little at a time whisking well each time. Add the yolks, mix again, and then stir in the grated peel and crushed seeds. Fold in the flour. Shape the dough into little ovals using two teaspoons and bake on a tray scattered with semolina for 20 minutes or until a light golden colour. Decorate with swirls of pink and white icing.
Makes about 40

OTTIJIET OR SESAME EIGHTS

400g plain flour
2 tsp baking powder
150g castor sugar or icing sugar
75ml olive oil
50g butter
Grated rind and the juice of 2 oranges and a lemon
2 eggs
Approx. 150g sesame seeds

Preheat the oven to gas mark 7/210ºC, until it is time to bake the biscuits, and then turn the oven down to gas mark 4/180ºC as you put the biscuits into the oven. Grate the lemon and orange rind and put it all in a bowl along with half the juice and the eggs and mix lightly.

Sieve the flour and baking powder into another bowl, and rub in the butter. Then stir the sugar and the oil and rub in briefly, just enough to mix the oil into the flour. Make a well in the centre, pour in the egg mixture and stir to combine and form dough. If the dough is dry add some more of the juice.

Knead lightly until the dough is smooth. Break off little lumps the size of a large walnut and roll into a sausage shape. Once it is the thickness of a finger, join the ends together and give the ring shape a twist to turn it into an eight and dip them into a pile of sesame seeds. Put them all onto a well-oiled baking sheet and bake for 25 minutes, or until they are a lovely deep golden colour. Cool on a wire rack and once cool store in an airtight container to preserve freshness.

Use a dry Martini instead of the citrus juice when the fruit is out of season.

ALMOND BISCUITS

2 egg whites
200g ground almonds
200g castor sugar
Grated rind of two lemons
Split blanched almonds or cherries to decorate

Heat the oven to gas mark 2/150ºC. Whisk the egg whites till stiff, whisk in the sugar. Fold in the almonds and lemon peel. Then either using two spoons or a piping bag put little rounds on an oven tray lined with rice paper, decorate the top with a split almond or a cherry and bake in the preheated oven for approximately half an hour to 40 minutes or till a lovely firm pale golden. Cool and store in an air tight tin till needed.

SOME MODERN BISCUITS

CRANBERRY BISCUITS

These biscuits make use of dried cranberries, the North American fruit that has quite taken Christmas by storm. They add a tangy bite and festive colour to these crisp little biscuits. Replace the cranberries with other dried fruit if you wish – but remember to chop up the fruit. Store the biscuits in an airtight tin and they will keep well.

100g butter
100g castor sugar
1 egg yolk
50g Good Earth dried cranberries – chopped up
Grated rind of 1 orange
1 tbs semolina
200g plain flour

Beat the sugar and sugar till white and fluffy. Drop in the egg yolk and beat till smooth. Add the cranberries, grated orange rind, semolina and flour and beat again to make soft dough. Roll it into a log, wrap it in cling film and refrigerate till hard. In the meantime heat the oven to gas mark 5/190ºC and line two baking trays with non-stick greaseproof paper. Then remove the hardened log of dough from the fridge and slice it up into biscuits, lay them on the prepared trays and bake in the preheated oven for about 15 minutes.

TANGERINE CRESCENT MOON BISCUITS

100g of butter
100g of castor sugar
250g of flour
1 small Malta-grown tangerine

To finish the biscuits
2 small Malta-grown tangerines and some icing sugar

Preheat the oven to gas mark 5/190ºC. Wash the tangerines and cut them in half. Remove the pips. Blend the tangerine halves until smooth. Add the sugar and blend again, then the butter and blend. Now do the same with the flour, to form dough. If the dough seems too soft, add a little more flour. Knead it briefly, roll it into a log shape and slice it. Shape the slices into crescent moons and arrange them on a well-greased baking-sheet. Bake them for 20-25 minutes or until they are golden. Leave them to cool on a wire rack.

Squeeze the two large tangerines and chop some of the peel finely. Stir icing sugar into the juice to make firm glace icing. Decorate the biscuits with zig-zags of icing.

LEMON BISCUITS

100g butter
100g soft light brown sugar
150g flour
Grated peel of 2 lemons
2 or 3 tbs of milk

Pre-heat the oven to gas mark 5/190ºC. Cream the butter and sugar together until light and fluffy. Beat in the grated lemon peel and flour and enough milk to make dough.

Knead briefly and cut into about 20 pieces, cut each of these into eight and roll them into balls. Arrange these into rings of touching balls on a well greased baking tray. Bake for 15 – 20 minutes until golden. Cool.

Make some runny glace icing with icing sugar stirred into the juice of the grated lemons. Dip the cooled lemon biscuits into this and leave to firm up before serving.

CHOCOLATE CHIP COOKIES

150g plain flour
½ tsp bicarbonate of soda
½ tsp baking powder
100g butter
50g soft light brown sugar
50g castor sugar
1 egg
175g chocolate chips or roughly chopped black chocolate

Pre-heat the oven to gas mark 5/190ºC. Cream the butter and sugar together until light and fluffy. Beat in the egg and when it is well amalgamated, beat in the flour and chocolate chips.

Spoon heaped teaspoons of the mixture onto a well greased baking sheet (or simply use non-stick greaseproof baking paper) and bake at gas mark 5/190ºC for 15 – 20 minutes or until a rich golden colour. Makes approximately 40; depending on the size of the biscuits – the smaller you make them the more you'll have.

N.B. Do not over crowd the tray as they
may spread and stick together.

ALMOND CAKE

This is my almond cake recipe that makes a lovely moist cake with excellent keeping qualities. The cake must be made a day before it is cut, so that the flavour and texture of the cake have time to mature. If you wish the icing to harden, then make the cake about three days before cutting.

To make the cake

500g ground almonds
500g castor sugar
75g flour
25g semolina
6 large or 8 medium eggs
Grated rind and juice of a lemon
Generous dash brandy
Generous dash rum

Preheat the oven to gas mark 3/ 170ºC and grease and base line a 26cm low sided non-stick cake tin.

Put all the dry ingredients in a bowl; add the brandy, rum, lemon juice and eggs and beat together till smooth and well combined. Pour into the prepared tin and bake for an hour and a quarter, but start checking it after an hour. The cake should be firm and springy when cooked and a skewer should come out clean when poked into the cake.

Allow to cool for about five minutes in the tin, then turn out onto a rack and remove the grease proof paper from the bottom of the cake. Cover it when cool.

To ice the cake

2 egg whites
500-600g sieved icing sugar
1 tsp glycerine
Tiny drop blue food colouring (optional)
6 tbs apricot or peach jam

Sieve the jam into a small pot, add 2 tablespoons of water and bring it to the boil and simmer briefly. Brush the hot jam over the cake and allow it to cool and dry while you make the icing.

Put the egg whites into a large bowl and whisk lightly until the whites are just frothy. Start adding the icing sugar a little at a time whisking well between each addition until you have thick icing that holds peaks well. Add the tiny drop of blue food colouring if you wish to highlight the whiteness of the icing, and the glycerine to keep it soft for longer. Spread the icing fairly thinly over the cake, smoothing it with a spatula.

Decorate with silver balls and any other decorations, like a ribbon tied around the side, or anything you may think suitable.

N.B. The quantity of icing is enough to cover the cake – you will need more for piping additional icing decorations.

A COUPLE OF MODERN CAKES

PISTACHIO AND LEMON CAKE

250g butter
250g castor sugar
4 eggs
The grated rind of 2 lemons
200g Good Earth shelled raw
pistachios, finely ground
50g Good Earth ground almonds
2 heaped tbs corn flour
1 tsp baking powder
1 tsp Good Earth nutmeg

Preheat the oven to gas mark 3/170ºC

Blanch the pistachios in boiling water
and when they are cool enough to
handle comfortably, remove the
brown skins. Dry the nuts well – on
an airy window sill or in a cool oven
and then grind them finely with the
corn flour and ground almonds.

Beat the butter and sugar together
till light and fluffy, beat in the eggs
one at a time, beating well until all
are well incorporated. Then gently
fold in the ground nuts, grated
lemon peel, nutmeg and flour
and make sure all is smooth.

Pour the batter into a well greased
and base lined loaf cake tin (26cm x
8cm 6cm) and bake for about ¾ of an
hour to an hour or till a skewer comes
out clean. Turn out when cool.

To finish
100g Good Earth shelled raw
pistachios, roughly chopped
100g sugar
The juice of 2 lemons
A little water

Put the sugar, lemon juice, and a little
water and bring it to the boil. Add the
nuts, stir, bring back to the boil for a
minute or two and pour over the cake.

DUNDEE CAKE

Its defining feature is a slightly domed top studded with neat concentric circles of whole blanched almonds. The almonds are arranged on the uncooked cake and become a warm, golden brown. Dundee cake is not an old cake. It is thought to have originated only in the 19th century, in the city of the same name, where it was made by the marmalade manufacturer Keiller. The left-over orange peel from marmalade-making was mixed into the cakes, which kept the workers busy when Seville oranges were not available for the main product. The cakes were glazed with orange syrup and sold on a widespread, commercial basis. Later versions of this cake came to be sold in decorative tins as an alternative to almond cake at weddings and other celebrations, like baptisms.

225g of softened butter
225g of soft brown Demerara sugar
The grated rind of 2 oranges
5 eggs
300g of sieved plain flour
1 tsp baking-powder
2 tsp ground mixed spice
750g of sultanas or mixed dried fruit
100g of chopped mixed peel (optional)
3 tbs of brandy
100g of whole blanched almonds for decoration

Beat the butter, orange rind and sugar together until the mixture is light and fluffy. Add the eggs one by one, beating well between each addition. If the mixture looks as though it is going to curdle, add a little flour with each of the eggs. Then fold in the rest of the ingredients. Spoon into a well-greased and lined cake-tin (20cm) and smooth the top with the back of a hot, wet metal spoon. Arrange the almonds neatly in circles over the top. Bake at gas mark 2 for two hours, then remove it from the oven and leave it to cool in the tin for five minutes. Turn it out onto a wire rack. Dundee cake improves considerably if it is turned upside down, pricked all over with a skewer and some good quality brandy is poured over it. Allow it to stand while the brandy soaks in, and then turn it right side up, wrap it well in cling-film, and keep it in a tin. The cake will be ready to eat in a week and will keep well for two months.

A sheet of home made pasta

PASTA AND A BURLY MALTESE OFFICER
Għaġin u ufficjal żorr

Cave dwellers or troglodytes were a fairly common feature of medieval Malta that thrived until the British period when such dwellings were outlawed and cleared out by the authorities. The remains of many cave dwellings can still be seen in quite a few places around Malta, but the best known is the Għar il-Kbir cave complex near Buskett. Troglodytes usually converted their caves into relatively comfortable places by building dividing drystone walls and carving shelves and cupboards into the walls.

Athanasius Kircher, a German Jesuit fascinated by cave dwellers, visited Malta in 1637 "as one of a group accompanying his Excellency Prince Friedrich Landgrave of Hessen." While here in Malta he spent a couple of days as a guest of the Grand Master at his summer residence Verdala Palace. During that time he was glad to be invited to view the troglodyte community at Għar il-Kbir and left a detailed account of their life there. He described how very organised they were, that they stored bread and cheeses in rock hewn cupboards, kept water in huge pottery jars, hung bundles of onions and garlic from the roof and even built ovens for baking bread in the cave. Cows, sheep, hens and donkeys were kept penned up in other parts of the well ventilated caves, and their dung was used as fuel.

Kircher described the troglodytes' eating habits with great interest;"they do not eat cow or sheep or chicken meat, since they keep this for sale to make much profit. They are satisfied to live on bread, cheese, milk, onions, garlic, and other vegetables. To demonstrate to me the truth of these facts the grand master asked to have a table laid out with all sorts of meat and all that which might be considered really excessive in a grand and delicious meal on one side, and cheese, onions, garlic, cauliflowers and food which they call macaroni, on the other. He then called the Troglodytes he had earlier asked to help in the kitchen. Immediately they turned away from the selected meats and did not even touch it. They turned to the food they were used to and with which they are satisfied. This they ate up in handfuls like hungry dogs."

It is a pity Kircher was so focussed on the cave dwellers' interests that he failed to list what constituted a grand and delicious meal in those days; however we are lucky enough to have quite such a vivid description of the troglodytes' favourite foods. The "hungry dogs" observation is a little unjust; it must have been the way pasta was eaten in those days as many travellers noted while travelling through southern Italy especially of lazzaroni or poorer class of Neapolitans and Sicilians.

Two hundred years after Athanius Kircher visited Malta, when George French Angus was "rambling" through Sicily and Malta in 1811 he described the way a Sicilian family ate their pasta, noting with surprise that they used their fingers as well as forks, "When seated, the good woman turned out a rotolo of maccaroni into a large dish, which I expected was intended for me, but to my surprise and astonishment, the whole family surrounded it instantly, and began to demolish it with wooden forks, cramming as much into their mouths at first as possible, and then dexterously pushing in the depending filaments with their fingers. This is the true Sicilian mode of eating maccaroni, though certainly not the most polite." [1]

Macaroni or pasta is frequently mentioned by travel writers describing Malta, they even ate it on board ships sailing here as Patrick Brydone did in June 1770". In spite of appearances, and our officer's wise prognostications, the wind changed in the afternoon, and we got under sail by six o'clock; we passed the Straits, and coasted along till eight, when we landed to cook some macaroni we had purchased of our sailors, and try if we could shoot something for sea-store, as we have still a long voyage before us."[2]

George French Angus, a more cheerful visitor, encountered macaroni in St Paul's Bay when he went by boat to visit the chapel there, "... we walked over the sand to the chapel of St Paul, which is said to be erected on the very spot where the natives kindled the fire when the apostle was shipwrecked on this island... on reaching the entrance of this chapel we paused, for instead of beholding St Paul in the doorway, we encountered a burly Maltese officer sitting at his dinner in the outer chamber of the sacred edifice, and doing ample justice to an enormous dish of boiled Macaroni. I bowed, and the officer looking up for a moment from his interesting occupation, returned my salutation." Unfortunately he doesn't mention whether the macaroni was served with sauce or not as he does when he writes about pasta in Sicily and says that it was "a dish of maccaroni, very nicely cooked, with the native appendage of Tomata sauce".

1   George French Angus, *A Ramble in Malta and Sicily,* 1841
2   Patrick Brydone, *A Tour Through Sicily and Malta: In a Series of Letters to William Beckford, Esq. of Somerly in Suffolk,* (1st ed.) 1773

TOMATO SAUCES

Once the myth that tomatoes are poisonous was dispelled tomatoes took hold of Mediterranean food and never let go. Pasta with tomato sauce is the very essence of a clichéd image of Mediterranean food; it is amazing to think that the first recipe did not appear before Leonardi wrote *L'Apicio Moderno* in 1790 and included a recipe for tomato sauce. The following are some of my favourite tomato sauce recipes.

SMOOTH RAW SUMMER TOMATO SAUCE

This delicate sauce must be made in summer when it is the tomato season and the flavour of summer tomatoes is unbeatable.

1 kg very red, ripe beefsteak
or field tomatoes
At the very least 5–6 tbs olive oil
Handful basil leaves
Salt and pepper

All that needs to be done is to blanch peel and seed the tomatoes, put them in the blender with the olive oil and basil and blend until perfectly smooth. In the meantime, boil the pasta in lots of salted water, sieve when cooked and pop it back into the saucepan. Pour the blended sauce over the pasta and stir well to mix. Serve drizzled with additional olive oil and sprinkled with salt and pepper.

This sauce matches beautifully with homemade *tagliatelli all' uova*, but if using bought pasta it would be best to use *spaghettini* or perhaps some commercially produced *pasta all' uova*.

CHUNKY RAW TOMATO SAUCE

1 kg ripe summer beefsteak, field tomatoes or really ripe *żenguli* ones
Garlic (The quantity used is optional)
2 handfuls torn basil leaves
At least 5 tbs olive oil
Salt and pepper
Flaked Parmesan cheese to serve

Peel, seed and roughly chop the tomatoes, put them in a bowl and stir in the rest of the ingredients (except for the Parmesan) and leave the tomatoes to marinate while you boil the pasta. Once the pasta has boiled, sieve it, put it back in the saucepan, pour over the sauce and stir to mix well and serve dressed with some more olive oil and the Parmesan flakes scattered over the top. Either penne or farfalle pasta would be best with this sauce, as would any short pasta, but penne or farfalle are best.

THICK TOMATO SAUCE

This tomato sauce is so full of flavour and rich it is simply irresistible.

2 kg tomatoes, preferably *żenguli*
garlic to taste
2 or 3 tbs olive oil
Pinch sugar
Pinch salt

Peel and crush the garlic and put it in a saucepan with the olive oil and barely simmer over the lowest heat possible just enough to warm the garlic and release the aroma and flavour. In the meantime, blanch and skin the tomatoes. Once that is done remove the calyx and chop them roughly. Then put them in the pot with the garlic and olive oil, add the salt and sugar, stir and cover the pot. Turn the heat up slightly and leave the tomatoes to simmer gently until the tomato sauce is thick and saucy. Serve as it is over hot pasta or blend for a smoother consistency.

LIGHT TOMATO SAUCE

This is a standard tomato sauce recipe that is extremely useful as it freezes very well and is excellent to bottle if you have freezer space problems.

Any amount of summer tomatoes
Some basil leaves (optional)
1 sugar lump (optional)

Cut all the tomatoes in half to check that they are good and then put them all in a saucepan that takes them comfortably add the sugar and basil if using. Bring the tomatoes to the boil and simmer, uncovered for about three quarters of an hour or until the tomatoes are very well cooked and soft enough to fall apart.

Put the whole lot through a food mill or pass purée and taste the sauce. If you would prefer a thicker sauce then put it into a clean saucepan and simmer gently until it is as thick as you like. Remember to stir it from time to time so that the bottom won't stick and burn.

This sauce may be used as it is or as a base to make many sorts of sauce like Norma, puttanesca, arrabiata, rabbit or Bolognese sauces and used to dress pasta dishes like gnocchi or ravioli. Freeze excess in suitable containers or bottle the sauce as follows: Pour the sauce into sterilised, well sealed jars. Then put them in a saucepan wide enough to hold the jars comfortably and deep enough to ensure the jars are completely immersed in water. Bring the water to a gentle boil very slowly and simmer them for ¾ of an hour. Allow the jars to cool down in the pot, then remove them from the water and a day later check that the jars are airtight. Store the sauce in a cool dark place for up to a year. Do not use if the seal is gone.

ROASTED TOMATO SAUCE

This is another easy way to make a delicious tomato sauce.

2 kg of tomatoes
A large onion, peeled
A head of garlic, peeled
A couple of chilli peppers (optional)
Basil leaves
Olive oil
Salt and pepper
1 tbs of sugar

Split the tomatoes in half and put in the oven dish with the garlic, onion and chilli. Pour over lots of olive oil, stir well, and add the basil leaves, salt, pepper and sugar and roast at gas mark 8 for an hour or until the tomatoes have begun to brown well. Remove from the oven, put through a food mill pass pure, and if it isn't as thick as you would like it to be then simply either put the strained sauce back in the washed oven dish and bake until it has reduced to the required thickness, or else put it in a sauce pan and simmer away the excess liquid until the sauce is as thick as required. This sauce freezes very well.

The pasta the burly guard in St Paul's Bay was enjoying was probably made in M. Pietro Paolo Agius' macaroni works where pasta was made on a quasi industrial scale. This factory was visited by George French Angus, "I went through this gentleman's macaroni works, which are very extensive, and there I saw the various processes employed in the preparation of this substance, which is one of the chief articles of food in the south of Europe.

The mills for grinding the corn are turned by mules, and numbers of miserable looking men and women are employed in forming the paste into an infinite variety of shapes which is then dried in the sun, and afterwards packed up for exportation."[1]

One shape that was well known in the 18th century and until quite recently was *fdewwex*. Ġużè Cassar Pullicino[2] wrote that Agius described *fdewwex* as "pasta to cook, much used by our farmers; a sort of tagliatelli." He said that the strands were about a hand span long and cooked with herbs, legumes and sometimes cooked in milk when it was called *Fdewwex mal-ħalib*, once very popular in rural areas. Joseph Aquilina wrote that *fdewwex* occurred in the saying *il-qarib mal-qarib bħall-fdewwex mal-ħalib* meaning family members stick together like *fdewwex* and milk, indicating that *fdewwex* cooked in milk was a very common combination and familiar to all, which is why it became part of an old proverb.

1   George French Angus, *A Ramble in Malta and Sicily*, 1841
2   Ġ. Cassar-Pullicino, 'Antichi Cibi Maltesi' in *Melita Historica: Journal of the Malta Historical Society*, 3 (1961) 2 (31-54)

MAKING PASTA

The standard equation for this dough is 1 large egg to every 100g. flour with a generous pinch of salt and a dash of olive oil. To make enough pasta for four generous helpings:

300g plain flour (preferable "00")
3 large eggs or 4 medium ones

Pile the flour up into a low mound on a work surface and make a wide hollow in the top. Crack the eggs gently into the hollow and begin to beat the eggs together with a fork, tipping in some oil from the edges of the mound with your other hand. If the dough seems at all dry add another egg. As the dough begins to thicken start to knead and carry on for at least 10 minutes, until the mass on the table turns into smooth, pliable dough. Add more flour if it is sticky.

Wrap the dough in cling film and rest it for at least an hour otherwise it will be difficult to roll out. Then, cut the dough into four chunks and start to roll out the first piece. The others must be kept covered to prevent the dough drying out. Roll out each using a pasta rolling machine or rolling pin until you have thin sheets of pasta. To make spaghetti, dust a sheet of pasta with some flour or semolina, roll or fold it up and cut across to make strands of pasta, opting for the right width to make *tarja*, *vermicelli, spaghetti, linguine, tagliatelli, papardalle* and so on up the scale. *Farfalle* are easy to make; simply cut the pasta into little oblongs and pinch together the longer edges – they look even better if you use a frilled cutter for the shorter edges.

Cook the pasta in a large saucepan of boiling salted water, calculating a minimum of a litre of water to every 100g. pasta, other wise the pasta will stick and ruin.

Variations: Puréed spinach added to the mix at the same time as the eggs makes green pasta, two fresh cuttlefish ink sacs makes jet black pasta, puréed dried tomatoes makes a reddish pasta, chopped herbs makes green speckled pasta – just carry on with ideas that include chilli pasta, black pepper pasta and so on. Simply add a favourite ingredient to the basic, fail-safe recipe above and create a new pasta dish.

freshly cut tagliatelle or fdewwex

**BARTOLOMEO SCAPPI 1570
"TO PREPARE A THICK SOUP
OF TAGLIATELLE"**

"Work two pounds of flour, three eggs and warm water into a dough, kneading it on a table for a quarter of an hour. Roll it out thin with a pin and let the sheets of dough dry out a little. With a cutting wheel trim away the irregular parts, the fringes. When it has dried a little, though not too much as it would break up, sprinkle it with flour through the sifter so it will not stick. Then take the rolling pin, and beginning at one end, wrap the whole sheet loosely onto the pin, draw the pin out and cut the rolled up dough crosswise with a broad thin knife. When they are cut, broaden them. Let them dry out a little and when they are dry, filter off the excess flour through a sieve. Make a soup of them with a fat meat broth or milk and butter. When they are cooked, serve them hot with cheese, sugar and cinnamon.

Cutting pasta into farfalle

CTIEB TAL CHCINA;
SECOND EDITION 1908
TRUMBUNI JEU FDEUUEX
BIR-RICOTTA FIL FORN

Ma nofs-artal trumbuni jew fdeuuex lesti nofs artal ricotta imhauuda ma erbhga baidiet, hacca giobon u ftit melh. Uara li tcun ghalleit il ghagin u icun bired, lesti forma tal-landa idlica taijeb bil butir, u itfa geuua figha il ghagin, li tcun imhauuad taijeb mar-ricotta u baid li tcun lesteit, fuku aghmel ftit butir iehor u kiegheda fil forn sa chemm tihmar. Jech trida fil meida min ghair il forma (chif hu xierak) biex tinkalghalech, roxx il forma bis-smid uara li kcun dlicta bil butir. Biex tinkalghalec bil heffa, dauuar sicchina bein il ghagin u il forma, akliba geuua id-dixx il ghandu jigi fil mejda, u tigha daktein fuk il kieh – arfa il forma bil mod u tcun lesta.

FDEWWEX BIĊ-ĊIĊRI

Leeks, chickpeas and pasta make for a delicious combination and a pleasant supper. The chickpeas combine with the wheat in the pasta to form a complete protein which is easy to digest. And it's quick to prepare, the ideal meal for a burly Maltese officer.

Wash three large Malta-grown leeks very carefully to remove all dirt and grit. Cut them into 1cm chunks and fry them in some good fresh olive oil until they are melting soft. Use tinned chickpeas to be quick: a 200g tin is enough. Rinse them thoroughly under running water in a sieve or colander to remove as much of that tinned taste as possible. Chop some lovage (karfus), a favourite herb of Roman and Medieval cooks and found in every one of the recipes in Apicius, and add it to the leeks along with the chickpeas. Stir in 250ml of vegetable stock and let the pot simmer for about 10 minutes. Meanwhile, cut some homemade dough into strips (use the recipe on the opposite page) and boil them in well-salted water for two minutes. Add them to the leek and chickpea sauce, and top with a grated Parmesan cheese. Serve immediately. You can use commercial pappardelle instead of homemade lasagne cut into strips.

Ġuże Cassar Pullicino cites a couple of different types of old fashioned pasta made in Malta in his article *Antici Cibi*[1]; one is *simara* made by peasant women who used to use *simara* or marine rush stalks to make pasta. They wrapped pasta dough around the reeds, allowed it to dry and then drew the reeds out to make hollow macaroni, making it lightweight and easy to digest, probably similar to modern *bucatini*. *Fettul* was another, translated by Joseph Aquilina as strips of flour paste twirled by one's fingers to give it the long and narrow shape of a ribbon such as *vermicelli* in the case of pasta.

kusksu pasta

KUSKSU

Kusksu is a very old sort of Maltese pasta described by Vassalli in his lexicon published in 1796 as "peperini, sorta di pasta fina," or a type of fine pasta, shaped like peppercorns. It is normally used in soup. To make a pot of kusksu to serve 4 – 6 people:

4 tbs Olive oil
1 large onion – peeled and finely chopped
3 or 4 cloves of garlic – peeled and crushed
3 tbs kunserva or 200ml chopped peeled tomatoes
200g kusksu pasta
400g shelled peas
400g podded broad beans (peel them if you wish)
2½ litres vegetable stock or water

To finish
Grated Parmesan to taste
Freshly ground black pepper
2 tbs finely chopped parsley

Fry the onion and garlic till soft and golden add the tomatoes or Kunserva and stir in. Add the vegetable stock or water and stir. Add the peas and broad beans and simmer for about 15 – 20 minutes. Stir in the pasta and season well, boil until the pasta is done. Serve hot, garnished with grated cheese, black pepper and parsley.

N.B. Watch the soup as it tends to stick to the bottom of the pot, and you may need to add a little more stock or water as the pasta swells considerably during cooking.

---

1   Ġ. Cassar-Pullicino, 'Antichi Cibi Maltesi' in *Melita Historica : Journal of the Malta Historical Society*, 3 (1961) 2 (31-54)

SOME MODERN PASTA RECIPES

SPAGHETTI RIZZI

The flavour of sea urchin roes is so pure that too many flavours simply detract from the delicate taste of sea urchins, so this pasta recipe uses few ingredients to highlight the flavour of the roes.

Rizzi or sea urchins – or even sea eggs – have always been popular in Malta. John Wignacourt describes how they were fished for in 1914, "the delicacy known as sea eggs, a kind of sea urchin, when deftly opened by the vendor ... should sell for several shillings each. I used to watch the men diving for them in front of my house in Sliema. Their baskets floated on the water and the captors would dive down at short intervals, staying under the water what seemed an interminable time, bringing up the little thorny prizes they had dislodged from its rocky dwelling. Private gentlemen skilled in this accomplishment seemed welcome guests at bathing parties where tea was provided."[1]

SPAGHETTI WITH SEA URCHIN ROE

400g spaghetti or bavette
2 large tomatoes
4 tbs olive oil
4 cloves garlic
2 sprigs marjoram and mint
2 pots sea urchin roes (*rizzi*)

Boil the pasta in plenty of well salted boiling water. In the meantime blend 1 of the pots of sea urchin roes (rizzi), the tomatoes, olive oil, garlic and herbs in a blender till smooth and well combined. When the pasta is *al dente*, save a mug of the boiling water and then drain the pasta. Toss the tomato mix through the pasta, add a little pasta water if necessary to loosen and make it all creamy, and then stir in the rest of the roes. Serve immediately.

---

1   John Wignacourt, *The Odd Man in Malta*, 1914

PASTA WITH BROCCOLI

This quick to prepare pasta dish pairs tomatoes and broccoli, two very healthy vegetables in a low fat dish.

300g short pasta – eg Penne, farfalle, etc
1 whole dark green broccoli, washed and cut into small florets
6 large or 8 medium tomatoes, skinned, seeded and diced
3 stalks fresh garlic, peeled, washed and cut up
2 leeks, peeled, washed and cut up
Extra Virgin Olive Oil
50g toasted pine nuts
Chopped fresh parsley and basil
A little Parmesan, freshly grated

Bring a large pot of water to a rolling boil, salt it well and add the pasta. Bring it back to the boil, then add the prepared broccoli, leeks and garlic after two or three minutes and carry on boiling it all until the pasta and vegetables are cooked but still al dente. Reserve a mug of the boiling water and drain the pasta and vegetables. Put the prepared tomatoes into the pot, add the pasta and vegetables and bring to the boil, adding a little of the reserved pasta water if it seems a little dry. Stir in the olive oil, pour the pasta into a serving dish and scatter it with the herbs, toasted pine nuts and freshly grated parmesan.
Serves 4

Variation: A couple of anchovies mashed into some olive oil and a shredded chilli or two stirred in at the end add great flavour.

SPAGHETTI AND ANCHOVIES

400g spaghetti
Olive oil
1 small chilli finely chopped (optional)
6 cloves garlic – peeled and crushed
10 anchovy fillets preserved in oil
2 tbs Maltese Marjoram – *merqtux*
3 tbs finely chopped fresh wild fennel

Make the topping
200g dry breadcrumbs
3 cloves garlic
3 tbs chopped parsley

This is quick to make and uses ingredients one usually has in the kitchen. While the water to cook the spaghetti is coming to the boil, stew the crushed garlic cloves and chopped chilli very gently in lots of olive oil until they are soft, stir in the anchovies fillets preserved in oil and dissolve them in the hot oil then add the *merqtux* (hardy marjoram) leaves and fennel, stir them in and remove from the heat. In the meantime fry the dried bread crumbs in olive oil with 2 or three crushed cloves of garlic and a tablespoon or two of finely chopped parsley till golden and crunchy. When the spaghetti has boiled remove a mug full of the boiling water and put aside. Drain the spaghetti, return it to the pot and add the garlic and anchovy mix and stir, add the mug of water and stir till well amalgamated and serve topped with the fried bread crumbs instead of grated cheese.

Variation: This variation is perhaps the most unusual and yet the most seasonal and delicious. Add the zest and juice of 2 large and juicy Maltese oranges to the pot of garlic and anchovies and stir in. Then peel away the zest and pith of another two or three oranges and cut out the segments making sure you leave behind the pith and seeds. Put the segments in a bowl and finish cooking and dressing the pasta as above, simply stirring in the orange segments at the end, just before topping the dish with the fried bread crumbs. Add Kunserva to taste to the mug of boling water.

ROSEMARY PESTO

This is dedicated to all lovers of the herb rosemary – I find that rosemary matches all sorts of food and adds an aromatic richness to everything. I like it in apple cakes and pies, with every sort of meat, even some fish. I make herbal infusions with it and add it to biscuit and bread dough – finely chopped of course. I would have bushes of rosemary and lavender growing in every corner of the garden – along with all other herbs of course – and enjoy their scented splendour all the time.

Boil some pasta, then reserve a mugful of the boiling water, strain the pasta and toss in the rosemary pesto, stirring in some of the mug of water to make the sauce creamy. Serve with freshly ground black pepper and extra cheese if necessary.

1 clove garlic, chopped
15 long sprigs fresh young rosemary, leaves picked off the branches
2 tbs chopped parsley
50g pine nuts
50g Parmesan cheese
Salt and pepper
Extra virgin olive oil

Put all the ingredients in a food processor and blend with enough olive oil till fairly smooth. Store this in a bowl in the fridge covered in a film of oil and some cling film. Use rosemary pesto as a pasta sauce, or to baste chicken and other meats before cooking. This sauce goes particularly well with a mix of potato and pumpkin gnocchi

ZALZETT SAUCE FOR PASTA

Zalzett (Maltese sausages) make a really rich and savory sauce for pasta that can be made very quickly. I use sausages made by Charles Butcher in Naxxar.

2 onions, peeled and finely chopped
Olive oil
Sugar
4 fennel and sage sausages
2 glasses red wine
2 bay leaves
4 short sprigs rosemary – very finely chopped
1½ kg peeled and purréed tomatoes

Simply fry the onions in olive oil till a rich golden colour and are just beginning to caramelise. Add the sugar, stir to dissolve and then peel and crumble the fennel and sage sausages into the pot. Fry around till nicely browned and add the red wine, bay leaves and rosemary. Once the wine has reduced, add kilo and a half puréed tomatoes and simmer till the sauce is thick and chunky. *Enough sauce for 500g pasta or for 4 people*

ANGELIC RAVIOLI

THESE ARE PERFECT FOR THE FESTIVE SEASON – WHEN ANGELS ARE AROUND AND ABOUT MORE THAN USUAL

These ravioli may be made up to two weeks before; open freeze them on a tray so that they do not stick together, then put them in a freezer bag and store them in the freezer and cook from frozen.

250g flour
100g – 150g semolina
4 or 5 large eggs

Pile the flour up into a low mound on a work surface a make a wide hollow in the top and crack the eggs gently into the hollow. Begin to beat the eggs together with a fork, tipping in some flour from the edges of the mound with your other hand. If the dough seems at all dry add another egg yolk or a little water. As the dough begins to come together, start to knead it and carry on for at least 10 minutes, until the mass on the table turns into smooth, pliable dough. Add more flour if it is sticky. The dough may be made in a food processor using the dough hook instead of making it by hand, follow the instructions above, just use the machine instead.

Wrap the dough in cling film and rest it for at least an hour otherwise it will be difficult to roll out. Then, cut the dough into four chunks and start to roll out the first piece. The others must be kept covered to prevent the dough drying out. Roll out each using a pasta rolling machine or rolling pin until you have thin sheets of pasta. Then, using an 8.5cm diameter frilled cutter cut rounds into the thin sheets of pasta dough, dot with the filling below; brush the edges with beaten egg, fold over and seal firmly.

Filling

300g ricotta
5 slices bresoala
100g fresh raw spinach
1 tbs chopped parsley
1 tbs grated parmesan
1 egg – separated
Simply stir all the ingredients together with a fork and use to stuff the ravioli above

To finish the Angelic Ravioli

12 cherry tomatoes
Extra Virgin Olive Oil
100g pine nuts
2 cloves garlic
100g Parmesan cheese
1 bunch parsley
Parmesan flakes and pepper

Bring a large pot of water to the boil and in the meantime roast or fry the cherry tomatoes till slightly softened and make the parsley pesto by blending the pine nuts, parmesan, olive oil, garlic and parsley together to make a smooth soft sauce. Then add salt to the boiling water and add 24 ravioli to the water and boil till *al dente* – either a couple of minutes if they are freshly made or a couple of minutes longer if frozen. Then drain them and arrange them quickly on each plate as follows: a cherry tomato for each angel's head, two ravioli for the wings and a triangle of parsley pesto for the dress. Drizzel the whole with fresh Extra Virgin Olive Oil and serve with a bowl of Pamresan flakes and the pepper mill to hand round. Serve 2 or 3 angels per plate.

THE GENERAL

THE TRAVEL MEMOIRS OF
GENERAL SIR GEORGE WHITMORE

EDITED BY
Joan Johnson

A watercolour of il-Hanzir tal-Erwieh by Sir George Whitmore (With thanks to Nicholas de Piro)

THE OLD PORKER
Skużi ħanżir

In the past *Skużi ħanżir* (like *skużi xkupa*) was the socially acceptable phrase used by country people to refer to a plain old pig (or broom) as Herbert Ganado explained in his book *Rajt Malta Tinbidel*. But, polite or not, it still meant pig which has always been the source of pork, a very popular meat in Malta and oddly enough, linked to 2 November or All Souls, a day when the souls' of all the dead are venerated.

The All Soul's Pig or *il-Ħanżira tal-Erwieħ* is an All Soul's Day custom that died out during the Second World War and was never revived. A pig, often donated by a generous family, was set free to roam the village streets for a year, enjoying all sorts of snacks, food and interesting left-overs fed to it by the villagers, while growing fatter and fatter until All Soul's Day. Then the pig was slaughtered and roasted at the local bakery or made into a soup called *Il-Borma tal-Erwieħ* or "The All Souls' pot".

In many of the villages, the All Souls' soup preparation was a communal effort, with many villagers joining in and peeling the vegetables for the pot and stirring the soup together, while in other parts of Malta religious communities took over, for example the Capuchin monks made the soup in Floriana. Then the poor of the village were gathered together and each received a plateful of nourishing pork. Sometimes the pig wasn't cooked but was sold instead and the money was given to the church for masses for the souls of all the dead.

This unusual custom is mentioned by Louis De Boisgelin *Ancient and Modern Malta* (1804) "The Maltese are remarkably sober; a clove of garlic, or an onion, anchovies dipped in oil, and salt-fish, being their usual diet. On great festivals, they eat pork. Hogs are very common in towns and villages; many of these animals belong to the church and different convents, and walk about the street both night and day, where they pick up sufficient nourishment. They are seldom molested, and never stolen."

Another long forgotten pre-war practise my mother-in-law remembers in Naxxar was a procession called *Għadd tal-Erwieħ* held on "All Saints Day" when beggars and other hungry people knocked on doors calling for *Karità! Karità!* while holding out bowls hoping they would be filled with some bread or flour, which they usually were. This may have its roots in the old practise of vowing to give some wheat to the poor in honour of the dead or in thanksgiving for a prayer answered.

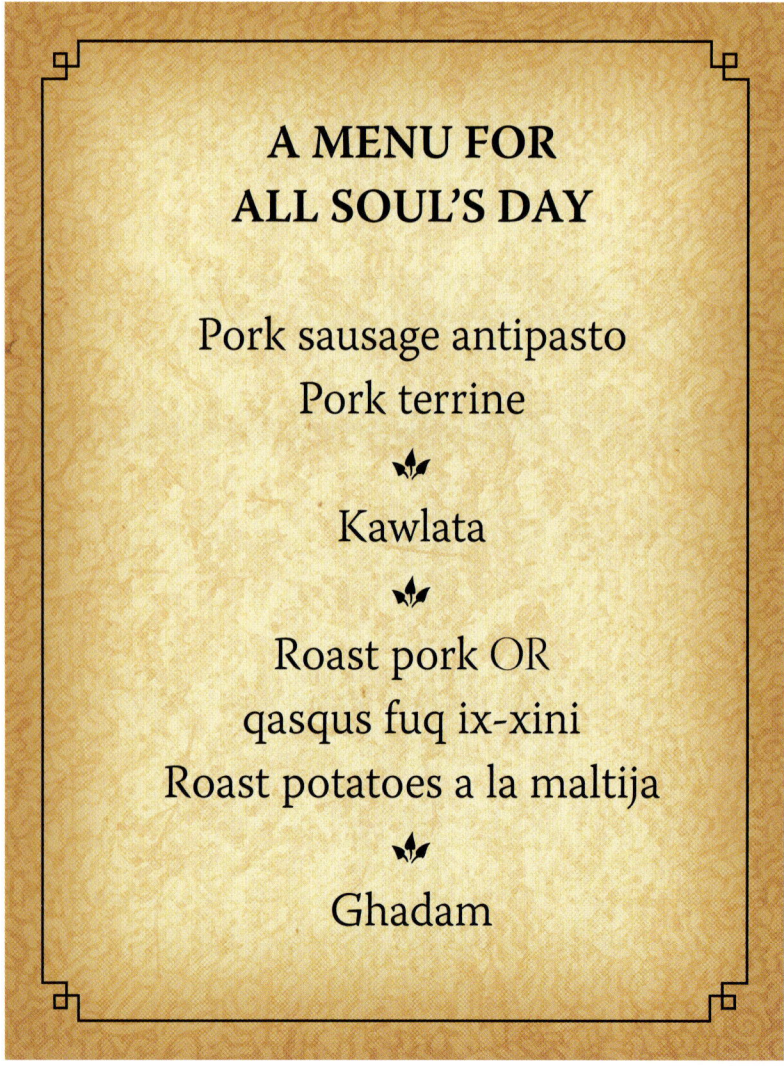

A MENU FOR
ALL SOUL'S DAY

Pork sausage antipasto
Pork terrine

❦

Kawlata

❦

Roast pork OR
qasqus fuq ix-xini
Roast potatoes a la maltija

❦

Ghadam

RAW ZALZETT

Eating raw *zalzett* isn't quite as dangerous as it sounds and in fact they are made to be served raw as well as cooked; the meat is cured so that it is safe to eat. I find these are the best ways to serve raw *zalzett*:

Peel the sausages and spread them on a bit of fresh bread, toasted bread or some galletti.

Serve the peeled sausages with some deep-fried bread dough, sprinkled with salt and fennel seeds.

Tuck some peeled sausage inside a bit of bread dough, deep fry and serve sprinkled with chopped fresh rosemary.

Sausages on galletti, sausages on fresh bread and sausage on deep fried bread dough.

PORK SAUSAGES

Zalzett Malti or Maltese sausages, like all sausages around the world, have been around for a long time. They are a positive consequence of efficient butchery; after portioning and jointing, the trimmings of meat are chopped or minced finely and mixed together with different herbs, spices and salt and stuffed into special tubular casing.

The traditional Maltese sausage mix has always been made up of minced pork, salt, black pepper and crushed coriander seed. Sometimes a little garlic and parsley is stirred in, for a special flavour but not always. Coriander seed is the defining flavour of Maltese sausages compared to some types of Sicilian sausages which, though similar to Maltese ones, are flavoured with fennel seeds. The casing used to make Maltese sausages was natural; this was carefully washed, turned inside out, scraped clean and washed again, then preserved in salt till needed when it was washed again. Nowadays a more hygienic synthetic sort of casing is used. In the past, customers generally had a favourite, trusted butcher who they would commission to fulfil a bulk order of sausages. In the days before refrigeration, the sausages were draped in muslin and hung in the *Tromba tal-Bejt* or stair head, where there was sure to be a cool draught that dried and preserved the sausages.

Maltese sausages suffer from a generally undeserved "too salty" reputation; this is probably because some butchers add too much salt to their sausage mix, so buy your sausages from a reputable butcher. Some people like to give the sausages a light boil to remove some of the excess salt before proceeding with their recipe. However, nowadays many butchers make a less salty version which is absolutely delicious; for example Charles Butcher in Naxxar makes a barbeque version of the traditional sausage recipe which is perfect. The original slightly salty version is often served raw and both sorts may be cooked in many ways. A sausage or two sliced up into a simple pork stew add tremendous flavour, some people like to crumble a couple of sausages into minestra, or simply split them and grill them and serve them with salad or roast the sausages cut into big chunks with small wedges of potatoes scattered with rosemary.

Leli and Victor Grech

ZALZETT FOCCACIA

500g plain flour
1 sachet instant yeast
A tsp salt
2 tbs fennel seeds or chopped fresh rosemary
Tepid Water – Approx. 350ml
3 peeled and very thinly sliced potatoes
3 or 4 *Zalzett*

Heap the flour up on a work surface or in a capacious bowl. Stir in the yeast, salt and fennel seeds or rosemary. Make a well and pour in enough of the tepid water to make dough. Knead it well for at least 10 minutes or until it is smooth and elastic. Leave to rise for ¾ of an hour to an hour or till doubled in size. In the meantime blanch the very thin potato slices for a couple of minutes, drain and put them in a bowl to one side. Peel the sausages and break them up into another bowl and put them to one side as well. Preheat the oven to gas mark 8/230ºC

Once the dough is ready to use just cut it into 3 or 4 pieces – do not knock it back roughly. Flatten and stretch then into roughly round shapes, drizzle with a little olive oil, and spread with the potato slices and crumbled sausage. Bake them in the preheated oven for at least 25 minutes or till golden and crunchy.

*N.B. crumbled sausage meat shrinks considerably so use
more sausage than you would think you need.*

Alternatively; omit the potatoes and knead the peeled sausages directly into the raw bread dough and leave the dough to rise and double in size. Then cut it into 5 pieces, shape them into rounds and flatten them out. Leave them to rise again for about half an hour then dimple it all over by pressing your finger tips gently over the surface. Then bake in the oven preheated to gas mark 9/240ºC for about 20-25 minutes or until golden brown all over. Serve drizzled with oil and sprinkled with fennel seeds and rosemary sprigs.

DRIED ZALZETT

Zalzett Malti are very easy to dry. Simply lay them out on a piece of greaseproof paper in the fridge; make sure they are in a single layer and are not too close together. Leave them, uncovered for approximately two weeks, turning them over every couple of days. They are ready to eat when they are shrunken, hard and semi dry, just like delicious salami.

Serve them as you would salami; thinly sliced as part of a selection of anti pasti or sliced up on galletti and served with drinks before a meal.

Toss thinly sliced dried zalzett in a green salad with croutons.

Use thinly sliced dried zalzett to fill a bread roll with some rocket and olive oil and so on.

PORK TERRINE

This pork terrine is a simple and rustic style terrine that requires little work and keeps in the fridge for up to a week. Although it is not typical of an All Soul's feast, the terrine recipe makes good use of pork meat. It is best matured for two or three days in the fridge before being served so that the flavours blend together.

Mix together the following ingredients for the marinade
75ml red Martini
50ml brandy
100ml white wine
1 tsp fresh thyme leaves
1tsp fresh rosemary – very finely chopped
12 bay leaves

Then put the following ingredients into a large, flat dish and pour over the marinade, cover with cling film and refrigerate for 24 hours:
500g skinned loin of pork – diced
500g belly of pork, boned and skinned – diced
300g cleaned chicken livers – diced
50g stoned prunes – roughly chopped (soaked separately in some brandy)
Large handful pistachios (shelled and kept aside)

To finish
200g whole, cleaned chicken livers
3 whole eggs
1 tbs flour
Seasoning
Grated nutmeg
24 slices streaky bacon, rinds removed

Fry the whole livers in a little butter just long enough to brown but not cook through and then put them to one side to cool. In the meantime drain the diced meats and reserve the marinade, mince or roughly blend the meats, stir in the eggs, flour and seasoning to combine, then add the prunes and marinade and mix well.

Hammer the slices of bacon between two sheets of cling film to flatten them out and then use them to line the base and sides of a loaf tin 24 x 9 x 10cm in such a way that the ends of the bacon slices overhang the sides of the loaf tin. Next, put half the meat mixture in the bottom of the lined tin, lay the fried livers on top then cover with the rest of the meat mix, press down firmly and enclose with the overhanging bacon. Bang the tin down on a surface to remove any gaps and cook Bain Marie (put into a roasting tin and pour enough very hot water into the tin to come half way up the sides of the loaf tin) for 2 hours in the oven preheated to gas mark 4/180ºC. Remove the dish from the roasting tin and leave to cool. Then weight down the terrine overnight in the fridge. The easiest way to do this is to cut out a piece of cardboard that will fit inside the rim of the dish, cover it thickly with foil, then place it on top of the terrine and place a few weights or unopened cans on top.

N.B. Some juices may over flow so put the loaf tin in a bowl or on a deep plate in the fridge to avoid a mess.

Serve the terrine with bread, toast, tomato chutney and salad.

TOMATO CHUTNEY

Chutney is a condiment made with a mixture of fruits and vegetables cooked and preserved with vinegar, sugar and a little salt. They have become an internationally popular preserve but originated in India, the name derives from the Hindu word *chatni*.

The Tomato chutney below is excellent served with meat, curries, cheeses, cold meats and salads.

2 kg skinned and chopped tomatoes
2 big onions, peeled and finely chopped
500g apples
200g sultanas
200g raisins
200g dates
1 litre cider vinegar
700g soft brown sugar
1 tbs salt
3 tsp yellow mustard seeds
2 tsp ground allspice

Put all the ingredients in a large wide pan and bring to the boil. Then turn down to a gentle simmer and cook slowly over a low heat, stirring every now and again for about two hours or until the chutney is thick and an even colour.

Pour into hot sterilised jars and screw on the lids. Label and store in cool place. Preferably allow the chutney to mature for two months before using it.

CAULATA

This recipe is taken from the second edition of *Ctieb Tal Chcina* written by "ELV" and published in 1908

Dan il platt li hu tant usat minna il Maltin ftit huma dauch li jaghmluh taijeb.

Hu caboccia, pastarda, zeug gidriet, zeug zfunnariet, neveuua, biccia kargha hamra u tnein jeu tliet patatiet, katta dan il haxix irkik ferm, itfa collox geuua lembia bl'ilma biex jitnaddaf taijeb, imbghad saffieh u itfghu geuua borma ta Franza (geuua borma ta Franza ghax qualunque haxix jehzien meta jtghalla gio borom tal-landa). Gio din il borma itfa ucoll mal haxix nofs-artal laham tal maijal daksxein grass, nofs-artal zalzett, nofs-artal laham tac-cianga, quart laham immellah, par sakain, (u min jggustagha uidna ucoll) tal maijal. Itfa ucoll mahhom dakxeinzerrigha tal buzbiez; ghatti collox bl'ilma u hallieh jaghli saghtein u nofs. Meta tcun lesta, u il haxix icun inhall collu, arfa il-laham b'furchetta u keghdu fi platt separate, u il caulata tigi fil meida f'supiera.

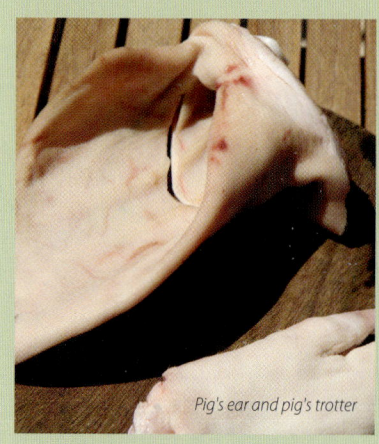

Pig's ear and pig's trotter

KAWLATA

2 or 3 tbs olive oil
1 large onion
A handful of peeled garlic
cloves (optional)
At least 3 stalks Maltese
celery called *karfus*
3 sprigs rosemary, stripped off the
branch and finely chopped
2 ripe tomatoes, peeled and seeded
3 large carrots
½ kg pumpkin
3 large or 6 small *qaraghbali*
½ a *qara twil* (when in season)
3 potatoes
½ a cabbage
½ a cauliflower
Chicken or vegetable stock (or water
and vegetable bouillon powder)
Salt and pepper
1 or 2 tbs Kunserva especially if
the tomatoes are winter ones
1 or 2 pork knuckles /xikel and/
or a couple of pigs trotters or
some meaty pork ribs
2 Maltese pork sausages – sliced up

First fry the pieces of pork in a little olive oil and finely chopped rosemary till golden. Then, remove the pieces of pork and add the onion, one of the sausages skinned and crumbled up, and the celery and cook till soft in the olive oil. Then dice the peeled and seeded tomatoes, add them to the onion mixture and leave them to dissolve into the onions. In the meantime, peel and chop the rest of the vegetables, adding them to the pot as you go, allowing them to release their juices, aroma and flavour. Then put the pork back into the pot, stir it around and add enough boiling water to cover the vegetables comfortably. Bring everything back to the boil, add salt and pepper, turn the heat right down to a gentle simmer for about and hour. Then, add the sliced up sausages and simmer for another half an hour to three quarters of an hour.

SERVE THE SOUP WITH SOME ROSEMARY TOAST MADE AS FOLLOWS:
Simply brush some slices of Maltese bread with olive oil and grill on a very hot griddle, on a barbeque or in a very hot oven until golden brown and crisp, then rub with fresh rosemary and garlic and scatter with some more finely chopped rosemary.

ROAST PORK

Pork is one of the easiest meats to roast; some cuts require long slow roasting, others respond to faster roasting while some cuts of pork are best braised or stewed.

Slow roasted shoulder is perfect when cooking for a large group; the meat should be lovely and juicy and so tender that it almost falls apart. Another cut that may be cooked slowly is *porchetta ala romana* – in this case the butcher will pull the belly part of the pork up over the loin so that the loin which tends to be rather dry will be kept moist while the meat is roasted.

ROAST PORK TO FEED A CROWD

A shoulder or leg of pork about 7 kg in weight
Coarse salt
Fennel seeds
Olive oil
Large bunch of rosemary and bay branches

Ask the butcher to trim the pork and score the skin for crackling. Pre heat the oven as hot as it can go while you rub and press fennel seeds and coarse salt generously into the slits in the skin. Put it into the extremely hot oven for at least half an hour or till the skin begins to crackle and bubble. Then open the oven, put the bay and rosemary branches into the bottom of the oven and turn the oven right down to gas mark 2 and leave the pork to cook slowly for the next 8 to 10 hours – either overnight for lunch or all day for supper. This recipe works every time and the meat is incredibly tender and covered in the most perfect, crisp crackling.
N.B. Roast a leg of pork in the same way

MALTESE ROAST POTATOES

Calculate 2 medium potatoes and ½ an onion per person.
Garlic (optional)
Fennels seeds
Coriander seeds (optional)
Fresh rosemary sprigs
Seasoning
Olive oil

Peel and slice up the potatoes and onions and a couple of garlic cloves per person, toss them together in an earthenware oven dish with olive oil, fresh rosemary, fennel seeds, coriander seeds and add a little water. Add salt and pepper and pop it into the oven for an hour and a half to two hours in a medium to hot oven.

Cooked by Mark Camilleri

PORK COOKED IN MILK

Although this is a traditionally Italian recipe it is so good and very easy to make that it is worth including.

2½ kg of pork loin, (de-boned and rolled)
½ tsp freshly grated nutmeg
Olive oil
50g of butter
1½ litres full fat milk
1 tbs Muscavado sugar
Four bay leaves
6 sprigs fresh thyme – leaves stripped from the stems
6 cloves garlic
2 sprigs rosemary
The grated zest of one lemon
Seasoning

Crush the garlic and mix it with the rosemary, a little oil and zest of 1 of the lemons. Push a knife through the pork and push in the lemon, rosemary and garlic mixture. Then rub the pork with the grated nutmeg, grated zest of the other lemon, thyme leaves, seasoning and sugar and leave it to marinate overnight or at least a couple of hours.

Then heat some olive oil and the butter in a cast iron casserole and gently brown the pork in it, turning it a couple of times until golden brown. Then add the milk and bring it slowly to a simmer, stirring to scrape all the burnt bits off the bottom of the pan. Then add the bay leaves, turn down the heat and put on the lid, tilting it slightly to allow steam to escape and the pork to cook very gently. Let it cook this way for about 2 hours, stirring every now and again to stop it sticking.

Carefully remove the pork from the pan and slice it up. Spoon out the crusty, milky curds from the pot, dividing them fairly between the plates, then generously spoon over the thinner milky gravy.

GĦADAM

Another traditional food prepared to celebrate the day were bone-shaped filled biscuits called *għadam*. These are still customary today, and no wonder as they are delicious. The biscuits are easy to make and resemble Easter figolli except that they are shaped like bones, as a cruel but sweet tasting reminder that the day is set aside to honour all the souls' of the dead. A less common variant of the bone shaped version is a skull and cross-bones shaped biscuit, made of the same pastry and filling, simply shaped differently.

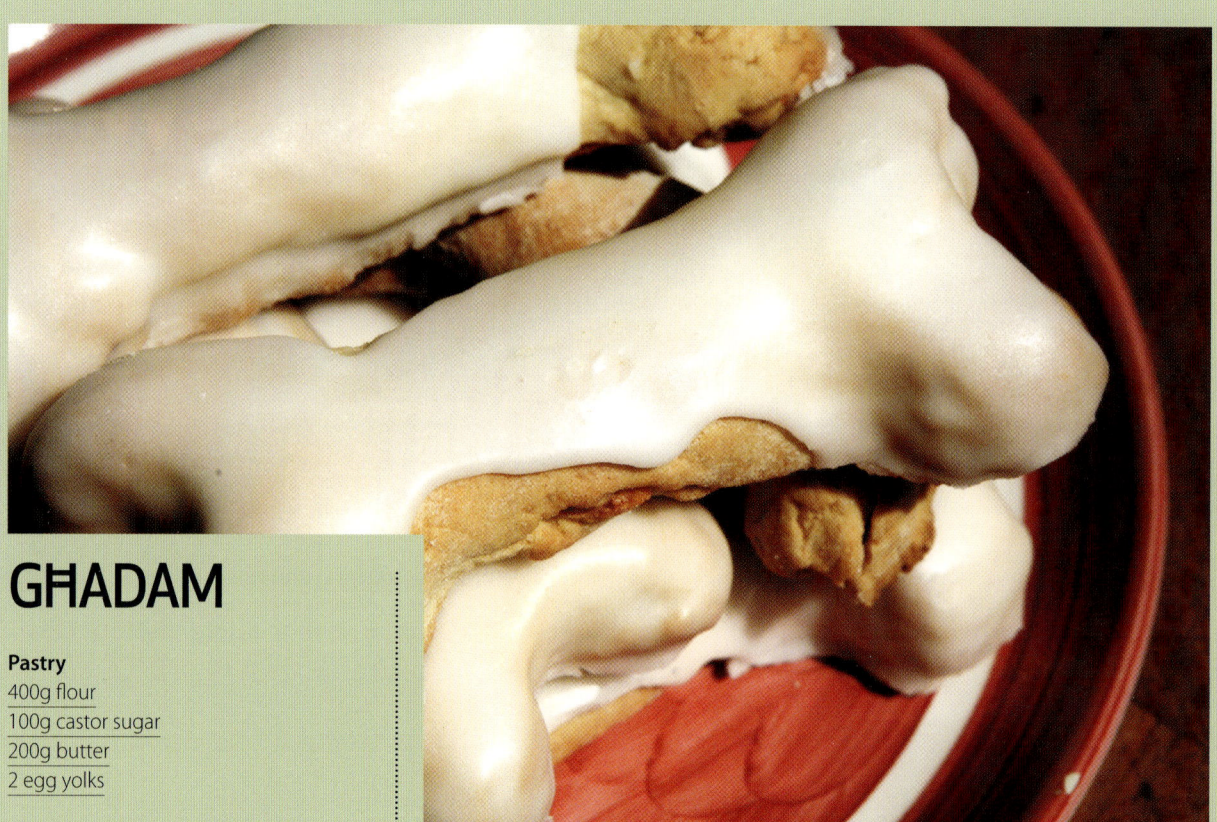

GĦADAM

Pastry
400g flour
100g castor sugar
200g butter
2 egg yolks

Rub the butter into the flour and sugar, make a hollow and add the yolks. Stir to make dough but if it is too dry still add either a dash of water or Dry Martini and knead briefly or until you have smooth dough. Put to one side while you make the almond filling.

Almond filling
300g finely ground almonds
300g castor sugar
Grated rind of a large lemon
2 egg whites

Stir together the dry ingredients and add the egg whites. Stir to make a fairly dry paste. Break off pieces and mould into classic bone shapes – a rod with a rounded edge split in two rounded knobs. Put these aside while you roll out the pastry. Cut the pastry into squares large enough to roll around the bone shaped bits of almond filling, and then wrap the filling up in the pastry, tucking it around to make a neat bone shape.

Lay the bones on a well greased or non-stick paper lined baking trays and bake at gas mark 5/190ºC for about half an hour or until they are golden brown. Then put them on a rack to cool. Ice the cooled bones with thick white glace icing, royal icing or coat in melted chocolate. The white icing is more realistic though, as old bones are said to be a greyish white…

A PORCINE FEAST

Pork was the star of a huge meal served on board HMS Assistance mentioned in Henry Teonge's diary and on the 4th February 1675 when Henry Teong was in Malta "this day dined with us Sir Roger Strickland, Captaine Temple, Captaine Harrice and on(e) gentleman more. Wee had a gallant baked pudding, an excellent legg of porke and colliflowers, an excellent dish made of piggs' petti-toes, 2 rosted hogg's head, 3 ducks, a dish of Cyprus burds, and pistachoes and dates together, and store of good wines.

TO MAKE ANY QUELCHECHOSE

To make a quelchechose which is a mixture of many things together; take the eggs and break them, and do away with half of the whites, and after they are beaten, put them to a good quantity of sweet cream, currants, cinnamon, cloves, mace, salt and a little ginger, spinach, endive and mary-gold flowers grosly chopt, and beat them all very well together. then take Pigs Pettitoes slic'd and grofly chopt, mix them with the Eggs, and with your hand stirre them exceeding well together; then put in sweet Butter in your Frying-pan, and being melted, put in all the rest, and fry it brown without burning, ever & anon turning it, till it be fryed enough ; then dish it upon a flat plate, and so serve it forth. Onely here is to be observed, that your Pettitoes must be very well boyled before you put them into the Fry-case.

15 This morning wee warp out of the harbour, with 6 merchantmen and a doggar, which wee are to convoy towards the Straits mouth. Here also wee tookin 2 mounths provision, and fresh water. And as wee goe out, wee meete 6 gallys of Malta, coming in in all their pompe, and they salute us, and wee them, and part. And heare at Malta (which was very strainge to mee) at this time of the yeare wee bought radishes, cabbidges, and excellent colly flowers, and large ons for Id. a peice.

'Mnarja' (detail), Antoine Favray

THE RABBIT HABIT[1]
Il-fenek u l-fenkata

D issatisfaction flavoured the air in late 18th century Malta; the people were hungry and "intrigues... were going on under the noses of the dulled and indifferent Knights." One group of imminently illustrious people went to supper in Floriana, "... on the last night of the year 1772, in the midst of all this suppressed excitement, a priest named Don Gaetano Mannarino was entertaining at his house in Floriana a select company of about forty Maltese, priests, soldiers, barbers and bakers, with a sprinkling of peasants. The appetising supper of steaming ravioli and fragrant stewed pork, washed down with plenty of wine, was served, he explained to celebrate the piety of his brother Don Paolo, who had vowed, if saved from a mortal illness to offer a procession, accompanied by music, to the church of St Publius in Floriana..."[2] but after a great deal of wine, the host and his guests were soon relaxed enough to plot rebellion. Drugging the *Porta Reale* (city gate) guards and all sorts of other ideas were finalised over supper, but the authorities seem to have got wind of the plans and the uprising had to be postponed.

'Baqra', Maltese rabbit stewing pot (from Palazzo Falson, Mdina)

1   Title borrowed from John Wignacourt, *The Odd Man in Malta*
2   E. W. Schermerhorn, *Malta of the Knights*

A SUPPER FOR REBELS

RAVJUL (RAVIOLI)

The recipe below is for standard Maltese ravioli filled with ricotta that are very popular today. Unfortunately, the type of ravioli served to Don Mannarino's guests is unspecified, and although his cook probably did use ricotta or soft Maltese sheep's cheese (ġbejniet) to stuff the ravioli, meat could easily have been used instead, as meat always conferred cachet to a celebratory meal in the past.

300g plain flour (preferably "00")
200g fine semolina
5 large eggs or 6 medium ones
2 tbs extra virgin olive oil

Pile the flour up into a low mound on a work surface and make a wide hollow in the top. Crack the eggs gently into the hollow and add the oil. Begin to beat the liquids together with a fork, tipping in some flour from the edges of the mound with your other hand. If the dough seems at all dry add another egg. As the dough begins to thicken start to knead and carry on for at least 10 minutes, until the mass on the table turns into smooth, pliable dough. Add more flour if it is sticky. Wrap the dough in cling film and rest it for at least an hour otherwise it will be difficult to roll out.

In the meantime make the filling
500g ricotta or 10 large fresh *gbejniet* (drained overnight in a sieve in the fridge)
3 egg yolks
Freshly ground black pepper to taste
3 tbs finely chopped parsley or marjoram (*merqtux*)

Put all the ingredients into a bowl and mix together with a fork until well blended. Put it in the fridge until required.

Then make the ravioli: Dust a large work surface with semolina and, using your longest rolling pin, start to roll out the dough until you have a large thin sheet of pasta like a piece of material; or use a pasta rolling machine if you have one. Then, using a ravioli or round cutter, cut circles into the dough and put spoonfuls of the filling in the centre of each round. Fold over each circle, carefully excluding any air bubbles and seal by moistening the edges and pressing them firmly together. Lay them on a tray dusted with semolina until it is time to boil them. Refrigerate them if necessary.

Drop them in boiling well salted water and boil them for 2 or 3 minutes, depending on how thick the pastry is; just bite the edge of one to find out if well cooked. Drain the ravioli and serve with sauce and grated Parmesan.

THE SAUCE

Tomato sauce is the most widespread dressing for ravioli today, but in the latter half of the 18th century tomato sauce had only just been invented. When Christopher Columbus brought tomatoes back to Europe they were first treated with suspicion and ignored – at best people thought they were some sort of an aphrodisiac, possibly detrimental to spiritual and physical health. This initial mistrust changed slowly and by the end of the 17th century tomatoes had been absorbed into Spanish and Italian cuisine to the extent that they featured in a cookbook by Antonion Lantini "Lo scalco alla moderna" 1692; but it was not until 1790 when Neapolitan chef Francesco Leonardi wrote *L'Apicio Moderno* that tomato sauce was paired with pasta. So unless Don Gaetano Mannarino's cook was innovative or completely up to date he probably served the ravioli with some of the gravy from the pork stew (below) and if he was dreadfully old fashioned he might have taken a leaf out of Bartolomeo Scappi's 1570 "Opera" or cookery book and served the ravioli with cheese, sugar and cinnamon. However nowadays most ravioli are usually served with tomato sauce (as in photo left) but may be presented with any sauce of choice.

TORTELLINI IN BRODO

Tortellini or capelletti in brodo are traditionally served on New Year's Eve in Italy, so perhaps Don Mannarino served these rather than ravioli to his fellow insurgents. The meat broth, made from beef and a "boiling" chicken, is the essential liquid in which the tortellini are cooked and eaten. "Tortellini are doomed to death by broth …" is the frequent lament of Italian culinary experts who have decreed that only an excellent home-made broth can enhance the intense flavour of the tortellini, while thin commercial broth ruins genuine tortellini.

Tortellini need a little patience to make as they are small but otherwise uncomplicated. Egg pasta is rolled out thinly, cut into small squares, dotted with filling, folded into a triangle, wound into a ring on the end of the little finger and the points pressed together. The shape is said to have been the creation of a Bolognese cook who dreamt he saw Venus rising from the waves, was inspired by her perfect navel and rushed into his kitchen in an frenzy of dazzled energy to recreate the divine belly-button as a pasta; a romantic legend for a beloved dish.

First make the stock
500g beef for soup
A couple of marrow bones
A boiling chicken
6 carrots
1 large onion
Salt
3 stalks celery
1 leek
1 small sprig fresh rosemary (optional)
1 small fresh sage leaf (optional)

Put all the ingredients in a large stock pot, bring it to a rolling boil, turn it down and simmer it for two to three hours. Then strain the soup, taste it to check for seasoning and chill till needed. Use the meat cooked to make the soup well marinated in an olive oil dressing in salads or chopped to make chunky sandwich fillings or in pies.

The pasta dough
300g plain flour (preferably "00")
3 large eggs or 4 medium ones
Semolina

Pile the flour up into a low mound on a work surface and make a wide hollow in the top. Crack three eggs gently into the hollow. Begin to beat the eggs together with a fork, tipping in some flour from the edges of the mound with your other

hand. If the dough seems at all dry add the other egg. As the dough begins to thicken start to knead and carry on for at least 10 minutes, until the mass on the table turns into smooth, pliable dough. Add more flour if it is sticky.

Wrap the dough in cling film and rest it for at least an hour otherwise it will be difficult to roll out. In the meantime make the filling as directed below. Then, cut the dough into four chunks and start to roll out the first piece. The others must be kept covered to prevent the dough drying out. Roll out each using a pasta rolling machine or rolling pin until you have very thin sheets of pasta.

Dust the sheets of pasta very lightly with semolina and cut them into small squares – approximately 3 cm square.

Put a small bit of filling on each one, and then fold the square over the filling to make a triangle, pressing the edges hard together to seal them. Pick each up by a corner, hold it in place between thumb and baby finger, grab the other corner, wind it round the fingertip and join the two corners under your thumb and press to stick them together, forming a ring. Lay them on a tray lightly dusted with semolina until needed. (refrigerate or freeze them till needed)

The filling
125g freshly grated Parmesan
100g lean pork
100g Parma Ham
100g Mortadella
1 egg
freshly grated nutmeg
butter

While the dough is resting, dice the pork and brown it in a pan for a couple of minutes. Put the pork in the blender with the Parma Ham and the Mortadella and blend till smooth. In a bowl mix the blended meats with the egg, cheese, nutmeg until smooth and chill till needed.

TO SERVE
Simply bring the soup to the boil and cook the tortellini in the soup till just tender, usually about 5 minutes. It depends how dry or frozen they are, if they are freshly made they will require less cooking. Then serve them in a little soup and offer round some freshly grated Parmesan cheese and the pepper mill.

MAJJAL GĦAD-DOBBU

BRAISED PORK

The term *għad-dobbu* is said to be derived from the French "en daube"[1] and as the prevalent influence on Maltese culture under the knights was French, it must have had some impact on the cuisine.

2 kg chunk of pork shoulder
2 pig's trotters (optional)
A couple of pork cheeks (optional)
4 onions
8 cloves garlic
250 ml chicken stock
500ml good white wine
6 sprigs fresh rosemary – finely chopped
6 sprigs fresh thyme – finely chopped
1 heaped tsp cinnamon
1 tsp ground coriander seed
1 heaped tsp grated orange zest
1 tsp sugar
Salt and pepper
Olive oil
Butter

Peel and slice up the onions thinly, put them in a deep casserole pot with the sugar, and cook them very gently in some butter and olive oil over a low heat till they are very soft and a very pale yellow. Peel and chop the garlic, add it to onions and cook for a little longer, taking care not to brown them at all. Then take them out of the pot, and replace them with the pork, pork cheeks and trotters, turn up the heat and brown the meat on all sides. Return the onions and garlic to the pot, add the herbs, cinnamon, orange zest, stock and wine and bring to the boil. Turn the heat right down and simmer the pork very gently for 2 ½ to 3 hours till it is meltingly soft and "fragrant". Check the pot at regular intervals and top up with a little stock or wine if seems at all dry.

SERVING THE PORK

Some boiled or mashed potatoes would be perfect with pork cooked like this, but not in 1772 as potatoes were still unknown in Malta. The potato plant was introduced to Malta by Bailiff Argotti in 1774, but farmers and cooks took little notice; they viewed the plant as decorative or possibly something to be grown by the dilettante farmer or gardener.

1   Elizabeth Shermerhorn, *Malta of the Knights*

The historian Carmel Cassar wrote that it was not until Alexander Ball introduced the potato as a cash crop and staple food around 1803 that potatoes took off. He chose a few farmers probably from the Zejtun or Axiaq area, and practically forced them to try out the new plants. The resulting crop was sold on the farmers' behalf by Ball to the Victualling Office at an extremely high price. Interestingly enough this account is echoed in the *Calendariu Tal-Bidwi Ghas-Sena 1850* published *Mis-Società Economico-Agraria* in which the author recorded that the first farmer to start to seriously cultivate the potato was Giuseppi Xicluna from Zabbar in January 1805 and that this first crop was very successful. Giuseppi Xicluna planted 24 *ratal* potatoes in his fields; harvested 12 *kantar* (or qantar) and sold them at 20 scut each qantar thus making the grand total of 240 scut. His success was such that other farmers started to grow potatoes and it soon became the cash crop it is today.

In keeping with the 18th century theme of the meal above, serve the pork with some boiled white beans and vegetables like cabbage and cauliflower for which Malta was renowned.

BEANS

250g of dried cannellini beans, soaked overnight or for at least eight hours
5 whole sage leaves + 2 extra finely chopped sage leaves
6 cloves of garlic
Olive oil
2 tbs of chopped parsley

Preheat the oven to gas mark 6/200ºC. Rinse the beans well under running-water then put them in an oven-proof casserole with a tight-fitting lid. Cover them with water, so that there is clear water to a depth of at least three centimetres above the beans. Add the whole sage leaves and the garlic, put on the lid and bring to the boil. Then tilt the lid so that there is some space for steam to come out, and let the mixture bubble fiercely for about 10 minutes. Preheat the oven meanwhile, then transfer the pot to it and carry on cooking for about 75 minutes or until the beans are soft and most of the water has been absorbed. Check every now and again to make sure the beans do not dry out before they are cooked and add a little boiling water if they are drying out too fast. Then remove the cooked sage, and blend half the beans. Stir the resulting puree into the rest of the beans, adding salt, pepper, the finely chopped fresh sage leaves and lots of olive oil. Serve with the pork or anything else.

Elizabeth Schermerhorn does not record what pudding Don Mannarino served to his guests; but a safe guess would be that one of Michele Mercieca's recipes was used as his book, *Libro di Secreti per Fare Cose Dolci di Varii Modi* was published in 1748 and was relatively recent. Most of the recipes are for ice-creams, but there are some recipes for biscuits, candied fruit and other things. As it was winter and probably rather cold, Don Mannarino's cook may have served the cake in the recipe below rather than ice-cream.

MODO DI FORNIRE UN PIATTO DI PANE DI SPAGNA
Lo formarete come vi piace sopra un piatto, poi le coprite con pasta di Marenche. Cioe assai meno zuccaro di detta pasta con passaretea setaccio zuccaro fino. Lo couerchio do forno di Campagna, li cocite cio foco moderato, sino che piglia un poco do colore. Poi freddo che sia lo potete servire in piu vole se volete.[1]

1   Michele Mercieca, *Libro di Secreti*

This interesting recipe is really very simple; a sponge cake is covered in marzipan and baked. The cake will taste much better if the sponge cake is flavoured with lemon or orange zest, sprinkled with some liqueur and brushed with jam before covering it with marzipan and baking it.

The *forno di Campagna* referred to in the recipe above is a "Dutch oven" which was a very strong, thick walled and thick based casserole dish with a lipped, tight fitting lid and feet. Cooks greased the casserole dish well and filled it with the food to be cooked, then placed it in the coals and covered the lid with coals. The feet allowed the Dutch oven to be set just above the coals and the lipped lid helped the coals piled on the top to stay there. This was the perfect answer for most households of the time as few people owned proper ovens.

All this fiery talk of frustrated nationalism and rebellion simmered down when Grand Master Ximenes came to power amid great hopes that his promises to be a "loving father"[1] to the nation and to address the food crisis would be fulfilled. One measure he adopted was to ban rabbit hunting completely for a while. This was a desperate bid to give rabbits breathing space to allow them to multiply with their usual efficiency and so restock the islands with inexpensive meat.

1   Schermerhorn

Unfortunately it was a short-sighted move "as hunting was among the pastimes to which the local clergy were most passionately addicted, and it came at a time when relations between the Order and the Bishop were at their worst."[2] The bishop, Monsignor Pellerano, was quick to complain about the rabbit hunting ban and the damage the rabbits were wreaking on his estate, so the Grand Master granted him permission to hunt in his possessions. This privilege was abused of course when the bishop gave others leave to hunt there.

So, into the stew pot of civil disobedience stirred by the clergy went rising prices, a severe lack of rabbit meat, cuts in salaries and other economic measures that all came to the boil in the form of a plot "planned to take place on the night of the 8th September 1775, a day which, since the year 1565, has always been marked by festivities and a great concourse of people assembling in Valletta from all over the island. It was so timed as to elude the vigilance of the authorities, *nel giorno della Vittoria, dopo l'Ave Maria*.[3] Which is when a group of priests, clerics and laymen led by Don Gaetano Mannarino occupied fort St Elmo and St James Cavalier and hoisted the Maltese Università red and white flag.

Hunters in Wardija, circa 1920. Thanks to Richard Ellis

This rebellion or Uprising of the Priests was as courageous as it was badly planned and did not last long. However, although the ring-leaders were executed or given long prison sentences, their efforts were not completely wasted. The authorities got the message and in 1776 there was the ultimate concession: hunting for rabbits with any sort of arms and equipment was allowed on public land.

This move was very well received as, apart from rabbit meat always having been very popular, hunting them kept rabbit numbers down and controlled the damage inflicted on crops, always a great concern to farmers as is so perfectly illustrated in the dialogue between a farmer and trapper recorded by Canon Agius De Soldanis in 1750 – just 25 years before The Rising Of The Priests.

2   Roderick Cavaliero, *The Last of the Crusaders*
3   P. Callus, *The Rising Of The Priests 1961*

The dialogue[4] takes place when a trapper, his ferret and his dog set off to catch rabbits and happen to meet a farmer on his way to Naxxar. The farmer advises the trapper to head out towards *Qbar il-Lhud, Mellieħa and Torri l-Aħmar* because he'd just heard about another hunter who caught 50 rabbits. The trapper is dismayed and asks the farmer whether he thinks there would be any rabbits left for him to catch. The farmer reassures him and claims that even though one thousand rabbits are caught daily, there are still so many rabbits in Malta that they drive everyone mad by feeding on the crops in the fields and he encourages the trapper to go and capture some rabbits. The farmer rounds off his part in the dialogue by asking the trapper to drop off a rabbit for him on his way home as, *af li naf nieklu!* or he would enjoy eating it.

Rabbit meat is at the heart of the secular part of the feast of Sts Peter and Paul, better known as *L-Imnarja*, held on 29th June at Buskett and Mdina. This was the most anticipated festival of the year for rural people, especially as there was so little to look forward to in their lives. The festivities proper commenced on the eve of June 29th when Mdina was illuminated by thousands of candles, flaming torches and oil pans. This must have been a magical, almost mystical vision when there was little if any light at night anywhere, and the Old City would have looked like a brightly lit bauble, suspended in the dark night sky to people, as they thronged towards Buskett to celebrate with good food, music and rustic singing and dancing. Then at dawn the following day, the people made their way from Buskett to Mdina Cathederal to High Mass followed by an afternoon of horse, mule and donkey races.

This festival has been firmly embedded in the Maltese cultural calendar since the Late Middle-Ages. Stanley Fiorini cites Mandati documents of the Università dating back to the first years of the 16th Century that record payment to people for preparing Rabat and Mdina for this important festival; there are payments made to people for renovating the streets like *La via di Sancta Agata* for the *Mnarja* bare-back races, levelling the squares where race horses, mules and donkeys were to be tied up and other documents showing that a "popular reward for the winners at the *Mnarja* bare-back races was some lance or a sword or a *rutella* – a round shield." [5]

In 1804 Louis De Boisgelin described how the old city was twice illuminated; he mentions the horse races, and how the crowd gathered and danced all night near a spacious grotto at Buskett. He described the music, the singing and the peasants dressed in their wedding clothes as they were the smartest clothes they owned, and how everyone sat in family groups under the trees and "partook of a meal, the principal dish of which was a pie"[6]. Unfortunately there is no way of finding out what these pies were filled with but it was likely to have been rabbit meat.

'Mnarja' (detail), Antoine Favray

4   Ġużè Cassar Pullicino, *Il-Kitba bil-Malti sa l-1870*
5   Stanley Fiorini, *The Mandati Documents at the Archives of the Mdina Cathedral, Malta 1437-1539*
6   Louis De Boisgelin, *Ancient and Modern Malta in 1804*

RABBIT PIE

I dislike watery pies that fall apart; I prefer firm and juicy pies that slice well. So this recipe makes a well flavoured solid pie that is perfect for rabbitty picnics and summer lunches.

1 rabbit – jointed
A little seasoned flour
White wine
6 bay leaves
10 cloves garlic – peeled and crushed
Olive oil
250g minced fatty pork
4 tbs chopped fresh rosemary
1 tbs chopped fresh thyme
1 tbs chopped fresh sage
50g minced bacon
2 onions – peeled and finely chopped
1 large aubergines – peeled and cubed
4 tomatoes – peeled, seeded and chopped
3 big potatoes – peeled and very thinly sliced
3 eggs
500g short crust pastry
1 extra egg – beaten

First salt the aubergines to draw out the bitter juices. Then dip the rabbit pieces in the seasoned flour and fry in olive oil till golden brown. Then add a little white wine and the bay leaves and leave it to simmer till it comes away from the bones quite easily. In the meantime prepare the rest of the ingredients: fry the onions and garlic till soft and a pale golden colour, remove to a bowl; fry the aubergine chunks till lightly browned and soft and remove to a bowl; then fry the bacon till lightly browned. Next, mix the raw pork with half the herbs and a little of the cooked onion, season well and add one of the eggs and beat it in well. Then take the rabbit meat off the bones and cut into bite sized pieces and mix with the rest of the cooked onions, the fried aubergines, the raw tomatoes, the herbs and 2 eggs mixed with some of the cooled rabbit cooking juices.

Then roll out the pastry and use it to line a 24cm pie dish. Line the base of the pastry with the paper thin slices of raw potato, cover these with a layer of the raw minced pork mix, top with the rabbit and vegetable mix and press down gently. Then cover it with the rest of the pork and then the rest of the potato slices. Press down gently again to flatten the surface. Brush the edges of the pie with the beaten egg, then roll out the rest of the pastry and cover the top of the pie. Seal the pie well by pressing down on the eggy edges, making a pattern with finger tips or fork. Cut some rabbit shapes out of the pastry trimmings and use them to decorate the top of the pie. Brush it all generously with the beaten egg and cook for about 45- 60 minutes in the oven preheated to gas mark 4 ½/185ºC.

Another, quicker and delicious way to make a rabbit pie comes from Mrs Maria Bondi in Victoria, Gozo. She simply bones some stewed rabbit and mixes the pieces of rabbit meat with the onions, garlic, peas and sauce from the stew, puts the savoury mix in the bottom of an oven dish, tops it with mashed potatoes and bakes it all till golden.

Other travel writers mention the festival, such as Richard Colt Hoare in 1790[1], "During the summer an annual festival is held here, by the peasantry of the island, who, with their brides, spend a most joyous day. According to description, the scene must be equally striking and agreeable. In the valley, beneath the Boschetto, is a large grove of orange trees, under each of which is a party of countrymen, with their wives, children, beasts, &c. attended by music, and forming numberless picturesque groups. Attendance at this festival is considered of so much importance by the females, that it is even said to form a clause in marriage contracts. At this revel jealousy is banished, and gives place to universal joy and content. Numerous parties from Malta crowd to witness such a scene of rural happiness, and enliven it by their presence."

The idea that mandatory attendance at L-Imnarja festivities was inserted into old marriage contracts may have its roots in the following verse. It forms part of the marriage contract burlesque called *Il-Qarcilla* performed during carnival.

"Ukoll taghmillu patt
Illi ghandu jehodha
l-Imnarja w San Girgor,
iqeghedha fuq il-hajt
u x'hin tispiedi l-festa
jixtrilha xriek qubbajt."[2]

'Mnarja' (detail), Antoine Favray

An agricultural show and competition were introduced in 1854 and they have become a permanent feature of the festival, encouraging more and more people to come to Buskett to visit the show, watch the races and "divide into companies and under the shades of the leafy orange trees in the beautiful garden, they seem quite happy in eating their sumptuous dinners, consisting chiefly of stewed rabbit, ham, pies, cheese and an allowance of common wine." as V Busuttil wrote in 1894. So by 1894 the pie mentioned in earlier descriptions had become stewed rabbit that 100 years later evolved again into the fenkata which is the rabbit dish enjoyed nowadays at L-Imnarja.

1   Richard Colt Hoare, *A Classical Tour Through Italy and Sicily*
2   Ġużè Cassar Pullicino, *Il-Kitba bil-Malti sa l-1870*

Fried rabbit

FENKATA

1 large tender rabbit (including
the kidney, liver and heart)
Olive oil
3 onions – peeled and chopped up
10 cloves garlic – peeled and crushed
Red wine
4 bay leaves
1 tbs chopped fresh rosemary
2 kg tomatoes, peeled and chopped up
1 tsp sugar
Salt and pepper

Cut the rabbit into potion sized pieces and fry with the liver and heart till browned in the olive oil, then remove and replace with the onions, sugar and garlic, add a little more oil and cook till soft. Then put the rabbit pieces, the kidneys and the heart back in the pot, stir and pour over the wine. Cook to evaporate a little; then add the tomatoes and herbs, season well and simmer till tender which should be about an hour and a half. Add the liver about 5 minutes before the end of the cooking time.

NB: some people like to add peas.

To serve
Take the rabbit pieces out of the sauce and keep it warm. Boil some spaghetti and serve it with the rabbit sauce, followed by the rabbit, chips and vegetables or salad.

Originally rabbit was stewed in a specially shaped pot called *Il-Baqra*. This barrel shaped pot has a square opening on the top and seems to be ideally shaped to hold a rabbit. It stands on 4 very short legs, designed to keep it steady over a fire, and there is a knob like handle to one side to facilitate handling. Later on cooks switched to using a *pagna* or earthenware pan while modern cooks use ordinary thick bottomed saucepans to cook rabbit in, but otherwise things remain the same and we generally eat rabbit cooked in garlic and wine, rabbit cooked in tomato sauce or rabbit stew.

Rabbit recipes feature in all Maltese cookery books; most of them fried in olive oil, garlic, bay leaves and white wine or simply stewed in tomato sauce. A typical rabbit recipe from *Ctieb Tal Chcina*, a cookery book written in 1908 is called *Fenec La Campanjola* or Country-style Rabbit possibly because cooking rabbit has always been connected to rural life.

FRIED RABBIT WITH GARLIC AND WINE

When a rabbit is young and tender it is best to cook it as simply as possible so the delicate flavour of rabbit is emphasized rather than masked. Fry the portioned rabbit in olive oil until it is a deep golden colour; and then add a couple of crushed garlic cloves, some fresh rosemary needles and a bay leaf. Season the pot, add some white wine (use red wine if you prefer) and cover. Leave it to simmer until the rabbit is tender; about three quarters of an hour if the rabbit was small, a bit more if it was bigger. This method of frying rabbit makes thin gravy; if you prefer a thicker sauce dust the pieces of rabbit lightly with flour before frying.

FENEC LA CAMPANJOLA
COUNTRY STYLE RABBIT 1908[1]

2 onions – peeled and chopped
Olive oil or fat
2 tomatoes
Some Maltese marjoram, mint, basil and parsley
4 bay leaves
2 glasses water 1 glass red wine or "imbit isued"
1 rabbit cut into portions
Potatoes
Seasoning

Fry the onions, herbs and tomatoes in some olive oil or fat in a *pagna* or thick bottomed saucepan till thick, then add the rabbit pieces, the water and wine and simmer till tender – about an hour and a half. Add some potatoes and season well about half way through the cooking time.

1   "ELV", *Ctieb Tal Chcina*, Second Edition 1908

RABBIT WITH GREEN PEPPERS

This is perfect in summer when peppers are at their ripest and adds interest to plain fried rabbit.

6 green peppers
6 or more cloves of garlic
Olive oil
6 tomatoes, skinned, seeded and chopped

Cut 6 large green peppers in half, remove the inner core and slice them up lengthways as finely as you can. Fry these gently in lots of olive oil, chopped garlic and salt until they are soft and barely browned, and then add the cooked green peppers to a pot of rabbit fried with garlic and wine (see above) and cook for an additional 15 minutes so that the flavours mingle well. Serve scattered with lots of freshly chopped parsley and 6 skinned, seeded and chopped ripe summer tomatoes.

Variation (1): Use coloured peppers instead of green ones. Add a handful of pre-soaked dry porcini mushrooms to the coloured peppers if you have them – and add their strained soaking water to the rabbit at the same time as the wine.

Variation (2): Cook 400g skinned broad beans with olive oil and garlic in the same way as the green peppers and then add them to fried rabbit as above.

RABBIT STEWED IN BEER

1 plump rabbit, jointed
Olive oil
1 heaped tbs flour
A little freshly grated nutmeg
1 large onion, peeled and thinly sliced
4 cloves garlic (or to taste)
12 stoned prunes
12 walnuts
1 bottle Farsons Lacto or red ale or similar dark beer

Fry the onion in the olive oil until just soft, then add the rabbit pieces and cook till the rabbit is golden brown. Sprinkle the flour over the rabbit in the pan and stir it in. Then add the nutmeg, garlic and stout. Allow it to bubble up, then give it a stir and if the sauce seems too thick add a little water or stock. Put it into an open proof casserole and braise in a slow oven 150ºC/gas mark 1½ for an hour and a half. In the meantime insert a walnut into each of the prunes and put them to one side. When the hour and a half is up add the prunes to the rabbit, stir and cook for another half hour.
Serves 6

Mashed potatoes are the perfect accompaniment to stews as the textures complement each other perfectly and the gravy melts into the potatoes, softening them and adding great flavour. Stir some grainy mustard into the mashed potatoes to add an unusual kick to the sometimes bland dish.

BONED AND STUFFED RABBIT BACK

This is a more unusual and rather extravagant rabbit dish as only the back fillets are used and each person will eat a whole fillet as a main course, or half of one as a starter. (Freeze the other portions of rabbit to use another day)

Rabbit back fillets
Fresh thyme
Salt and pepper
About 6 lettuce leaves – thick central rib removed
4 grilled and skinned coloured peppers
1 clove of garlic – crushed and chopped up
1 lightly beaten egg
The juice and zest of one lemon
3 heaped tbs of fresh breadcrumbs
Olive oil
4 bay leaves
A dash of brandy
250ml of dry red wine
150ml of chicken stock
1 tbs chopped parsley

First, using a well-honed filleting knife, cut along the rabbit's spine, cutting away the meat on either side of the back bone so that you end up with two fillets (or take the easy way out and ask the butcher to do it for you). Put the fillets in between two sheets of cling-film and strike them with a meat-hammer them until they are thin and flat.

Remove the cling-film and sprinkle the meat with fresh thyme leaves, grated lemon zest, salt and pepper. Place on each fillet a large, clean lettuce leaf and top with the grilled and skinned coloured peppers, and a crushed and finely chopped clove of garlic. Now mix together the lightly beaten egg, the lemon juice, the fresh breadcrumbs, thyme, salt and pepper, and pour this over the rabbit and topping, pressing down gently. Roll the rabbit fillets tightly round the filling, and carefully secure them with tooth picks. Fry them in olive oil with bay leaves, garlic and thyme until they are golden. Remove the rabbit rolls to an oven-proof dish, and deglaze the pan in which you have just fried them, using a dash of brandy, dry red wine and chicken stock. Reduce the liquid by boiling it for a couple of minutes, and then pour it over the rabbit. Drizzle with olive oil, season and roast in a medium to hot oven for 20-30 minutes until browned and sizzling. Make some gravy, using the pan juices. Serve the rabbit sliced to show off the layers inside, with the gravy and sprinkled with chopped parsley.

RABBIT WITH MUSTARD

1 rabbit cut into portions
A little flour
Olive oil
4 slices chopped back bacon
1 chopped onion
3 bay leaves
3 sprigs rosemary
500ml white wine
6 tbs wholegrain mustard
200ml fresh cream

Dust the rabbit with flour and fry in olive oil with sliced back bacon and the finely chopped onion. When golden add the bay leaves, rosemary and white wine. Cover and leave it to simmer until the rabbit is tender; about an hour if the rabbit was small, a bit more if it was bigger.

Then remove the rabbit pieces to an oven proof serving dish and keep warm. Add 4 tablespoons wholegrain mustard to the pan juices with 200ml cream and stir well. Pour over the rabbit and roast in a very hot oven for 5 minutes. Serve.

RABBIT WITH OLIVES

This makes a great main course that is satisfyingly tasty and easy to prepare.

1 rabbit cut into portions
200g plain flour
Seasoning
3 tbs sugar
3 tbs wine vinegar
1 large onion finely chopped
3 or 4 cloves of garlic
2 tbs chopped capers
250g pitted and chopped Maltese olives
4 carrots, peeled and sliced up
6 stalks Maltese celery

Dust the rabbit pieces in seasoned flour and fry them in olive oil till golden brown. Then sprinkle the whole lot with the sugar and cook for a couple of minutes until dissolved then pour over the wine vinegar and allow it to evaporate. Place the lid on the pan and put it to one side. In the meantime fry an onion, some garlic, three carrots sliced up, a tablespoon of chopped capers and 250g chopped and pitted Maltese olives in olive oil along with 6 stalks chopped Maltese celery, fresh rosemary and bay leaves until everything is a soft and pale golden colour.

Pour this aromatic mixture over the rabbit pieces in the pan and carry on cooking at a slow and gentle simmer in the covered pot, adding enough white wine and stock to be able to simmer the rabbit in a sauce. It needs at least an hour and a half to cook to tender perfection. This may be finished off in a low to medium oven in a covered casserole if necessary but take care it does not dry out and top up with wine or water if it seems dry half way through cooking.

RABBIT WITH BACON AND ARTICHOKE HEARTS

1 rabbit cut into portions
Olive oil
1 knob of butter
125g minced bacon
1 onion – peeled and finely chopped
2 leeks – peeled and finely chopped
2 spring garlic or 4 cloves garlic – chopped
6 artichokes
½ a bottle white wine
2 heaped tbs finely chopped fresh rosemary
6 leaves finely chopped fresh sage

First make the artichoke hearts as follows: cut away the tough outside leaves and stringy parts but leave a couple of centimetres of stalk on the artichoke. Peel the stalks to reveal the tender inner part, then cut off the tops of the leaves that are left on the artichoke and remove the choke with a strong teaspoon. Once the hearts are ready, rub them with the cut side of a lemon as quickly as possible and then put them in a bowl full of acidulated water (water, lemon and parsley stalks) to prevent them discolouring. Quarter them lengthways before using them in this recipe.

Then, once the hearts are ready fry the bacon in a little olive oil for a minute or two, then add the onion, leeks and garlic, add the butter and carry on frying very gently till the onions and leeks are very soft. Remove from the pan, add a little more oil, turn up the heat and brown the rabbit pieces. Then return the onion and bacon mix to the pan, add the herbs and artichoke hearts and stir in. When everything is hot add the wine, season well and braise gently for about an hour and a half or until the rabbit is tender.

RABBIT IN CAROB SAUCE

This is a richly flavoured rabbit dish inspired by rabbit in a chocolate sauce. The marinade tenderises the meat and the orange, rosemary and carob add delicious taste to the otherwise rather bland rabbit meat.

1 rabbit – jointed
½ a bottle red wine
4 sprigs fresh rosemary
4 strips orange zest
4 bay leaves
1 onion – peeled and sliced thinly
4 or more cloves garlic –
peeled and crushed
Dash balsamic vinegar
Olive oil
1 tsp sugar
Salt and freshly ground black pepper
4 carrots, scraped and sliced
3 flat tbs carob flour blended
with a glass of red wine

Marinate the rabbit pieces in the wine, rosemary, bay leaves and orange zest in the fridge for at least 12 hours, turning the rabbit pieces once or twice. Then remove the rabbit from the marinade, pat it dry and fry in a pan with a little olive oil till golden brown. In the meantime, fry the onion and garlic in a casserole in a little olive oil till soft and golden, then add the sugar and the balsamic vinegar. Add the fried rabbit pieces to the casserole and cook for few more minutes, add the carrots and carob flour and red wine mix and leave to cook for a moment or two while you deglaze the frying pan with the marinade, then pour it into the casserole, cover and leave it to simmer very gently for about an hour and a half over a low heat. Season well before serving. Serve with potatoes roasted with onions, garlic, bay leaves, fennel seeds and rosemary. *1 whole rabbit serves about 6 people.*

RABBIT TERRINE

This is a delicious terrine that has a light gamey flavour. It is certainly worth making and it keeps in the fridge for a week and freezes well for a couple of months. The only difficulty lies in boning the rabbit and quail but Charles Butcher in Naxxar does this if you ring and order it a day or two beforehand.

1 fresh, medium sized, tender rabbit
1 quail
400g fatty pork – minced once
400g lean pork – minced once
50g soft pork fat – minced once
1 tbs juniper berries
15g porcini
1 rabbit liver
10 prunes – chopped
4 cardamom pods – lightly crushed
10 Bay leaves
1 flat tsp ground allspice
3 tbs very finely chopped fresh rosemary
250ml whisky
3 large eggs or 4 small ones

First cut all the meat off the rabbit and quail; keeping the rabbit saddles (back fillets) and quail breasts whole, and dice the rest of the meat. Then, in a large shallow dish arrange all the different meats, the dried porcini, juniper berries, chopped prunes and rabbit liver so that they are still separate. Then scatter with the allspice, crushed cardamom pods and bay leaves, pour over the whisky and leave to marinate covered in the fridge for 18-24 hours.

Once the meats are well marinated remove them from the fridge and allow them to come to room temperature. Then butter and base line a 30cm loaf tin and then cover with the slices of bacon. Remove the bay leaves and cardamom pods from the dish of meat and, in a large mixing bowl, mix the minced and diced meats together with the prunes and juniper berries, then add the eggs and mix well so that they are all combined evenly. Divide this mixture into three equal parts spread the bottom of the prepared tin evenly with the first third. Then roll the rabbit saddles in the chopped rosemary and lay them neatly down on the meat. Cover them with the second third of the meat and press down gently to remove any air bubbles. Then lay down the quail breasts, the rabbit liver and porcini and cover with the final third of the meat. Bang down to eliminate any air bubbles and cook Bain Marie (in an oven dish with warm water to come ¾ up the side of the tin) in the oven at gas mark 3 ½ /170ºC for 1 ¼ hours. Cover the top of the terrine with something that fits neatly on top and weight it down with weights while it cools and firms up. Then remove it and chill in the fridge for at least 12 hours before serving.

COFFEE AND RICOTTA CAKE

For the cake:
8 eggs
200g castor sugar
200g plain flour
2 level teaspoons baking powder
4 tablespoons of olive oil
6tsp instant coffee

To finish:
300ml strong coffee mixed
with100 ml Brandy
600g ricotta
150g black chocolate – grated
150g castor sugar
100g flaked almonds – toasted
200g black chocolate – melted

First make the cake:
Separate the eggs and put the yolks in one bowl and whites in another. Whisk the whites until stiff and then add the sugar bit-by-bit, whisking well in between each addition until all the sugar is incorporated. Melt the coffee in as little hot water as possible, just enough to make a loose paste. Stir it into the egg yolks and oil and mix them together till smooth. Then add it to the egg white and sugar mixture and whisk it in as lightly as possible, just until all is well blended but not collapsed. Then gently fold in the flour and baking powder. Divide the batter between 3 well-greased, base lined 20cm sandwich cake tins and bake at gas 5 /190ºC for about 20 minutes or until springy and just golden. Turn out onto a wire rack and cool.

To finish the cake:
In the meantime prepare the filling by beating the ricotta together with the sugar, grated chocolate and toasted flaked almonds and keep cool. Then pour the brandy and coffee mix into a bowl. Next dip or brush the cakes lightly in the coffee and brandy and sandwich them together with the ricotta mixture. Keep in the fridge until needed – it keeps well for a couple of days. Then, just before serving it, cover the cake with warm melted chocolate.

Living memories

This section is the fruit of shared memories, collected from friends and relatives. They are all about great meals shared with family and friends during times of happiness. There are dark memories of hunger , fear and terrible discomfort during the Second World War when Malta just about survived. The chapters in the section are inspired by the lovely people who so kindly shared their memories with me.

CTIEB TAL CHCINA

(IT-TIENI EDIZIONI)

MIZIUD B'ERBGHA U TLETIN RICETTA GIODDA

MINN

E. L. V.

— • —

"Omnibus placere non possumus"

— ◇•◇ —

MALTA

A. C. Aquilina & Co. *Librari-Edituri.*
58D. Strada Reale, il-Belt.

—

1908.

The front cover of an old Maltese cookery book

THE FIRST HALF OF THE 20TH CENTURY
L-ewwel nofs tas-seklu għoxrin

Urban Maltese food and cooking in the first half of the 20th century offers a sharp contrast to modern life. Ingredients were very simple; almost everything was local, seasonal and fresh. In towns fishmongers brought their catch to the door; herdsmen drove their goats door to door selling milk directly from the udder to the jug; bread men delivered bread and farmers sold vegetables, live poultry, rabbits and eggs from carts laden with their produce "when the huckster comes round with his cart you will see quite a medley of animals in these small cages, fowls, pigeons and rabbits, living happily together, but little knowing how closely their fate resembles those of the French aristocrats on the tumbrils."[1]

Indrin, a vegetable vendor in 1921, photographed on Tower Road, Sliema by my grandfather Henry Ferro.

Fridges and freezers were unheard of, at best some households enjoyed the luxury of an icebox, which was a zinc lined box kept cool with huge straw and salt wrapped ice blocks that were brought round by the ice-man who called *tas-silġ hawn*. Meat bought from the sawdust strewn butcher's shops would have been stored "on the ice", or in a *guardacarne* or meat safe, which was a wooden, wire gauze covered box for storing perishables in. People who did not have such useful gadgets kept butter and other fresh goods in a metal bucket or string bag which was hung in the well to keep cool.

---

1   John Wignacourt, *The Odd Man In Malta*, 1914

Thanks to Michael Diacono

Invitations and menus from the first half of the 20th Century

Dry goods like pasta, rice and flour as well as tinned food, oils and other necessities were purchased at grocery shops that were generally much smaller than their modern counterpart, except for some of the Valletta shops; "The Valletta shops fall into several classes. There are the quite English ones, like the Junior Army and Navy Stores and Mortimer's, where you can get anything at a fixed price: large Maltese emporia like Paris house (La Ville de Londres) crowded with faldetta'd women dallying with flowery hats; small Maltese shops, largely of the huckster type, the owners of which are often, so 'tis said, and probably with truth, fabulously rich; and Indian bazaars where you can buy kimonos, Japanese slippers ..." [1]

---

1   *Ibid*

The Valletta market *Is-suq* in Merchant street was the Mecca for serious food shoppers; it teemed with stalls, their holders all vying with each other for customers from the moment doors were opened at dawn till they closed late in the evening. Bustling business went on all day, perishables like fish, meat and butter were still bought daily by weight and wrapped in greaseproof paper to be taken home; one had to shop carefully as "sometimes cheeky stallholders added water to things like Kunserva to make it heavier." Customers often returned in the evening to buy something for supper as the means of keeping food fresh were so limited; Katerin, the Briffa Brincati's cook for example, went to the market most evenings to buy fish because, as Mrs Antoinette Samut said "my father always ate fish and salad, sometimes with spinach or asparagus for supper". The best of fresh Maltese produce was sold here.

Maltese merchants supplied consumers with imported goods like lard, chocolate and sugar from Belgium, Brazilian coffee, Danish butter, Egyptian flour and fruit, English condensed milk, French wines, Italian olive oil and pasta and so on which made cooking a little tastier and more interesting. Innovative items like tinned and powdered foods were probably available in Malta earlier than in other, similar areas of the Mediterranean as Malta was part of the British Empire. So much so that there were three tomato processing factories in Malta in the 1930's, Vernon's, Canaries' and Coleiro's – although Stockdale reports that almost the whole production was consumed by British garrison cooks. In 1915, John Borg M.A., M.D., wrote, "Tomatoes are grown very extensively to meet the large local demand, and to supply material for the manufacture of sauce. The local tomato is large and flat, more or less ribbed, almost free from acidity, and is very early and productive. Smooth skinned tomatoes have been introduced lately, and are being increasingly cultivated for the canning industry."

This was a time when distinction between the social orders was tremendous, a time of atrocious poverty. There were great differences in the diet of the urban working-class, the rural poor, the various middle classes, and the upper class. Mothers right across the social spectrum were haunted by the spectre of high infant mortality. Women were much preoccupied with feeding up their babies in the hope of deflecting the ever-present threat of tuberculosis, rheumatic fever, polio, the influenza, and other murderous diseases.

In more affluent households meals were more formal and far heavier than they are today. All meals were served in the dining room; the table was spread with a starched white cloth and matching napkins, laid with silver posati or cutlery, good china and glasses. Very often little dishes of nibbles were set on the table containing some anchovies or herrings, some olives and roast nuts, especially at supper time. Water was served in a crystal jug and wine in a decanter, although whether wine was served at every meal or not depended on each family's own likes and dislikes.

A selection of crystal decanters

BREAKFAST

My aunt Rita Ferro neé de Giorgio remembered that "Breakfast was always served at table in the dining room, the table was laid with a cloth, napkins and proper crockery and one had whatever one wished. My father always had brown bread, butter and marmalade with coffee for example, but if one wanted some fruit or an egg or something else you simply had to ask." Other families enjoyed different sorts of breakfasts, eggs were popular, bread was spread with homemade jams, chocolate or honey, tea, coffee and chocolate was drunk hot in winter or cold in summer. Cheese and gammon was a winter favourite, in Mrs Samut's family a leg of gammon was kept in a pantry adjacent to the dining room in the guardacarne.

GAMMON

Soak one whole gammon leg as instructed by the butcher, usually overnight including one change of water. Next morning, put it in a large ham pan and cover it with cold water. Bring it slowly to a rapid boil. Skim off any grey scum that may form and add 2 apples, 2 oranges, an onion, two cinnamon sticks, a tablespoon of cloves and a tablespoon of peppercorns and turn it down to a gentle simmer and cook it gently for about three hours. When it is cooked, drain away the water and carefully peel away the rind while it is still quite hot, taking care to remove only the skin and not the fat. Prepare a piece of greaseproof paper by scattering it with an equal amount of brown sugar and breadcrumbs and the roll the still warm ham in it on the fat side. Then pick up any bread and sugar left on the paper and press it onto the skin. Score the sugary ham fat in a diamond pattern and insert a whole clove into the centre of the little diamond shaped squares. Roast the ham for half an hour at gas mark 8/220ºC or until it is nicely browned. Allow it to cool then cover with cling film and store in the fridge (or guardacarne!) until required. Serve carved into thin slices

LUNCH

Lunch followed a rigorous three course rule and was served at noon sharp in most households. It was usually a three course meal: a first course which was normally soup, rice or some form of pasta, this was always followed by some kind of meat; beef, chicken or pork accompanied by potatoes and vegetables, then the cheese platter and a sweet little chaser of pudding or fresh fruit. Puddings were popular, especially Maltese trifle or soufflé, home-made ice-cream made from evaporated milk or *pudina tal-biskutelli*. The style was plain and simple; the purpose was nourishing food, there was little fiddling and exotic foods were limited to things like bananas.

BRODU
TAL-FALDA

Falda or thin flank is a popular cut of meat used to make a delicious soup. Ask the butcher to cut a deep slit into the meat to make a sort of pocket to stuff with ingredients as follows.

1 whole "*falda*"
450g minced beef and pork
50g finely chopped ham (optional)
1 egg
1 heaped tbs finely chopped fresh parsley
1 onion or leek finely chopped
A little butter
½ tbs finely chopped fresh rosemary
1 tsp chopped fresh thyme leaves
6 carrots, peeled
1 large whole peeled onion
1 tomato – chopped
Either a chunk of beef rib ends
and/or some marrow bones

Put the large chunk of beef rib ends, the marrow bones, the carrots and whole onion, chopped tomato, Maltese celery and enough water to cover it all generously in a large stock pot and bring it all to the boil. In the meantime, fry the chopped onion or leek in a little butter till soft, taking care that it does not brown at all. Then mix the minced meat with the ham, egg, parsley, rosemary and thyme, add the buttery onion or leek with the butter, season the mixture well and use it to stuff the flank. Seal the open end of the meat with a skewer or stitch it up and lower it into the boiling soup.

Turn down the heat and gently simmer the soup for about two and a half hours, then season to taste and serve as follows: Carefully take the meats and vegetables out of the soup and arrange on a serving plate, cover and keep warm. Serve the soup as a first course, perhaps with some small pasta shapes added to it or some of the vegetables chopped up in it. Serve the meat as the second course with some, *Zalza Ħadra*, boiled potatoes dressed in olives oil and herbs and other vegetables.

TOMATO SOUP
VERSION 1

5 large garlic cloves
5 tbs olive oil
2 kg of ripe summer tomatoes
2 tsp sugar (optional)
½ litre cool water or vegetable stock
2 or 3 tbs semolina
Good handful basil leaves
6 slices Maltese bread

Peel and finely chop the garlic, put them in a large pot and stew gently in the olive oil till soft but not coloured. While the garlic is stewing in the oil, peel, seed and chop the tomatoes and add to the garlic and oil. Season lightly and leave to cook over a very low heat for about 35-30 minutes. Add the cold water or the cold vegetable stock and while the soup is cool, add the semolina and stir while you bring it back to the boil. Do not add the semolina to hot soup as it may form hard little lumps and spoil it. Then simmer the soup for another 15 minutes.

Serve garnished with shredded basil leaves, croutons and a generous dash of olive oil. To make croutons cube up some bread and either fry it in olive oil or toss the cubed bread lightly in olive oil and then put the bread in an oven dish and roast till golden brown
Serves 6

TOMATO SOUP
VERSION 2

This makes a much lighter soup than the first recipe and it is quick and easy to make.
2 kg ripe tomatoes
3 carrots
1 large onion
2 stalks Maltese celery – karfus
1 tsp sugar
1 tsp salt
500ml vegetable stock

Put all the ingredients in to a large pot, bring to a boil and simmer for about ½ an hour or until the vegetables are all soft. Put through a food mill or pass- purée until smooth. Check the seasoning and serve. If the soup seems a little too runny turn down the heat and thicken it with a little beurre manie – in other words – rub 25g butter and 1 heaped tablespoon flour together , then drop the crumbly mix into the soup and stir it in till dissolved; bring the soup back to the boil and stir till thickened slightly.
Serves 6

ZALZA ĦADRA, SALSA VERDE OR GREEN SAUCE

This is excellent served with cold fish, cold beef, potatoes and all varieties of summer vegetables. *Zalza Ħadra* is a literal translation from the Italian Salsa Verde (green sauce) in more ways than one as the two sauces are very similar. One version or another of *Zalza Ħadra*/Salsa Verde has been enjoyed for hundreds of years and it is interesting to read about the various refinements made to the sauce through the centuries. The first known recipe comes from Apicius' *De re coquinaria* where the cook is instructed to "Take a loaf of Alexandrian bread without the crust, dunk it in water and vinegar. Put in a mortar pepper, honey, mint, garlic leaves, salted cow'-milk, water and oil. Place the container over snow and serve."

In *Opera dell' arte del cucinare* published in 1570 Scappi's recipe for Green Sauce requires that slices of toasted bread are pasted in the mortar with parsley, spinach, sorrel, burnet, rocket and mint. Once this is well ground, the sauce is seasoned with pepper, salt and vinegar so that it is well blended and will not require straining. Scappi recommends the addition of almonds or hazelnuts, but should the cook wish the sauce to be green they must be omitted.

In the Maltese cookery book *Ctieb Tal Chcina* published in 1908 there is whole chapter dedicated to sauces – three of these resemble our modern *Zalza Ħadra*. The one that is precisely like *Zalza Ħadra* is *Zalza tat-Tursin* (parsley sauce) – in this recipe the leaves of a whole bunch of parsley are plucked off the stalks and then they are pasted in a pestle and mortar together with a clove of garlic, pepper, salt, a chunk of crust less bread soaked in vinegar and some oil until everything is smooth and moist, adding more oil as necessary. The author of this book suggests that this sauce is served with boiled meat or fish.

Many people make *Zalza Verde* in the same way as the recipe for Parsley Sauce above, while the recipe below makes a tastier, richer *Zalza Ħadra*.

The inside of 2 thick slices of Maltese bread, soaked briefly in a bit of vinegar and water, squeezed dry and mashed

6 tbs fresh herbs like parsley, mint and merqtux, finely chopped

2 tbs olives, stoned and chopped small (optional)

2 tbs capers, rinsed, squeezed dry and roughly chopped (optional)

2 cloves garlic, peeled and crushed

Olive oil

Salt and pepper

Put the mashed bread into a bowl and add all the other ingredients and mix well until you have a very moist mixture. Pour olive oil all over the top of the mixture and store in the fridge until needed.

Variations

Popular additions include a couple of anchovies that should be boned, mashed or chopped and simply stirred into the sauce along with all the other ingredients.

Another addition that makes the sauce more refreshing but less green is as follows: Peel and seed a large ripe and juicy summer tomato and then sieve the seeds into the bread mixture. While the seeds are sieving chop the tomato flesh into dice and add to the Salsa Verde.

In the days before importation of foreign meat, cuts of meat like lucerto or silverside were much more popular than they are today. Lucerto was particularly popular and was usually braised as it tends to dry out easily as it contains little fat.

ICE-CREAM

My 96-year-old Great Aunt Margaret clearly remembered ice being ordered from the butcher. It was delivered on the back of a cart in huge compacted blocks, wrapped in sacking or straw. They used this ice in their icebox, which was used to keep food cool, the origin of the term "on the ice" found in so many old recipe books. They also used the ice to make ice-cream.

It is difficult to imagine how cooks of the past managed to make ice-creams without the aid of electric freezers, as the melting qualities of the summer sun are legendary. But one of my father's susters made it sound very simple when she described making ice-cream in a *Buzzun* or *bezzun* (an ice pail). This was a wooden tub that had another smaller thick metal bucket sitting in it. Chipped ice was packed tightly into the larger tub, sprinkled at intervals with sea salt to keep it from melting. This was because salty water, once frozen, melts at a lower temperature than ice and so keeps the ice from melting too soon. The smaller metal bucket sat in the ice and became very cold. A handle was attached to it and, once the inner bucket was full of the ingredients required to make the ice-cream, it was churned until the ice-cream was ready. My father, her youngest brother, was always willing to churn away for ages to enjoy the privilege of licking the paddles once the ice-cream was ready and the paddles lifted out. This type of ice-cream was left in the *buzzun* to keep it from melting before it was eaten.

Coffee shops at the ferries in Sliema were the purveyors of ice-creams in the early years of the last century. They used a *buzzun* similar to the domestic version but much bigger and strong-armed ice-cream makers shook the tub rather than stirred it. They served their ice-cream and granita with special biscuits called *krustini* that were longer and thinner than the usual sort and lightly flavoured with lemon rather than nuts. Buying an ice-cream from one of the coffee shops was considered to be a treat and not an everyday occurrence.

'Buzzun' old fashioned hand powered ice-cream machine (from the old priory in Mdina)

OLD FASHIONED ICE-CREAM

I am sure this recipe will bring back memories of tinned milk ice-cream for many people. I ate lots of it throughout my childhood, but for some reason not since. It may be the unappealing idea of eating frozen tinned milk – all misplaced because this is a lovely ice-cream that is made without the aid of an ice-cream machine or lots of freezing and whisking. Before you start, chill a tin of milk overnight, otherwise it will not whisk up as easily.

1 large tin full cream evaporated (tinned) milk (chilled overnight)
3 tbs castor sugar
The juice and zest of 2 small, green summer lemons
3 tbs honey

Whisk the very cold tinned milk till it thickens, then add about two or three tablespoons of the lemon juice and whisk. The milk will thicken considerably, then add the sugar and carry on whisking till really thick. Very lightly fold in the grated lemon zest and the honey just enough to combine everything and pour into a paper or stretch & seal, lined loaf tin and freeze. To serve, unmold and serve in slices.

VARIATIONS
This ice-cream is very nice when *either*:
Some crushed, sweetened strawberries are carefully stirred into the half frozen ice-cream (add cointreau to the strawberries for a grown up treat).

***Or* some crushed praline made as follows:**
100g whole blanched almonds (or hazelnuts)
150g granulated sugar
2 tbs water or lemon juice

Put the sugar and water into a large frying pan and when everything has dissolved add the nuts and boil it all till the sugar turns a deep dark brown. Pour it out onto some dampened grease proof paper and allow it to cool and harden. Then cover it with a thick layer of paper and crush with a mallet till it is all crumbled. Fold it gently into the half frozen ice-cream (this is for people with strong teeth).

BUDINA TAL-BISCUTTELLI

This recipe comes from Ctieb Tal Chcina by E.L.V. (2nd edition 1908)

Hu sitt biscuttelli, chissirom becijec u xarrabom giol halib. Lesti apparti erbgha baidied, erbgha imgharef zoccor mishuk, ftit zbib sultana u daksxein koxra tal-lumi. Hauuad collox taijeb u itfa zeug tazzi haib; u meta il biscuttelli isiru minghair ghokod, kieghed gio dixx tal budini midluc bil butir u kieghed cellox fil forn ghal sigha.

Break up 6 biskuttelli and soak them in milk. Then, in a separate bowl, prepare 4 eggs, 4 tablespoons crushed sugar, some sultanas and some grated lemon rind. Mix everything well and add two glasses of milk; and when the biskuttelli are smooth, put everything in a well greased pudding bowl and bake for an hour.

This pudding's popularity has been eclipsed by the one below:

MALTESE BREAD PUDDING

1 slightly stale loaf of Maltese bread
125g butter
125g sugar
4 or 5 tbs cocoa
400g sultanas and raisins
100g chopped almonds
2tbs marmalade or chopped candied peel
1tbs finely chopped tangerine peel (use preserved if fresh is unavailable)
4 eggs
A generous dash brandy or whisky
2tsp mixed spice

Soak the loaf of Maltese bread in lots of water for about an hour. Then preheat the oven to gas mark 6/200ºC and grease an oblong oven proof dish – approx. 30 x 22 x 5cm. Put the water-logged loaf into a sieve and carefully press out as much of the water as possible. Put the soggy bread into a large mixing bowl, add the rest of the ingredients and mash and mix with your hands till everything is smooth (a little messy, but amusing and children love to muck in and mush away).

Spread it out in the prepared oven proof dish and smooth the top. Bake for approximately one to one and a quarter hours or till firm and crisp on top.

Serve it warm or at room temperature straight from the dish. This version of bread pudding is not an elegant pudding made to be served at the end of a meal; it is more like a cake enjoyed at teatime or as a sweet snack and is a popular addition to school lunch boxes.

FISH ON FRIDAY

Fridays – and Wednesdays in most families – were fish days. The choice was restricted by the season and the weather. *Bakkaljaw* or a "modern" dish like *pulpetti tas-salamon*, (made with tinned or salted salmon as fresh salmon was almost impossible to come by in Malta in those days), was served if the was sea was rough or fresh fish was quite simply unavailable. Eggs and cheese were popular ingredients on fasting days. *Ġbejniet* and ricotta were always easy to come by and good stores like Wembley Stores in Valletta sold other foreign cheeses like Parmesan, Gorgonzola and Emmenthal.

BAKKALJAW OR SALT COD

Bakkaljaw or salt cod needs to be prepared carefully to be really good. The main thing is to soak it for about two days, changing the water and rinsing the fish regularly to remove as much of the salt as possible and to rehydrate the fish.

There are many different ways of cooking the prepared fish: Normally the fish is simmered till tender, the bones removed, and then the fish is dressed with a dressing made by whisking together crushed or chopped garlic, finely chopped parsley, grated lemon zest and juice, and olive oil. The dressed fish is served with boiled potatoes and cauliflower.

Another way with *bakkaljaw* is to simmer it until just tender, bone it and then finish cooking it for the last five or ten minutes in tomato sauce flavoured with onions, mint, merqtux, capers and olives. Serve with boiled potatoes and green salad.

Children love it if simmered *bakkaljaw* is drained, boned and cut it into chunks, then dipped into semolina and fried till crisp. Serve with a green salad.

TEATIME

The vast majority of people in Malta enjoyed an afternoon siesta, to the extent that Sir Harry Luke remarked that "from twelve to three o'clock, one would suppose the island was deserted."[1] Tea was served afterwards, at about four o'clock; it was often a little meal in itself, where the family sat down to tea, bread and jam, biscuits and cakes. English afternoon tea, an innovation in pre-world war two Malta, was fashionable with the ladies of the time. At a formal tea party most of the cakes and sandwiches were homemade but some special items were bought from some of the best confectioners of the time. *Pasti* or pastries and *biskuttini* came from Indri Bonaci, as well as Venchi triangular chocolates and special green cakes named after the famous aviator Lindberg. Blackley's Bakery specialized in English style confectionery; they made excellent meringues and cakes and their walnut topped chocolate cakes, cream puffs and fancy tea breads were particularly popular. Zerrek and Bisazza were two other well-liked Valletta confectioners and bakers, especially renowned for their ice-cream. Tea, made from tea-leaves was served in delicate china from a silver tea pot and a good hostess invariably offered coffee as an alternative.

Teatime in Mdina 1914. My grandfather is in the centre, then left to right his sisters Dora and Margaret, his brother Bill and Teddy and his grandmother Enrichetta and cousin John Pullicino.

---

1   Sir Harry Luke, *Malta an Account and an Appreciation*

TANGERINE SUGAR OR PRESERVED TANGERINE PEEL

This is an easy way to preserve tangerine peel, useful for cooks who like to add a tangerine flavour to cakes and biscuits.

Make layers of very fresh finely chopped tangerine peel with castor sugar, pressing down with the back of a spoon on each layer. Make sure the peel is well covered with castor sugar on each layer, otherwise it will go off. Once the sugar turns a pale orange colour and looks moist, store it in the fridge. Tangerine sugar keeps for at least two years, stored in the fridge. To use the tangerine sugar; either add a spoonful or two of the sugar for a mild flavour or some of the chopped peel for a stronger flavour to the dough or cake before baking.

TORTA TAT-TAMAL U ĠEWZ
Date and walnut tart

400g Good Earth stoned dates
200g Good Earth shelled walnut halves
3 tbs preserved tangerine peel (or fresh)
A generous tot anisette (or more)
300g plain flour
150g butter
Cold water to bind

Sieve the flour into a bowl and rub in the butter. Make a well in the centre and add the egg and water and stir together to make pastry. Knead lightly to form a ball. Put to one side while you make the filling. Put the dates into a thick bottomed sauce pan and cook gently, stirring and adding enough water till they melt into a soft puree. In the meantime grind up 125g of the walnuts and stir them into the now soft, almost creamily smooth dates. Add the tangerine and anisette and stir in. Taste the mixture and add a little more of anything you particularly like. Use the pastry to line an approximately 24cm flan dish and add the filling. Make a criss-cross pattern on the top of the filling using strips of left over pastry and put the rest of the walnut halves in each of the squares. Bake in an oven pre-heated to Gas mark 6/200ºC for approximately 35 minutes or till golden.

SINIZZA

Sinizza is a delicious Maltese cake that traditionally consists of a light Swiss roll filled with sweetened ricotta, flavoured with candied peel, candied fruits and nuts, and rolled in puff pastry and baked in a hot oven till the pastry is golden and crisp.

To make the sponge
4 eggs
100g castor sugar
100g plain flour
½ tsp baking powder

Preheat the oven to gas mark 5/190ºC. Whisk the eggs until thick and foamy, add the sugar a little at a time, whisking all the time. Then sieve the flour and baking powder and fold it in carefully.

Spread the mixture over a well greased and lined baking tray approximate size 25cm x 25cm and bake in the preheated oven for about 15-20 minutes or until golden and springy. Turn it out onto a cotton cloth and roll it up, taking care not to press or squeeze it. Leave it to cool down inside the cloth while you prepare the filling.

To prepare the filling
3 tbs jam
300g soft ricotta
50g black chocolate
Whisky

Chop up or grate the dark chocolate and stir it into the ricotta. Unroll the sponge slowly and gently and sprinkle it with whisky, spread with jam, top with the ricotta and chocolate mixture and roll it up again.

To finish it off
1 packet x 250g frozen puff pastry
1 egg

Preheat the oven to gas mark 7/210ºC, then either roll out the pastry or buy the ready rolled sort. Lay the sponge roll on top of the pastry seam-side up and lift up the pastry to completely cover the roll. Seal the edges and trim off the excess pastry and brush with the egg beaten lightly with a little water. Bake in the oven for 20 – 25 minutes till golden and crisp. It is important to cook the pastry well to avoid soggy pastry inside the sinizza.

Serve warm or at room temperature – if there are leftovers store them in the fridge in hot weather as the ricotta may turn sour.

TORTA TAL-MARMURAT

This traditional Maltese sweet tart is a perfect cold weather dessert or teatime treat. It is equally delicious served warm or at room temperature.

200g plain flour
100g butter or 75ml olive oil
1 egg
Water

Sieve the flour into a bowl and rub in the butter or oil till the mixture resembles bread crumbs. Add the egg and enough water to make dough. You may need a little more water or flour if the dough is too dry or wet. Flatten this slightly with your knuckles, then fold it in half and flatten it again, do this three or four times until the dough is fairly smooth but do not overwork it as this makes it tough.

Preheat the oven to gas mark 6/200ºC and leave the dough to rest while you make the filling.

The filling
200g ground almonds
100g chopped candied peel
1 heaped tbs marmalade
100g soft brown sugar
1 tbs cocoa
75g black chocolate – grated
1 tsp mixed spice
3 large eggs or 4 small ones

Put all the dry ingredients into a bowl and stir them together. Add the eggs and mix well.

To assemble the tart: roll out the pastry thinly and use it to line a loose bottomed, 24cm non-stick fluted tin, arranging the edges so that there is a proper border. Spoon the filling into the pastry case and smooth it with the back of a spoon. Put the tart into the oven and after 15 minutes turn the temperature down to gas mark 3/160ºC for approximately another 20 – 30 minutes or until the pastry is a golden colour.

To finish the tart
100g black chocolate

Melt the chocolate and when the tart is cooked spread it over the hot tart.

GRAPEFRUIT AND APRICOT TEABREAD

A teabread is always nice to serve at teatime. This version makes use of grapefruits which give the cake a nice sharpness that contrasts very well with the apricots. Serve it buttered if you wish.

200g dried apricots (soaked overnight)
2 fresh Maltese grapefruits
300g self raising flour
1 flat tsp baking powder
100g butter
100g castor sugar
2 eggs
5 tbs milk
1 tbs brandy
6 or more sugar lumps to decorate
(crushed with a mallet)

Drain and chop the apricots roughly. Grate the zest from both the grapefruits; then squeeze one and peel the other grapefruit and chop up the flesh. Put the apricots, the grapefruit pulp, juice and zest in a bowl and set to one side. Put all the flour in a big bowl, rub in the butter, stir in the sugar and the rest of the ingredients and stir in well till smooth. Put it into a base lined well greased large loaf tin and scatter the surface with the crushed sugar lumps. Bake in the oven preheated to gas mark 3/160ºC for about and hour and a quarter or till an skewer pushed into its centre comes out clean. Turn out, cool and serve sliced and lightly buttered.

LOST CONFECTION

CITRATA

This wonderfully named large biscuit was "as big as a plate" as Mrs Antoinette Samut described it, she said that when she lived in Valletta as a child in the 1920s her sister would go and buy Citrata from Zerrek's confectionery. She remembers it was one of her favourite treats; a sweet and buttery, crumbly citrus flavoured biscuit that was shaped like a Maltese Cross and outlined in white icing. Herbert Ganado mourns the disappearance of these biscuits that he has "never seen since".[1] Mrs Samut couldn't quite put her finger on the quality of the texture of the biscuit; it was a cross between almond biscuit and shortcake, she recalled.

My grandfather and his sisters ready for bed, 1910

SUPPER

Children had supper earlier than their parents, and it was generally a simple meal; eggs in the form of a *barbuljata* or a lightly boiled egg with toast soldiers, perhaps a little beef tea or *tarja bil-butir* were popular choices for a meal before bed. Adults had supper later on, as Mrs Laura Pullicino put it, "in quiet elegance"; somehow evoking in that short phrase, the serenity of evenings before television invaded our houses. The food was fairly routine and was usually some soup or ravioli, a cooked salad, or *lenticchie u tarja*, and some fruit was a typical quiet mid-week winter supper; in the summer, different salads were served, they were made up of different things, sometimes cooked, sometimes raw *qarabali, fażola, tomatoes* were popular as was a squash stew.

---

1   Herbert Ganado/Michael Refalo, *My Century (Rajt Malta Tinbidel)*, vol 1

SQUASH STEW

1 onion – peeled and finely chopped
½ a long gourd/*qara' twil*
250g orange pumpkin/*qara' hamra*
250g white pumkin/ *qara' tork*
2 large courgettes/*qaraghbali*
4 potatoes
Seasoning
Thyme leaves – approx. 1 tbs
Olive oil

Fry the onion gently in olive oil while
you peel and chop the rest of the
vegetables into chunks. Then toss them
in the onion mixture and fry for about
2 or 3 minutes, add a little water some
more oil, some salt and pepper and the
thyme leaves. Cover the pot, turn the
heat down and leave it to cook over
a low flame for about ¾ of an hour.

LENTICCHIE U TARJA

200g lentils
1 large onion, peeled and finely chopped
1 carrot, peeled and finely chopped
1 chilli, seeds removed and chopped
3 stalks *karfus*/Maltese celery finely chopped
1 clove of garlic, peeled and crushed
1 tomato, finely chopped
1 tbs finely chopped fresh rosemary
 Olive oil
500ml chicken or vegetable stock
Salt and black pepper
400g tarja pasta

Fry the onion, carrot, celery, chilli and chopped garlic in the olive oil till very soft
but not browned. Then add the chopped tomato and fry for a further minute or so
then add the chopped rosemary and the lentils, stir and add the stock. Then cover
and simmer for about half an hour or till lentils are soft. Keep an eye on them and
check occasionally to make sure the lentils don't dry out too much, adding a little
more water if necessary. Then, once the lentils are soft, remove and puree half of
them, return the purée to the pot and keep warm.. In the meantime cook the tarja
in plenty of well salted boiling water till al dente and drain. Just before serving mix
the hot lentil sauce into the tarja and serve with an extra drizzle of olive oil.

ENTERTAINING

The emphasis was on simplicity as this was a time of austerity; a period troubled by a huge economic collapse that stunned a world recovering from a devastating world war and balanced on the brink of another. True, everyone was still "bright and gay" but there was little true affluence, especially when compared to the amazing choice available today. When people entertained at home it was generally on a small, intimate scale, a few close friends and family would have been invited to lunch, tea or dinner.

This interesting photograph was taken by my grandfather in 1927. His sister Josephine is first left, then my grandfather reading the paper, his mother is on the right while his sister Margaret is playing the piano. The room is lit by gaslight and the photograph required a 10 minute exposure.

"AT HOME"

Many ladies sent "At Home" cards round to friends and relatives and this meant that the lady of the house was at home on that particular day to welcome visitors, so other ladies would drop in to chat, play the piano or harp and generally spend time together, discussing the

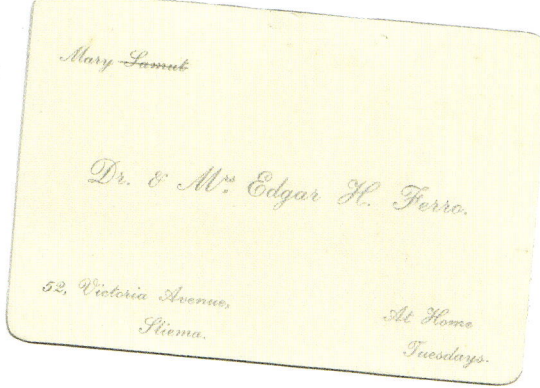

latest "on-dits", new books, the latest opera or play, wedding, books and generally setting the world to rights. There would be tiny savouries, petit fours, little almond biscuits and similar nibbles served with tea, coffee and of course rosolin. Brightly coloured, variously flavoured and often overly sweet, rosolin was liqueur served in special tiny silver cups and was very popular. One lady who remembers her mother's at homes remarked that they were all very fat, perhaps as they ate too many of the goodies on the following pages.

Ladies off to an 'at home' in the first years of the 20th Century.

MINI RICOTTA TARTLETS

Basic recipe for pastry

300g Plain flour
150g butter
A pinch of salt
Cold water

Sieve the flour into a mixing bowl, add the butter and rub it in. Make a hollow in the top and add the cold water mixture and stir until dough is formed. You may need a little more water or flour if the dough is too dry or wet. Flatten this slightly with your knuckles, then fold it in half and flatten it again, do this three or four times until the dough is fairly smooth but do not overwork it as this makes it tough. Leave the pastry to rest for half an hour.

The filling

500g ricotta
1 chopped red chilli
4 tbs chopped parsley
4 tbs grated parmesan
2 eggs
Asparagus spears
Cherry tomatoes
Chervil

Mix together the ricotta, chopped chilli, parsley, Parmesan and eggs with a fork until smooth. Put to one side while you roll out the pastry and cut out little rounds. Press them into a patty tin and fill with the ricotta filling and decorate each with an asparagus spear, quarter of a cherry tomato and a sprig of chervil.

Bake at gas mark 4/180ºC for about ½ an hour or until a golden and crisp, then take them out of the oven, remove from the tins and cool on a rack.

COCONUT MACAROONS

These crunchy biscuits take minutes to make and cook and are a pleasant alternative to the more common almonds macaroons.

2 egg whites
175g castor sugar
175g desiccated coconut

Whisk the egg whites till frothy, then add all the sugar and whisk again till the mixture is smooth and shiny. Remove two heaped tablespoons of the coconut, and put it into a bowl. Add the rest to the mixture and whisk till well combined. The mixture should be firm enough to shape teaspoonfuls of the mixture into little balls quite easily. If the egg whites are large, then you may need to add a little more coconut. Then roll the balls in the extra coconut and lay on a tray lined with non-stick baking paper or rice paper and bake in the oven preheated to gas mark 4 ½/185ºC for about 15–18 minutes or till golden brown. Cool on a rack and serve with tea, coffee or ice-cream or store in an airtight container.
Makes 24 medium sized macaroons

COFFEE AND ALMOND BALLS

100g ground almonds
100g castor sugar
1 egg white
2 or 3 tbs ground coffee
Cocoa powder

Put all the ingredients into a bowl and mix them well together with a fork to make a firm but slightly sticky dough. If the dough is too dry add a tiny dash of brandy; if too wet add more ground almonds. Then roll them into balls, toss lightly in cocoa powder and serve in little paper cases.
NB. Less egg white is required when you double or triple the receipt. Makes approximately 12.

ALMOND MACAROONS

250g whole almonds – skins on
2 tbs semolina
1 tbs honey
1 egg white
200g castor sugar
2 tbs Amaretto liqueur
Some extra whole almonds for decoration

Grind the whole, unskinned almonds till fine. In a separate bowl, whisk the egg white till frothy, then add the sugar and whisk in till thick. Then add the almonds, semolina and honey and whisk till combined, then fold in the liqueur. Roll into walnut sized balls, stick a whole almond on top and arrange on a baking tray lined with rice paper or non-stick baking paper. Space them out as they flatten during baking.

Bake them in the oven preheated to gas mark 5/190ºC for about 10 minutes. Cool and store in an airtight container till needed.

N.B. if you have a bitter almond tree in the garden, then replace 25g of the almonds in this recipe with some bitter almonds to give these biscuits a delicious flavour. Makes approximately 30.

IMQARET

Make these traditional fried pastries smaller than usual to serve at parties as large chunky ones are difficult to eat and look clumsy.

First make the filling
250g dates – Stoned and chopped
Grated zest of I large tangerine
2 tbs Anisette (or Sambuca)
2 tbs icing sugar

Melt the dates in a saucepan with about 4 or 5 tablespoons water. It should take about 4 minutes. Then stir in the other ingredients and taste, add a little more Anisette or tangerine if necessary. Put to one side to cool while you make the pastry. *N.B. If you can't find tangerines use some tangerine liqueur instead.*

Make the pastry
250g plain flour
75g butter or 50ml olive oil
Enough water to bind

Rub the oil or butter into the flour and make dough with water to bind. Rest the pastry for quarter of an hour, then cut it in half and roll both halves out into a rectangular shape. Spread the filling onto one side of each of the rectangles and fold over the pastry, sealing the edges well. Cut these at an angle to make imqaret. Then either brush them generously with oil and bake them in a hot oven at gas mark 6/200ºC for approximately 20-25minutes, turning them half way through baking if necessary, or simply deep fry them

These are best eaten hot although the baked ones are just as good at room temperature. Makes 12-15.

old silver rosolin cups

PEACH BRANDY

This liqueur is ideal to make when peaches are in season.

750g peaches
250g sugar
1 vanilla pod – split and cut up
1 bottle brandy

Slice and cut up the peaches and put them in a very large jar. Crack the peach stones, remove the kernels, peel them and add them to the peaches along with the sugar and vanilla pod. Stir well and pour in the brandy.

Close the jar and put in a dark, cool place for two weeks to infuse. Sterilise one or two bottles – either use a commercial sterilising fluid or simply wash them well and heat them in the oven at gas mark 3/180ºC for 20 minutes.

Then strain the liqueur through muslin, allowing it to drip through without pressing as that will make it cloudy and form a thick layer of sediment. Pour into the prepared bottles, seal and mature for a month before serving.

ROSOLIN TAT-TUT

500g black mulberry tree fruit *(tut)*
Approx. 400ml 95% pure fruit alcohol (use *Eau de vie* if unavailable)
600g of sugar
600ml of water

Put the black mulberry tree fruit *(tut)* in a large, clean jar and pour on the alcohol until the fruit is covered. Cover the jar tightly and leave it in a dark, cool place for at least two weeks. When the two weeks are up, dissolve 600g of sugar in 600ml of water, then bring the pan to a rolling boil for a minute or two and turn off the heat. Leave the syrup to cool completely. Strain the alcohol into a jug and mix it with the syrup. Pour this into a sterilised bottle. Allow it to settle for two months. Serve it chilled in liqueur glasses.

LUNCH PARTIES AND COCKTAIL PARTIES

A typical lunch party would definitely start off with a soup and have included favourites like dentici served with mayonnaise in summer or some sort of chicken or meat as a main course in the winter. Puddings were extremely popular as people were not as figure conscious as they are today and really enjoyed their food. Of course the language question filtered down into the sort of food that was served; some families enjoyed Italianized Maltese cuisine, while others preferred a more Anglicised twist to their menus.

This was the way people entertained at home at that time. More formal or official dinners were fairly frequent and held at hotels or places like Casino Maltese. These were generally held in honour of an important visiting dignitary or to celebrate or commemorate some memorable event. The food served at such meals was much more elegant and sophisticated on the whole as the cooks were usually more skilled and more often than not professional chefs trained in Haute Cuisine. Cocktail parties caught on in 1930's Malta and were very popular; drinks and cocktails were served along with some roasted nuts and a few canapés but little else as these were cocktail parties in the true sense.

STUFFED OR DEVILED EGGS

These are simple to make and were very popular. Mrs Josephine Burridge neè Pullicino remembers them being served at her parents' parties and said that the family cook decorated them to look like little sailing boats by sticking a rice paper "sail" onto a parsley-stalk "mast" that went into the yolk.

Hard boil enough eggs for the guests – 1 each – pop out (remove) the egg yolks to a small bowl and mash with a fork. Add mayonnaise, dijon mustard, sweet paprika, dill, chives, finely chopped parsley, salt and pepper and mix well. Fill the empty egg white shells with the mixture (piping recommended!) and garnish the tops with a small bit of caviar on a tiny coffee spoon.

To have perfectly centred yolks: Lay the eggs on their sides in a container and chill in the refrigerator for about a week, turning them on their axis every day or two. This also helps the cooked eggs to separate more easily from the shell membrane as very fresh eggs are impossible to shell neatly.

SAUSAGE ROLLS

Although sausage rolls are a little unpopular nowadays, possibly due to the fact that they are usually greasily made, badly cooked and often soggy, back then they were one of the most popular nibblers on the tray.

It would have been difficult to get hold of the bright pink sausage meat that is used to fill them nowadays; in those days what they did was split well made *zalzett Malti* and use that as a filling instead.

BOMBI TAR-ROSS ŻGĦIR or ARANCINI

Traditionally arancini are stuffed with a rich, very thick meat sauce or cheese, but anything can be used. In spring and summer seafood like cooked shrimps or octopus makes a delicious change or some chopped seasonal vegetables like aubergine stewed in tomato sauce; ingredients like mushrooms, ham, ricotta and spinach are perfect on autumn days. Make these as small as possible to serve at parties; they may be difficult to stuff when they are very small, so mix the filling and rice together and proceed according to the recipe.

The basic recipe is as follows
400g Arborio rice
1 glass white wine
1½ litres stock
1 onion
Generous pinch saffron threads (see note)
20g butter
2 tbs olive oil
2 tbs freshly grated Parmesan
1 large egg

Fry the onion in the olive oil until soft, add the Arborio rice and stir it around then add a glass of white wine and the saffron threads. Cook, stirring till absorbed, and then add the stock a ladleful at a time, stirring until each has evaporated until the rice is cooked and the stock used up. If the rice needs a little more cooking and the stock has finished, add boiling water in the same way. As soon as the rice is ready add the parmesan and butter, stir and allow the rice to cool slightly then beat in the egg and carry on cooling. The rice should be tepid not cold when used as it is difficult to shape when cold.

NOTE: Saffron imparts a delicate, delicious flavour and colours arancini perfectly but it is an expensive spice. You could substitute powdered saffron or leave it out for an everyday version of arancini.

In the meantime prepare one or two (or all) of the fillings below:

MEAT FILLING

1 onion, finely chopped
Olive oil
1 or 2 cloves of garlic, crushed
400g minced beef
1 tbs very finely chopped fresh rosemary
2 bay leaves
2 glasses red wine
300 ml tomato sauce
4 tbs good quality *Kunserva*
(tomato concentrate)
Seasoning
100g fresh or frozen peas

First make the sauce: Fry the onion in olive oil till golden and soft, add the finely chopped rosemary, garlic and minced beef. Fry until the meat is lightly browned then add the red wine, bay leaves and simmer briefly. Pour on the tomato sauce and *kunserva*, then season it and leave it all to simmer on a low heat for about an hour until the sauce is nice and thick. Add the peas half way through cooking if you use fresh ones, otherwise add them at the end if you use frozen ones, otherwise they will overcook.

AUBERGINE FILLING

1 aubergine
Olive oil
3 tbs *kunserva*
2 tbs chopped basil
A dash white wine
1 clove garlic
1 big ball mozzarella

Peel the aubergine and garlic, dice it small and fry in some olive oil till browned; then add the wine and *kunserva* and cook till soft. Stir in the basil and season well. When the mix is quite cold, cube up the mozzarella and stir it in.

RICOTTA AND SPINACH FILLING

300g ricotta
150g raw spinach, borage or nettle leaves, washed and squeezed dry
50g freshly grated parmesan
1 or 2 tsp chopped red chilli

Make sure the greens are dry, then chop them finely and stir into the ricotta, add the chilli and parmesan and stir well to combine.

CHEESE FILLING

50g pecorino – diced
50g mozzarella – diced
50g Parmesan – grated
1 tbs chopped parsley
A little black pepper

Mix all the ingredients together.

TO FINISH THE ARANCINI
Prepare the following:

Approx. 2 litres sunflower oil for deep frying
3 eggs, seasoned and lightly beaten in a shallow dish
Approx. 200g flour, in a flat dish
Breadcrumbs, in another flat dish
A bowl of water
Lots of Kitchen roll

First wet your hands (to stop the rice sticking) then take a large tablespoon of the rice and put it in the palm of your hand; then make a hollow in the centre, fill it with your chosen filling and close up the hole with a little more rice. Roll the stuffed rice ball in the flour, then in the egg, then in the bread crumbs, patting and pressing gently as you go, making sure the ball is neat and round. Put the ball on a plate, ready to be fried when the rest are ready.

When all the arancini are prepared, heat the oil in a deep saucepan that is wide enough to hold about four arancini easily and when the oil is hot enough to brown a cube of bread in a couple of minutes, start to cook the arancini about 4 at a time until they are a deep golden brown. Drain on kitchen roll and serve as soon as they are ready.

Makes about 12 medium ones and 20 small ones.

My grandfather, left, with his parents and sisters off to lunch in Mdina 1910.

A TYPICAL SUNDAY LUNCH PARTY MENU

Soppa "Julienne"
or
Cream of Tomato soup

❧

Bomba rar-ross
or
Salmon Mousse

❧

Cervellini Dorati

❧

Cold dentici and mayonnaise
Dressed potatoes
Boiled qaraghbaghli (marrows)

❧

Soufflé
or
Steamed Pudding Maltaise

❧

Coffee and petit fours

CERVELLINI DORATI

2 pork brains
2 eggs
2 tbs very finely chopped parsley
A little flour for dusting
Seasoning
Oil for deep frying

Prepare the brain as follows: Wash the brains in cold, running water and remove any tiny bits of bone, membrane and blood vessels. Soak them in cold water for an hour and then blanch them in lightly salted water with a teaspoon of vinegar and a bay leaf for a couple of minutes. Drain them.

Separate the eggs and beat the white until stiff, then add the yolks and whisk them in. Stir in the parsley and season it all well. Fill a sauce pan with some oil and heat it, in the meantime dust the slices of brain in the flour, dip them in the egg and drop the in the boiling oil a few at a time. Cook till golden, then remove and drain them on kitchen paper and serve while hot and crunchy.

SOPPA "JULIENNE"

1 kg beef shin and a couple of marrow bones
2 leeks
1 onion
5 carrots
5 stalks and leaves Maltese *karfus* type celery
2 sprigs thyme
A tsp of *Kunserva*
Seasoning
Tiny meat balls – optional

Put the ingredients into a deep stock pot, just cover with cold water and bring to the boil. Skim off any scum that may rise to the surface and simmer for about two or three hours and then strain it. Put the meat and boiled vegetables in a bowl and keep to serve dressed with olive oil and lemon juice at another meal with *salsa verde* and boiled potatoes.

This meat broth is used to prepare Soppa Julienne simply by cutting some carrots, leeks, courgettes, a few peas and other seasonal vegetables into slivers (julienne) and simmering them in the broth until tender. Then add some pastina and boil till just done. Serve the soup with a light dusting of chopped parsley.

BOMBA TAR-ROSS

300g rice
Bolognaise sauce (made with 300ml tomato sauce and 300g minced meat)
6 chicken livers – cut in half
Dash of brandy
75g frozen peas
2 tbs chopped parsley
4 tbs grated Parmesan
1 egg
100ml milk or cream
300ml smooth tomato sauce

Parboil the rice, drain it and put it to one side. In the meantime toss the chicken livers in a little butter and olive oil till browned but not cooked through, then add the brandy to the pan and bubble. Stir the livers into the rice along with the rest of the ingredients and pour the mixture into a well greased, base lined pudding bowl and smooth the top. Cover the bowl with grease proof paper and tie it around the bowl. Top this with foil tucked tightly around the grease proof paper. Put it into a large saucepan filled with enough water to reach half way up the pudding bowl, cover the pot and steam for ¾ an hour. When it is cooked through, remove the foil and greaseproof paper, invert it onto a plate and serve coated with the tomato sauce.

N.B. Take care the pot does not boil dry. If the level of water drops – top it up with boiling water – not cold water to keep the temperature even or it will not cook properly.

COLD DENTICI AND MAYONNAISE

Poach a large dentici, approximately 2 kilos for 30 minutes in some water, white wine and herbs. Allow it to cool in the poaching liquid, then lift it out carefully and serve it whole, decorated with some lemon quarters, herbs and lettuce and mayonnaise – preferably homemade as follows.

The yolks of two eggs (whisked)
250ml of olive oil
Sea-salt, chives (chopped)
Hardy marjoram/*merqtux* (chopped)

Add the olive oil to the whisked yolks, a little at a time, whisking in between each addition, until the oil is thoroughly incorporated. As the mixture thickens and grows you can add the oil a little faster, but always whisk well. Lastly, scatter on the herbs. You can whisk by hand with a balloon whisk, or use a food processor. If you don't like the strong taste of olive oil, use a mild vegetable oil instead. If the mayonnaise seems too thick before the oil has been used up, whisk in a little of the egg white. If the mayonnaise curdles, don't despair. Just start again with two fresh yolks, and use the curdled mayonnaise instead of more oil.

STEAMED PUDDING MALTAISE

This very English pudding that was very popular, and still is with the older generation, is given a Maltese twist by using oranges and honey.

150g butter +extra for greasing the bowl
150g castor sugar + an extra tbs
The grated peel and juice
of 2 Maltese oranges
A slice of an orange
3 eggs
200g sieved self raising flour
3 tbs milk
Maltese honey

Beat the butter and sugar together till white and creamy; add the grated peel of the oranges and start to add the eggs one at a time, beating each egg in very well before adding the next. Then fold in the flour and milk gently till well mixed. Grease and base line a pudding bowl, sprinkle with the extra sugar and lay down a thin slice of orange, then pour in the cake mix and smooth the top. Cover the bowl with grease proof paper and tie it around the bowl. Top this with foil tucked tightly around the grease proof paper. Put it into a large saucepan filled with enough water to reach half way up the pudding bowl, cover the pot and steam for ¾ an hour. In the meantime pour the orange juice into a small pot and add the honey and melt gently. When the pudding is cooked through, remove the foil and greaseproof paper, invert it onto a plate, pour over the orange and honey and serve it hot.

When the chicken broth was served Nicholas shouted above the din whether anyone wanted to add a fresh egg to the soup ... Baked macaroni and chicken followed in quick succession. We were served a meat dish and when it was time for ricotta pie ... I was served a huge chunk and tried to avoid looking at the soufflé that followed. ... What could I do but accept a large helping of soufflé.

Herbert Ganado/Michael Refalo, *My Century (Rajt Malta Tinbidel)*, Vol 3

SOUFFLÉ

"Soufflé" or Maltese trifle is made by layering sponge, vanilla custard, sponge, sweetened ricotta, sponge, chocolate custard, sponge and so on. The sponge is brushed with some rum and jam, the ricotta is flavoured with chopped chocolate, candied peel and toasted almonds and the custard is perfect and homemade. Maltese Soufflé is similar to the Italian Zuppa Inglese made in Emilia-Romagna where it has layers of sponge and different coloured custard or crema pasticciera – chocolate and vanilla. A soufflé is firmer and better looking when made with crema pasticciera but many people prefer to use custard because it makes the soufflé softer and juicier.

1 sponge cake

Make this using the usual sponge cake method comprising the following ingredients: 6 eggs, 200g sugar, and 200g flour. Bake and leave to cool in the switched off oven so that the sponge is slightly drier than usual. (N.B. do not burn it). Then, when it is cool, slice it up fairly thinly.

One amount crema pasticciera or custard (see recipe opposite)

For the ricotta filling
500g soft ricotta
50g toasted flaked almonds
100g grated black chocolate

Mix all the ingredients together

To assemble
Jam
Approx. 100ml brandy or whisky
2 tbs castor sugar
50ml boiling water

Stir the castor sugar into the boiling water till it dissolves, then add the brandy or whisky and stir. Make layers in a deep pudding bowl as follows: cover the base with a layer of sponge cake slices, sprinkle or brush with brandy, spread with jam and then pour over some of the vanilla custard. Cover with slices of sponge cake, spread with jam and sprinkle generously with brandy, then spread over about half of the ricotta. Then sponge cake, jam, brandy, cover with chocolate custard, sponge and so on until you have used up all the ingredients taking care to ensure that the last layer is sponge. Cover the top with cling film and chill overnight.

First melt the butter in a little saucepan, then remove from the heat and put to one side. Then whisk the eggs till very thick and foamy, then split the vanilla pod and scrape the seedy inside into the eggs and whisk in. Then start to add the sugar a little at a time, whisking in between each addition until all the sugar has been added. Then sieve the flour and baking powder together onto a paper and start to fold in as follows: first fold in about one third of the flour, then one third of the melted cooled butter, then the next third of the flour, and then the next one third of the butter and so on until all is used up.

Then pour the mixture into a well greased and base lined 23cm cake tin and bake for about 40-45 minutes at gas mark 4/180ºC or until golden and well risen. Remove from tins and cool.

Crème patisserie
1 litre full fat milk
4 eggs
150g sugar
125g plain flour
200g black chocolate

Bring the milk to the boil, and in the meantime, beat the eggs and sugar till well combined and slightly thickened. Then sieve in the flour and beat again till smooth. Then, very slowly, pour in the milk, beating all the while. Clean the pot and return the creamy mass to the pot and bring to the boil, stirring all the while. It will thicken

quickly, but it may turn lumpy so keep stirring vigorously, especially as it starts to come to the boil. Then remove from the heat and add the chocolate and beat till it is melted into the cream.

Ricotta
1 kilo Maltese ricotta
Freshly ground coffee to taste
Icing sugar to taste
A very generous dash of whisky
100ml fresh cream
Beat the ingredients together till smooth

Syrup
50g sugar
100ml coffee
100ml whisky

Melt the sugar in the coffee, bring it to the boil, remove from the heat, cool slightly and add the whisky.

Once all the separate components are ready – line a large bowl with cling film and starting with a layer of sponge slices which must be drizzled with the whisky and coffee syrup make layers as follows: drizzled sponge – chocolate cream – drizzled sponge – coffee flavoured ricotta – drizzled sponge – chocolate cream and so on until all the ingredients have been used up, Then cover it with cling film and refrigerate for at least 24 hours. Then turn it out, top with a little whipped fresh cream and scatter with toasted flaked almonds.
Serves about 16 – 20. It depends on the size of the slices

CAPPUCCINO SOUFFLÉ

This version of "soufflé" resembles the traditional version in that it features sponge layered up with both custard and ricotta; other than that that the taste is very different, the chocolate and coffee flavours are reminiscent of a cappuccino. This is my more modern version of the more traditional pudding.

Sponge cake
8 eggs
250g castor sugar
½ a vanilla pod
250g plain flour
1 tsp baking powder
100g butter – melted

CHRISTMAS SOUFFLÉ

The Christmas soufflé was served in a silver entrée dish, but may be made in any low sided dish, preferably a glass one so that the pretty layers are visible.

Sponge cake made with 6 eggs
500g ricotta
100 – 150g finely chopped dark chocolate
100g finely chopped candied citrus peel (preferably homemade)
1 tbs sugar
Whisky
150g green marzipan

Slice up the sponge cake to make a layer in the bottom of the bowl. Sprinkle generously with whisky. Mix the ricotta with the sugar, chocolate and candied citrus peel then spread it over the sponge cake layer. Cover this with another layer of sliced sponge cake and sprinkle it all with whisky. Roll out the green marzipan and lay it neatly over the top of the sponge cake layer. Just before serving the pudding, whisk up a tin of milk (ideal milk or similar) with a squeeze of lemon and sugar to taste until very thick and spread it over the top. This topping, called *fior di latte*, was very popular at the time but modern tastes may prefer whipped cream instead.

Some people liked to make a bulkier version of this by repeating the layers and preparing it in a high sided bowl

CHRISTMAS LUNCH – HERBERT GANADO – 7 YEARS OLD (1914)

The meal was served with traditional pomp and ceremony. Two tureens were brought in …. Soup was followed by Timpana, at which Grandmother's cook always excelled. Turkey was next. The bird was brought in on a huge dish, its tail feathers arranged like a fan and to give colour, decorated with crinkled paper. … Uncle Alfred uncorked a bottle of rum, liberally poured it over the pudding, lit a match and blue violet flames rose around the pudding. … Grandmother's lunches unlike those at Granny's house, had a distinct English flavour about them.

Herbert Ganado/Michael Refalo, My Century (Rajt Malta Tinbidel), Vol. 1

Between the second half of the 19th century and the first half of the 20th century, the Maltese Christmas table evolved into something very unusual indeed: a mix of English and Sicilian festive fare that has been woven into a Maltese Christmas.

A traditional Maltese Christmas lunch is often a marathon meal of heroic proportions. It starts off with drinks and little appetisers: nuts, olives, smoked salmon, Parma ham, tiny crostini topped with a little liver pâté as well as sweet nibbles, like stuffed dates, marrons glacé and chocolate truffles. The meal begins with a small bowl of soup, made from the neck, wing-tips and giblets of the main course – the turkey – and carrot, onion and celery. A dash of sherry might be added to give it a more festive flavour. Then there is the timpana, best served in small portions but eaten in huge quantities nonetheless. Turkey follows, though before World War II it was often a goose for the well-to-do and a chicken for the less so. Gammon is sometimes served along with the turkey, giving an alternative to those who are not too fond of the big bird. The traditional Maltese Christmas sweet is the qagħqa tal-għasel, but this has become everyday fare available in supermarkets. The British legacy of mince pies and plum pudding remain with us strictly at Christmas. A different kind of peculiarly Maltese Christmas dessert is the soufflé, which is nothing like a French soufflé but is similar to the Italian *zuppa Inglese.*

Cooked by Mark Camilleri

CHRISTMAS TIMPANA

The dish must be lined with short crust pastry, filled with penne mixed with a rich bolognaise sauce dotted with little pieces of chicken liver and boiled eggs, bound with eggs and cheese and topped with flaky puff pastry all baked till golden and crisp.

1 lot short crust pastry
made with 300g flour
1 lot puff pastry made with 200g
flour + I beaten egg to glaze
500g penne

For the sauce
1 onion, finely chopped
Olive oil
1 or 2 cloves of garlic, crushed
500g minced beef
1 sprig very finely chopped rosemary
2 bay leaves
1 glass red wine
700ml tomato sauce
150g chicken livers, cleaned cut in half
3 or 4 lightly boiled eggs
5 raw eggs, lightly beaten
5 heaped tbs grated Parmesan cheese
Seasoning

First make the sauce: Fry the onion in olive oil till golden and soft, add the finely chopped rosemary, garlic and minced beef. Fry until the meat is lightly browned then add the red wine and bay leaves and simmer briefly. Pour on the tomato sauce, season and leave it all to simmer on a very low heat for about an hour.

In the meantime fry the prepared chicken livers till browned on the outside but still blood-red inside and boil the eggs for about 3 minutes, just so that they are firm enough to peel as both of these will need to cook further inside the Timpana.

Then, boil the penne till extremely al dente, drain well and stir in the sauce, add the beaten eggs, grated cheese, liver and eggs. Allow the mixture to cool. Then pour it into a dish lined with short crust pastry. Top it with puff pastry and brush with a beaten egg. Cut the left over pastry into shapes and decorate the top, brush with the rest of the beaten egg and bake at gas mark 4 ½ /185ºC for about an hour to n hour and a quarter or till golden, crisp and firm.

If chicken livers and eggs are unpopular with children, only put them in one half of the Timpana and mark the top with a pastry tick to indicate where they are and the plainer half with a pastry cross – meaning nothing there (my mother's trick).

As the era came to a close and the world once again descended into the horror of war, entertaining at home became the exception rather than the rule because of the disruption of war and the infamous food shortages that crippled Malta for the next few years.

CHRISTMAS PUDDING

There are few secrets to making a perfect Christmas pudding: obvious ones include a recipe that really works and top quality ingredients. However, the crucial trick is to steam the pudding for a minimum of eight hours initially and then for another five hours on Christmas morning – this practically ensures excellence. My recipe uses butter rather than the more traditional suet, making the pudding healthier and much tastier. I have made puddings using this recipe ever since I started making Christmas pudding and they are always delicious.

100g coarsely grated carrot
100g pitted pruned – chopped
350g sultanas and raisins
25g chopped candied peel
125g butter
125g soft dark brown sugar
2 eggs
50g fresh brown bread crumbs
175g flour
1 tbs mixed spice
200ml Guinness
100ml brandy
Juice and grated zest of two oranges and a lemon
2 tbs black treacle

Put all the prunes, raisins, sultanas and candied peel in a bowl and cover with the brandy, juice and zest for at least 24 hours. Beat the butter and sugar until light and fluffy. Add the eggs one at a time, beating well after each addition. Add the rest of the ingredients and fold in until well blended. Cover and leave in a cool place overnight.

Next morning prepare the pudding basin – simply carefully grease and base line a 1.5 litre bowl and cut out two circles of greaseproof paper with a border 2.5cm wider than the bowl's rim.

Then stir the pudding – each member of the family should give the pudding a stir and make a Christmas wish – then pour the pudding into the bowl and smooth the top. Cover the bowl with a double layer of the prepared grease proof paper and tie it around the bowl. Top this with foil tucked tightly around the grease proof paper. Invert a plate over this and tie it in place with a tea-cloth.

Put this in a large saucepan filled with enough water to reach half way up the pudding bowl and steam for at least eight hours.

N.B. Take care the pot does not boil dry. If the level of water drops – top it up with boiling water – otherwise fluctuations in the temperature will result in a soggy pudding and the distinct possibility of a burnt pot.

Allow the pudding to cool, then replace the foil with fresh foil and store for up to a month in the fridge. If you want to make it earlier – then put it in the freezer after

the month is up. If you forget to make the pudding in time to allow a month's maturing don't worry, the pudding will still taste good – I've made it a week before Christmas and it still tasted scrumptious.

On Christmas morning put the pudding in a saucepan filled with enough water to reach half way up the pudding bowl and steam for at least five hours. Then unwrap it and turn it out onto a stout plate, remove the base paper and take it to the Christmas table and allow the man of the day to flame the pudding with brandy (watch your eyebrows). Serve the steaming hot pudding with brandy butter.

To make brandy butter: Beat equal amounts of butter and icing sugar till very pale and fluffy, then beat in brandy to taste – be generous otherwise it will just taste like butter icing. Some people like to add cream or almonds; but I prefer it without, just with lots of brandy. A scraping of nutmeg over the top looks pretty and adds flavour – but it isn't vital.

My father, my mother and myself

GROWING UP IN THE 1960s AND 70s

Tea with my great-grandmother at San Pawl tat-Tarġa

Some memories are like butterflies; brilliantly coloured and as light as air. Flitting away on the breeze, difficult to catch and leaving a smear of powdery colour, an impression of patterned wings. Others are clearer, brought into sharp focus by scents, sounds or tastes that bring in their wake a flood of emotion.

Food has always inspired me and I was very young when this trait showed its greedy hand. My mother often teasingly recalled that as soon as I learned to pull myself along the floor (I was still too young to crawl) I made my way to the kitchen, sat up and opened the kitchen cupboard where the biscuits were kept and pulled out the tin of Peek Freans biscuits. Deeply disappointed that I couldn't open the tin, or so the story goes, I started to cry and was given a biscuit by my fond mother.

Chocolate and jam are the stars of my earliest food recollections and are entwined with memories of my Hungarian Great Grandmother, who died when I was four. More often than not, she would bring me a little bar of chocolate wrapped in paper decorated with an Alpine scene complete with a cow when she visited us, and I loved that chocolate almost as much as I loved her. We, too, went to see her at San Pawl Tat-Targa where she lived with my Grandfather in a lovely old house where Grandpa grew lots of fruit and lovely roses and carnations. There was a special peach tree in the courtyard; Grandpa had grafted it so that white peaches grew on one side of the tree at the beginning of summer while yellow peaches ripened on the other side later in the summer. We would have tea there, with buttered bread and jam, cakes and biscuits but the best part of it all was choosing the jam; Granny would pick me up and take me into her larder which was full of jars of jam and other goodies and I was allowed to chose the jam for tea.

PLUM OR APRICOT OR PEACH JAM

1 kg fresh, ripe plums or apricots
or peaches (stoned weight)
1 kg sugar
The juice of one lemon
½ a glass of water

Wash the plums or apricots or peaches
and split them in half, remove the
stones and chop the fruit very roughly.
Put the fruit in a jam pan, (a very wide,
low-sided large pan) with the lemon
juice and glass of water. Bring the fruit
slowly to the boil then turn the heat
down and simmer until the fruit is soft
and cooked, stirring it every now and
again to make sure the fruit doesn't stick
to the bottom of the pan and burn.

Once the fruit is soft and cooked through (you should be able to squash the fruit
easily with the back of a wooden spoon and the skin should be tender), turn down
the heat and add the sugar, stirring until the sugar has dissolved completely. If the
sugar isn't completely dissolved before you bring the jam back to the boil it may
crystallise during storage. Once the sugar is dissolved, bring the jam back to a rolling
boil and cook for at least 15 minutes, stirring every now and again. Then test the
jam for setting in this way: put a spoonful of jam on a saucer, allow it to cool for
about 15 seconds then push the back of a spoon through the little pool of jam. The
surface should wrinkle up. If it doesn't, then carry on boiling the jam until setting
point is reached, it shouldn't need any more than another few minutes boiling
otherwise it may overcook, darken and the sugar caramelise, losing much of the
true fruit flavour. When the jam is ready to pot, pour it into the hot, sterilised jars
and screw the lids on tightly. The jam will keep for at least a year if not longer.

To sterilise jars: Wash them and then put the jars in the oven at gas mark
3/150ºC/325F for 20 minutes and boil the lids for 10 minutes.

NOTES:
*Sometimes it is worth cracking the plum or apricot or peach stones to extract the kernel
within. Peel these carefully and add them to the jam; it enhances the flavour beautifully.
Add a couple of tablespoons of finely chopped thyme or rosemary or a split
vanilla pod at the same time as the sugar to give the jam exquisite flavour.
A dash of brandy is excellent stirred into the peach jam in the last two minutes of
cooking – not to the plum or apricot jam as it somehow does not match at all.*

FIG AND LEMON JAM

This jam is a vast improvement on typical fig jam which is usually cloyingly sweet. There may seem to be a huge amount of lemons in the recipe, but they add the sharp tang necessary to emphasis the fig taste and balance out the sweetness while helping the jam set better. The lemons are best sliced as thinly as possible, either using a mandolin or electric slicer so that they become very tender through the cooking and melt into the jam, adding texture to the jam which might otherwise resemble a paste rather than a jam.

This jam is very good made with the figs that ripen in June, the *bajtar ta' San Ġwann*, **but it is just as good if not better made with any of our later Maltese figs, especially the black ones called** *farkizzan*.

1.2 kg figs
6 local lemons
12 sprigs fresh rosemary
900g granulated sugar

Slice up the figs thickly or quarter them. Slice the unpeeled lemons paper thin and remove the pips. Strip the needles from the rosemary sprigs and chop them up roughly. Weigh out the sugar carefully. Once everything is prepared, layer up the ingredients in a large glass bowl, starting with the figs, covering them with the lemons; then sprinkle on the rosemary and cover with some of the sugar. Carry on in this way until all the ingredients are used up but make sure the last one is a layer of sugar. Cover it with cling film or some kind of a lid and stand in a cool place for about 24 hours – if you intend to leave it for longer refrigerate it for up to 48hours.

Pour the fruit and sugar mix into a large saucepan and cook over a low heat until the lemon peel is soft and the syrup thick and setting into jam. Spoon the jam into sterilised jars (see above) and screw the lids on tightly to seal. In times when it was difficult to obtain new lids paper was used instead as follows: Greaseproof paper circles the diameter of the jars were cut out and, dipped in brandy and placed on the jam. Then larger circles were cut out, the edges dipped in lightly beaten egg white and then pressed over the jar and held in place to stick down tightly.

This should make approximately 8 to 10 200g jars Serve as all other jams; use on bread and toast and to fill tarts and cakes or wrap up prettily and give away as a present. Try using the jams in one of these recipes

JAM BISCUITS

250g plain flour
125g butter
1 egg
125g castor sugar
Pinch cinnamon
A variety of Jams
Mascarpone

Cut the butter into the flour and then rub in briefly until
the mixture resembles coarse bread crumbs and stir in
the sugar and cinnamon. Add the egg to make dough,
add a little water if it seems too dry or a little flour if too
wet. Knead briefly till smooth and put aside for half an
hour so the pastry will rest and be easier to use.

Roll out the pastry and cut out circles. Lay them out on a well
greased or lined baking tray and bake at gas mark 4/180ºC for
15 -20 minutes or until golden. Cool them on a rack and then
sandwich them together with a little jam and mascarpone.
If you intend to keep them longer than an afternoon omit
the mascarpone as it will sour and spoil the biscuits.

JAM TARTLETS

200g plain flour
100g butter
25g icing sugar
A little cold water to bind
Jam

Sieve the flour into a large bowl and chop the butter into it. Then
rub the butter into the flour till it resembles coarse bread crumbs,
then stir in the icing sugar till combined. Next add cold water
and stir till it comes together to make dough. Knead briefly and
leave it to rest for 20 minutes before rolling it out. Use it to line
12 small tartlet tins, then weigh them down with a crumpled
piece of tin foil and bake blind for 15 minutes or till golden.

In the meantime warm up some peach, plum or apricot jam with
a little water, give it a quick boil and then use it to fill the tartlets.

My great aunts Dora and Margaret

My Great Aunts Dora and Margaret often had us to tea; they lived in Balluta Buildings and their dining room was huge and the furniture dark and old. There were foxes and ducks carved into the side boards which always looked as though they were glaring at us and struggling to break free. But the tea table made up for the furniture; it would be laden with lovely things like meringues, biscuits and cakes made by Aunt Margaret who was a great cook; but very old fashioned. This meant we all had to adhere to the rule of a piece of bread and butter, then a piece of bread and jam and only then some of the goodies ranged around the table on pretty plates. Luckily enough Aunt Margaret usually served buttered baguettes (bzitzen) sliced thin and buttered lightly, so not all that filling.

Aunt Margaret buttered the bread quite differently to usual; she never cut and then buttered the bread as people normally do. Instead she first buttered the cut side of a loaf and then sliced it; so the lovely, fresh bread could be cut thinly and as it was already buttered, the problem of flattened and torn bread was avoided.

NUT AND JAM TART

200g plain flour
50g ground almonds
½ a vanilla pod
150g butter
50g icing sugar
1 whole egg + 1 egg yolk
(keep the white to use later)
250g jam/marmalade
150g walnuts or blanched
almonds – roughly chopped

Stir the flour, icing sugar and ground almonds together and then scrape the insides of the vanilla pod into the flour. Chop the butter into the flour and rub it in until it resembles breadcrumbs. Stir in the whole egg and egg yolk to make dough and knead briefly. Then leave it to rest for half an hour. Then roll it out and use it to line a 23cm flan dish, brush the edges and sides with the lightly with the egg white and fill with the jam. Scatter over the roughly chopped nuts and bake for about 40 minutes or till it is lovely and golden.

PLAIN MERINGUES

Meringues are always popular and although they are simple to make, keep in mind that they soften very quickly in damp weather (or when a south wind blows). It helps if the meringues are left to cool completely in the oven and then transferred immediately to an airtight tin to be removed just before serving. My great Aunt Margaret made excellent meringues and served them in spring with strawberries and cream in big glass bowls. The teaspoon of corn flour in the recipe is her addition, and it is an excellent idea as it stabilises and helps the meringues cook well without affecting the taste at all.

4 egg whites
200g castor sugar
1 tsp corn flour

Mix the corn flour and sugar together. Whisk the egg whites till it holds peaks, and then whisk in the rest of the sugar a spoonful at a time until it is stiff and shiny. Put tablespoonfuls of the mixture onto baking sheets lined with non-stick baking paper and bake at gas mark ½ /110 C for about 2 hours or until the meringues are dry and come off the paper easily. Serve the meringues as they are or:

*   With some whipped cream and fresh strawberries
*   Dip the bottom of the meringues in some melted black chocolate
*   Beat some mascarpone with some chopped frozen raspberries and icing sugar and a dash of cointreau to make instant ice-cream. Use it to sandwich the meringues together.

PISTACHIO MERINGUES

4 egg whites
200g castor sugar
1 tsp corn flour
175g Good Earth raw shelled pistachios – ground up roughly

Mix the corn flour and sugar together. Whisk the egg whites till it holds peaks, then whisk in the rest of the sugar a spoonful at a time until it is stiff and shiny and then fold in about 100g of the pistachios.

Put tablespoonfuls of the mixture onto baking sheets lined with non-stick baking paper, sprinkle over the rest of the nuts and bake at gas mark ½ /110ºC for about 2 hours or until the meringues are dry and come off the paper easily..

Makes about 24 – 30 meringues – depends how big or small the spoonfuls are; you could make tiny little ones which would double production.

VARIATION: For chocolate meringues – stir two or three tablespoons ground up black chocolate into the egg white and sugar mix instead of the pistachios. Don't mix it thoroughly – just enough for a few chocolate swirls and then proceed in the same way as above.

FAIRY CAKES AND BUTTERFLY CAKES

These are often called cup cakes, probably because they are made in little paper cups; I simply prefer the name fairy cakes and find it far more appealing, as do little children who so love fairy tales.

200g butter
200g sugar
4 eggs
200g self raising flour – sieved

Then choose one of the following to flavour the cakes
Either grated lemon or orange rind
Or 1 heaped tbs sieved cocoa
Or 50g chocolate chips
Or 50g frozen blackberries or blueberries
Or the seeds of a vanilla pod
Or 1 tsp instant coffee dissolved in a little hot water
Or a pinch of crushed saffron threads and poppy seeds

Beat the butter and sugar till light and fluffy, then beat in the eggs one at a time, beating well in between each addition. Then gently fold in then flour and the flavour of your choice till all is smoothly incorporated and spoon the batter into paper cases and bake at gas mark 4/ 180ºC for about 20-25 minutes or till risen, golden and firm. Remove from the oven and cool on a rack and ice with some glace icing made by dissolving icing sugar with enough water to make a soft paste. Flavour or colour the icing to match the flavour of the cakes.

To make butterfly cakes simply slice off the top of the fairy cakes, split the disk of cake down the middle and cut a tiny notch into the curved sides to make "butterfly wings". Cover the wings with glace icing (mix icing sugar with a little water to make paste) and sprinkle them with coloured hundreds and thousands. Next prepare some butter icing by beating together 150g butter and 200g icing sugar till light and fluffy, flavoured to match the little cakes. Then cover the "cut off" top of each fairy cake with the butter icing and stick the two "wings" in at an angle.

TANGERINE CAKE

This is delicious when tangerines are in season. The sweet citrus flavour of tangerines comes out perfectly as the best flavour is in the soft, sweet skins which melt away into the sugar when processed as described below.

6 eggs
150g castor sugar
150g plain flour
1 tsp baking powder
3 fresh, Maltese tangerines
2 tbs Olive oil

Peel the tangerines and grind the skins with the sugar in a food processor. Use the segments in a different dish or simply eat them. Preheat oven to gas mark 4 ½ – 5/185ºC.

Once the sugar is ready, whisk the eggs until thick and then add the sugar bit-by-bit whisking well in between each addition. Once all the sugar is incorporated, sieve in the flour and drizzle in the olive oil and fold it all in very gently till the flour is well incorporated.

Pour the mixture into a well-greased cake tin and bake for about 20-25 minutes. Turn out and cool on a rack.

To finish the cake
2 fresh, Maltese tangerines
Castor sugar to taste
A little water
A dash whisky

Peel and sliver up the peel of 2 tangerines and put them into a little saucepan – add the juice of the tangerines (squeeze in another two or three tangerines if they are small), add castor sugar and some water to taste, bring it all to the boil and once the sugar has dissolved add a dash of whisky and pour over the hot cake, spreading out the slivered peel as you go.

CHOC SWIRL CAKE

This light and easy to make cake is always very popular. It is a cross between a light sponge cake and a pound cake but contains only half the butter usually used in a pound cake. The chocolate and butter add lots of flavour, keep the cake moist and preventing it from drying out.

4 eggs – separated
200g sugar
100g butter
150g black chocolate
200g self raising flour – sieved

Preheat the oven to gas mark 4/180ºC. Grease a ring shaped cake tin very well. Melt the chocolate bain-marie (in a bowl suspended over a pot of barely simmering water). Melt the butter in a small saucepan, then remove it and allow it to cool. Whisk the egg whites till stiff, then start adding the sugar a little at a time and whisking it in between each addition. Once all the sugar has been incorporated and the mixture is thick and glossy, drop in the yolks and whisk briefly, just till they are fully incorporated. Then, using a large metal spoon, fold in the flour and melted butter in alternate goes. Once this is all incorporated, add the cooled and melted chocolate, stir two or three times and spoon into the greased ring mould. Bake in the preheated oven for approximately 45 minutes or until a skewer comes out clean. Turn out and serve as it is as the swirls are so pretty, otherwise, if you prefer ice the cake with either chocolate glacè icing or melted chocolate with a little butter added to stop it hardening completely.

LEMON DRIZZLE CAKE

This pretty fluted cake is intensely lemon flavoured and decorated with a lemon drizzle to make a refreshing and very light cake.

200g butter
200g castor sugar
2 big Maltese lemons
4 eggs
200g self raising flour

Preheat the oven to gas mark 4/180ºC. Grease and base line a fluted cake tin very well. Grate the zest off the lemons and squeeze them, put the juice in a bowl and put to one side to use later in the lemon drizzle. Beat the sugar, lemon zest and butter until light and creamy; add the eggs one at a time, beating the mixture well in between each addition. Sieve in the flour and fold in gently with a metal spoon. Pour into the prepared tin and bake for approximately 45 minutes or until a skewer comes out clean.

To finish off the cake
Juice of two lemons (see above)
150g castor sugar
Another lemon
Icing sugar

Put the juice and castor sugar into a small saucepan and dissolve, add two or three tablespoons water, bring it to the boil and simmer for two or three minutes. Then when the cake comes out of the oven, turn it out on to a plate and prick it all over the top of the cake. Carefully pour over the lemon drizzle and leave it to cool. Then, once the cake has cooled down, use a zester to make long strips of zest and put this to one side, squeeze the lemon and make glace icing with the icing sugar and juice and pour it over the cake so that the icing coats the top and dribbles over the edges in-between the flutes. Decorate the top with the strands of lemon zest.

CHOCOLATE CAKE

There are hundreds of chocolate cake recipes in the world; all of them sound delicious and most of them probably work well. I like to suit chocolate cakes to occasions, moods and weather.

A chocolate sponge is a light version of a cake: Lightly fold 150g cooled melted chocolate into a sponge mixture made with 6 eggs. There is no need to fold it in thoroughly; swirls of chocolate are more attractive. Then simply cover the cake with the chocolate ganache recipe below or sieve over equal amounts of icing sugar and cocoa.

This is my favourite chocolate cake recipe
3 eggs – separated
125g sugar
125g butter
150g dark chocolate
125g plain flour sieved with 1 tsp baking powder

Preheat the oven to gas mark5/190ºC. Melt the chocolate bain-marie (in a glass bowl suspended over a pan of barely simmering water) and then stir in the butter till melted. In the meantime, whisk the egg yolks and sugar till thick and foamy in one bowl and in another bowl whisk up the egg whites. Once the chocolate and butter mixture is ready, add it to the yolks and whisk, then fold in the flour with a metal spoon, and once that is smooth fold in the egg whites. Pour into a well greased 20cm cake tin and bake for approximately 45 minutes or firm and springy in the centre. Cool in the tin before turning out and covering the top with freshly made chocolate ganache (see below).

CHOCOLATE GANACHE

Chocolate ganache is a treat for chocoholics. It is unbelievably rich, smooth and chocolaty. It is ridiculously easy to make and although it is not absolutely essential, try and use chocolate with a high percentage of cocoa solids – it makes all the difference to the taste.

150ml fresh cream
150g dark chocolate

Break the chocolate up into squares and drop them into a saucepan. Pour over the cream and heat gently, stirring with a whisk until the chocolate has melted. Remove from the heat and carry on whisking until it is thick and glossy, a couple of minutes. Either use this to pour over a cake immediately or pour it into a bowl and store it in the fridge. (Allow it to come to room temperature before using to spread on cakes and things.)

Teatime was at the heart of children's entertainment in those days; we celebrated most things at teatime, especially birthdays with a tea party full of games, food and a magician. My mother organised excellent birthday parties; we would play all sorts of exciting games like musical chairs, musical bumps, pass the parcel, another which involved a race blowing up paper bags and bursting them as fast as possible which was such fun. Then we would go into the dining room for tea where there were sandwiches, jellies, biscuits, popcorn, "twistees", smarties, fairy cakes, meringues, various cakes and the birthday cake. After tea and blowing out the candles and making a wish there would be "Von Fred" the most popular magician of the time. The trick I really looked forward to (he was at almost all of our parties so we all knew what was coming) was the one where he made milk pour out of someone's armpit. One year, a naughty little boy sneaked into the room where all of Von Fred's magical things were and set a couple of pigeons and a rabbit or two free. Von Fred was very cross, but still managed the put on the show. Everyone loved Von Fred.

My memories of childhood summers are caught frozen in little vignettes; the relief of my hot feet scampering over cool, tiled floors, or wearing light cotton dresses and playing never-ending games chasing cousins and friends all over the place. The days seem full of endless sunshine, we spent them on the beach, swimming and eating *ħobż biż-żejt* that had been stored in sun warmed tins so that it was warm, soggy and lightly dusted with sand, but somehow so delicious. I remember the feeling of frustration at being called inside to supper and bed, just as it was getting really dark and interesting outside, just as the games of hide and seek in the dark, squashed sardines or murder in the dark were getting really competitive, there was Mummy's voice, the one that had to be obeyed, calling one inside to supper.

TARJA BIL-BUTIR

Tarja (very fine Maltese pasta similar to angels' hair pasta) was a frequent fixture of my childhood supper menu. The name of the pasta points to the Arab origin of pasta as the name *tarja* is similar to "tria" and comes from the Sicilian name in dialect for the same sort of pasta.

It was served in different ways; most usually as *tarja bil-butir* or "*Tarja* butter and cheese". This is made as follows: simply boil the pasta till still *al dente*, then take a mug of the boiling water, drain the rest and finally toss the drained pasta with butter, grated Parmesan cheese and a little of the reserved boiling water till the butter and cheese melt into a sauce. Serve immediately.

ĦOBŻ BIŻ-ŻEJT

Really fresh crusty Maltese bread,
Ripe and juicy summer tomatoes
Mint, basil and Maltese marjoram (*merqtux*)
Sea salt and freshly ground pepper

Cut the tomatoes in half and slice the loaf of Maltese bread into thick slices. Rub the cut side of the tomato over the slices of bread hard enough to stain the bread a lovely tomato red without flattening the bread entirely.

Pour a generous amount of olive oil into a saucer and dip each slice of bread, tomato side down, into the oil and lay the slices of bread on a plate, season them and scatter with herbs. Some people like to cut up the used tomato halves and divide the pieces around on the slices of bread.

N.B. During the winter months simply substitute the tomatoes with good quality kunserva – sun dried tomato paste.

MOLLY CARUANA DINGLI'S PULPETTI TAT-TARJA

400g *tarja* pasta
4 eggs
3 tbs grated Parmesan cheese
4 tsps cornflour

Boil the *Tarja* pasta till *al dente*, in the meantime beat the eggs, cheese and corn flour together in a bowl. Then drain the pasta well, add it to the egg mixture and stir it in. Then heat some butter and oil in a frying pan, and twirl the pasta round a big fork to make patties and fry till golden on both sides. Serve immediately.

FROĠA

The word *froġa* simply means omelette; the sort of omelette is designated by the descriptive word that follows, such as *froġa tal-pastard* or cauliflower omelette. According to "E.L.V", the author of *Ctieb Tal Chcina* first published in 1898 an omelette or *froġa sempliċi* was made by separating 4 eggs and beating the whites lightly, and then beating the yolks with a pinch of salt and some finely chopped parsley. Then fold the whites into the yolks and fry the mixture in hot fat, turning it over once, until it is golden on both sides. Slide it onto a plate and serve. A cauliflower omelette is made in the same way with the addition of some boiled mashed cauliflower; aubergines, marrows and bits of ham may be substituted for the cauliflower with success.

However to the vast majority of people *froġa* really means *froġa tal-għaġin* or spaghetti omelette. This is a very useful way to use up left overs; either left over pasta or sauce. Any sort of pasta may be used but the best kind is Maltese pasta called Tarja which is the thinnest pasta available similar to angels' hair pasta. A *froġa tal-għaġin* is so good that it is sometimes worth cooking more pasta than is necessary so that there will be enough leftover pasta to have a *froġa* at the next meal; or boiling up some pasta, especially if you have some left over sauce to use up. The same thing is made in Italy, but there it is called frittata di spaghetti.

To serve 4
400g pasta (leftover or just boiled) with sauce or plain
Some sauce (optional)
5 eggs
4 tbs grated Parmesan or to taste
2 tbs chopped herbs (basil, parsley)
Olive oil

Beat the eggs together lightly in a large bowl together with the cheese and herbs, stir in the pasta and mix well. Heat the oil in a large frying pan and pour in the pasta, pressing down with the back of a fork. Cook till golden on the bottom, then turn it over and carry on cooking till golden and crisp on both sides. Serve immediately.

N.B. If you are nervous about flipping a froga try either of these two solutions: Either put the frying pan under a hot grill and cook the top of the froga till golden or slide the froga onto a plate, then invert it back into the frying pan, uncooked side down and carry on cooking till golden.

MALTOVA OR PASTINA

Pastina is the name of tiny little pasta shapes; they usually come in stars, rings, or tiny balls and are cooked and served in broth. More often than not an egg lightly beaten with a little grated parmesan and finely chopped parsley was added to the soup to make *stracchiatelle*.

500ml good beef or chicken stock
A couple of handfuls of "pastina" pasta
1 egg
½ tbs grated parmesan
½ tbs finely chopped parsley

Beat the egg, cheese and parsley together in a little bowl and put to tone side while you boil the *pastina* in the broth. Once the *pastina* is cooked, turn the heat right down and stir in the egg mixture and switch off the heat immediately as the egg will be rubbery if overcooked. Serve immediately.

CHICKEN NOODLE SOUP

Some chicken stock must be made first, ideally from the carcass of a roast free-range chicken to make what we call *Brodu tal-Qafas* in traditional Maltese cooking. If you are short of a carcass or two, lightly roast about a dozen chicken wings and use them instead. Simply simmer the chicken carcass or wings in 2 litres of water with any dripping left in the roasting pan, a couple of carrots, some Maltese celery (karfus) and an onion for an hour and a half and the broth is ready to use.

Chicken broth made as above
1 onion, finely chopped
2 zucchini – *qaraghbali* cut into julienne strips
1 carrot cut into julienne strips
A generous pinch saffron threads, crushed
50g (or to taste) tarja, capellini or filini d'oro pasta
Finely chopped parsley and mint

Strain the broth, taste it, season it well and save the little bits of chicken meat left on the bones or wings. In a clean saucepan fry the onion in a little oil till soft, and then add the saved chicken meat and the prepared vegetables. Fry them while stirring the pot for a couple of minutes, then add the stock and bring to the boil. Add the pasta and the saffron and simmer for as long as it takes for the pasta to cook, then serve scattered with the chopped herbs.

SCRAMBLED EGGS

Scrambled eggs are the easiest and quickest way to cook eggs. They are best scrambled in a little butter with a tiny dash of milk or cream, but taste very good and are healthier when simply scrambled with a little olive oil instead. Scrambled egg are easily turned into Balbuljata or Maltese scrambled eggs by first frying a finely chopped onion in the butter with a little olive oil, then adding a deseeded and chopped tomato before stirring in the eggs and scrambling them as usual. Serve Balbuljata scattered with chopped mint, freshly ground black pepper and toasted Maltese bread.

SCRAMBLED EGGS

4 big eggs
Seasoning
25g butter
A generous dash of cream (optional)
A little chopped mint (optional)

Beat the eggs lightly together with a little seasoning, just enough to blend the whites and yolks. Melt the butter in a small frying pan and just as it begins to bubble, pour in the eggs and stir with a wooden spoon. As the eggs begin to coagulate, quickly add the cream, stir and when they are creamy and beginning to set spoon onto a plate, top with the mint and serve immediately. Do not overcook the eggs as they will become nasty and rubbery.

Variations: Convert this simple children's supper into a deliciously indulgent light supper for adults in this way – stir in some slivered smoked salmon at the end of the cooking time and replace the mint with some dill, then serve the scrambled eggs topped with a little caviar on buttered toast. Or more simply stir in the roe of some sea urchins for a summery version, as pictured below.

GĦAĠIN TORK OR GRIEG

This traditional dish features as a popular supper in the repertoire of traditional urban Maltese dishes. Its name is a curiosity; there seems to be no connection to Greece or Turkey where they seem to prefer to eat lamb rather than pork. However, there is a tenuous connection to the pasta rather than the meat; during the early part of the Knights rule in Malta "Turkish" ships used to smuggle pasta into Malta as there was such demand for it – and "Turks" enjoyed eating it themselves – in fact a Moslem prisoner called Memi Rais regularly sent out to buy pasta which he cooked and ate in his cell in the Inquisitors prison.

250g minced pork
50g minced bacon
2 sprigs rosemary – chopped
2 cloves garlic – peeled and finely chopped
1 small onion – peeled and finely chopped
A glass white wine
200ml chicken stock
25g butter
A little olive oil
Seasoning
1 lump or tsp sugar
½ tsp cinnamon
1 tsp fennel seeds

Melt the butter in a little olive oil, add the finely chopped onion, garlic and sugar and cook gently till they begin to soften then add the cinnamon. Add the bacon and cook for a minute or two, then stir in the pork and cook till lightly browned. Then add the wine, stock and rosemary, bring to the boil and simmer till thick.

Bring a large pot of salted water to the boil, add the pasta and boil till *al dente*. Drain, stir in the sauce made as above and top with some freshly grated Parmesan if liked.

The sauce may be served with any shape of short pasta, but the traditional choice is *żibeġ* which translates as "beads" and refers to the shape of the pasta. Although this shape of pasta is generally served in *Minestra* or vegetable soup its use in this dish is mandatory. Nowadays most commercial pasta commonly available on the market is Italian and the closest equivalent shape to Maltese *żibeġ* is *ditaloni*.

RICOTTA PIE

This pie is very easy to make and is always very popular. Replace some or all of the ricotta with fresh *ġbejniet* for a lighter version of the pies below. To ensure success when using fresh *ġbejniet*, always drain them in a sieve for a couple of hours or overnight in the fridge.

The pastry
250g plain flour
125g butter
A generous pinch of salt
1 tsp of oregano
The grated rind of one lemon (optional)
Water

Rub the butter into the flour and stir in the salt, oregano and grated lemon peel, if you are using it. Add enough water to make dough and knead it lightly by folding it and pressing it down a couple of times, then shape it into a ball and set it aside while you prepare the filling.

The filling
500g of ricotta
3 or 4 eggs
Three heaped tbs of parmesan cheese (grated)
500g of fresh spinach
½ tps of nutmeg (grated)
2 tbs semolina

Wash and dry the spinach thoroughly. Finely chop it and add it to the ricotta. Stir in the rest of the ingredients and beat it with a large fork until the mixture is smooth. Do not over process the mixture as this will make it heavy and rubbery.

To finish the tart
2 handfuls of basil leaves
2 handfuls of pine nuts
Olive oil

Then roll out the pastry and use it to line an 23cm ovenproof flan dish. Pour in the filling, smooth the surface and scatter it with the pine nuts. Drizzle on some olive oil. Bake the tart at gas mark 5/190ºC for 45-50 minutes, or until the filling has risen and turns golden, and the pastry is golden and crisp. Scatter the basil leaves over the tart just before serving it. You can also put a pastry lid on it before backing, and turn it into a pie. For this, leave out the pine nuts. You will need to increase the quantities in the pastry recipe.

To vary this recipe
Either leave out the spinach and add a little more grated cheese and two or three tablespoonfuls of chopped parsley, or replace the spinach with silver beet leaves, finely chopped beetroot tops, borage or nettle leaves, and carry on in the same way.

Either grate in a couple of raw marrows(qaraghbali) or add some shelled broad beans and peas, instead of the spinach, stir them into the ricotta with a little chopped parsley, and top the tart with a generous layer of sesame seeds

Make sweet versions of this tart by using sweet pastry and replacing the cheese and spinach in the ricotta either 6 tablespoonfuls of chopped black chocolate, 3 tablespoonfuls of chopped candied peel and five heaped tablespoonfuls of vanilla sugar. Scatter the top of the tart with flaked almonds rather than pine nuts and bake in the same way. Or give the sweet tart a citrus zing by grating in the zest of 2 Maltese oranges or lemons, adding a little of the juice, 6 heaped tablespoonfuls of sugar and a topping of flaked almonds. Bake it in the same way and dust it with icing sugar just before serving.

MEAT PIES

400g flour
200g butter
A pinch of salt
Water to bind

First make the pastry. Put the flour into a bowl, cut in the butter and rub in lightly to ensure it is all evenly distributed. Make a well in the centre and pour in enough water to bind and stir until dough is formed. Flatten this slightly with your knuckles, then fold it in half and flatten it again, do this three or four times until the dough is fairly smooth but do not overwork it as this makes it tough and difficult to use.

Leave the dough to rest for quarter of an hour as this helps it to relax and makes it easier to roll out.

500g raw minced meat – a mix of beef and pork is best
3 medium sized peeled and raw potatoes – diced fairly small
1 medium peeled and finely chopped raw leek or onion
1 tbs finely chopped fresh rosemary
1 tbs finely chopped fresh sage
A little freshly ground black pepper and salt

Mix all the raw ingredients together. Roll out the pastry and cut out large circles. On each circle lay some potato, onion meat and herbs, Season well and fold over, crimping the edges well and bake at gas mark 5/190ºC for about 35-40 minutes or till golden. Makes about 15 depending on the size of the circles used.

Food, like fashion, changes all the time. In the 1970s cooking was all about recreating the foods discovered while travelling; the feel of French bistro food at home, like onion soup for example, or gooey fondues that evoked Alpine chalets and skiing trips, while Alfredo's spaghetti carbonara, made with cream, eggs, Parmesan and bacon, conjured up happy Roman holidays. The only problem this involved was getting hold of those "glamorous" ingredients to cook with back in the heyday of bulk buying and shortages.

Avocado pears, for example, were exclusive and hard to come by back then, so an avocado pear vinaigrette was considered to be the height of sophistication, as was a prawn cocktail – often made with tinned or frozen shrimps rather like plastic pink commas in an equally pink sauce. Starters like "garlic mushrooms" were popular as mushrooms were equally rare in the Malta of those days and we were easily pleased.

In fact one of the first memories to spring to mind when remembering my teenage summers in the 1970s is a 7-up float.

Off to Comino. My father (right) and Aunty Terry (left)

7-UP FLOAT

A 7-up float is made by pouring a soft drink like 7-up drink over one or more scoops of ice-cream. The ice-cream, being less dense than the carbonated drink, floats giving the drink its name. The most popular combination was vanilla ice-cream and 7-up, although in theory anything could be used – a scoop or two of lemon sorbet drizzled with a little limoncello and soda might be a more interesting, adult version of the rather white, sickly authentic 7-up float.

SHRIMP OR PRAWN COCKTAIL

Summer is the best time of year to make this properly as the wonderful red Mediterranean prawns are in season and nothing is as good as these perfect prawns. You will need approximately 125g of these prawns to make a shrimp cocktail as a starter – if this is to be served as a main course salad then double or triple the amount.

500g fresh red Mediterranean prawns
Olive oil
2 cloves garlic – peeled and crushed
A tot whisky
1 large cos lettuce *(hass twil)*
Lemon juice
½ a cucumber, peeled, deseeded and finely diced
250ml mayonnaise – bought or home-made*
1 tbs tomato ketchup (Heinz)
A little Tabasco sauce

Wash the prawns then fry them in a little olive oil and the crushed garlic. When they just about begin to cook – the prawns start to change colour – pour over the whisky, stir around gently for another minute or two and they will be ready. Do not over cook them as they will dry out.

Then put them to one side to cool down while you prepare the salad. First wash and dry the lettuce and shred finely – the best way to do this is to roll up the leaves like a cigar and shred then across the width, then they are ready to be tossed in a little olive and lemon juice. Divide this between four cocktail glass and top with the prepared cucumber.

Mix the mayonnaise with the ketchup, Tabasco sauce and a little of the pan juices and put in the fridge while you shell the prawns. Then stir the prawns into the sauce and divide them equally between the glasses of salad, arranging them on top of the salad. Serve well chilled.
Serves 4

* To make the mayonnaise: Whisk up two egg yolks and then add 250ml olive oil drop by drop whisking all the time. Once this is thick, season it with some dry mustard powder, a dash of lemon and salt and pepper.

VANILLA FUDGE

This creamy fudge has a lovely old-fashioned taste that brings back childhood memories of sweet-shops. It is soft and smooth and flavoured with vanilla. Replacing the castor sugar with brown sugar will give a darker colour.

You will need

150ml of tinned milk
100ml of fresh milk or fresh cream
300g of soft brown sugar
150g of castor sugar
a vanilla pod (split in half)
50g of butter

Put the tinned milk, fresh milk or cream, split vanilla pod and sugars into a deep saucepan over a low heat. Stir until the sugar has dissolved. Then add the butter and stir until it too has dissolved. Turn up the heat and boil the mixture, stirring frequently, until it is thick and has reached the 'soft ball' stage. Test for this by dropping a little fudge into a bowl of water. If it forms a soft ball it is ready. Otherwise, and more accurately, use a sugar thermometer and cook the mixture to 115C. Have patience, this takes a little longer than imagined, but if the right temperature isn't reached the recipe doesn't work out and what you will get is a greasy, chewy mass. When the right point has been reached, turn off the heat, lift out the vanilla pod and press out the last drops of vanilla flavour from it between two spoons.

Stir the mixture briskly until it is really thick and smooth. This takes two to three minutes. Pour it onto a greased baking-sheet or over the bottom of a greased roasting-tin. Leave it to cool and then cut it into little squares. Decorate a plate of vanilla fudge with the cooked vanilla pod. Good Earth stocks vanilla pods, but if you are unable to find any, use half a teaspoonful of vanilla essence instead – but the flavour of vanilla pods is so much better than essence and this makes all the difference. If you wish, you could scrape the inside of the vanilla pod out into the sugar before cooking and push the scraped-out pod into a jar of sugar to make vanilla-sugar. To vary this recipe, add chopped nuts or some chocolate or granules of instant coffee, or a few rum soaked raisins and finely chopped dates.

WARTIME FOOD AND VICTORY KITCHENS

The manifold hardships suffered by the Maltese during the worst years of WW2 are manifest; incessant bombing and crushing shortages of every possible commodity affected the whole population and the situation was almost unbearable. It is difficult, if not impossible for people today, surrounded as we are by a surfeit of commercial bounty, to even begin to imagine the horrors of hunger.

Malta was under siege. Most provisions came by sea and as the axis forces blew convey after convoy of commodity laden ships out of the sea the situation deteriorated alarmingly and starvation loomed. It became harder and harder to find basic supplies and to make matters worse the armed forces were running desperately low on fuel and ammunition and could only fire a restricted number of rounds at enemy bombers and send up fewer and fewer fighter plane sorties to protect the convoys which was cruelly frustrating.

Many shops closed or were simply blown out of existence – although some wittier retailers posted humorous notices on bomb blasted shop fronts like "even more open than usual" and worked on in crumbling buildings selling from an ever diminishing stock supplemented by meagre rations.

Vegetable vendor's carts disappeared from the streets as supplies were requisitioned to be rationed and although hoarding was outlawed, shortages had been apparent as soon as the war broke out as people panicked and quickly stockpiled goods to see them through the coming times of trouble. Long, boring queues sprung up everywhere and housewives had to stand in line to buy powdered eggs, bread, kerosene, milk, water and everything else – even matches were rationed. Soon, just like the old Soviet joke, no-one went out without a shopping bag just in case an opportunity to queue appeared out of the blue.

This was 1942 and Malta was the most bombed place on earth at the time – and survival was paramount in most people's minds. Rations were barely adequate; creating ideal conditions for a thriving black market where wealthy customers paid shocking prices for something extra, while the rest subsisted on meagre rations. One fresh egg for example cost half a crown – inconceivably expensive at a time when wages were very low and families large, so most people resorted to powdered eggs.

Reports of suspected black markets deals were rife; my mother-in-law Guza Cremona who lived in Naxxar during the war, remembers that a greengrocer in St Lucy Street deflected police suspicion during a raid on her shop by sending them on to my mother-in-laws's aunt Zarena, who kept pigs in the alley opposite the shop. The greengrocer told the police that she had seen a cart suspiciously full of fodder going into Zarena's alley – the ruse failed as the pigs were licensed as was the fodder, however they found and confiscated two precious sacks of black market flour bought, ironically enough, from the greedy grocer opposite.

Some of the black marketeers cheated – anything to make a little more money. When Salvu Camilleri from Naxxar bought a sack of potatoes for 18 pounds (a fortune at the time) from a profiteer known as Ic-Cijc, he took them home to his wife who started to spread them out on the cool cellar floor so that they would keep better – only to find that the bottom half of the sack was full of soil rather than potatoes. Salvu was a tough man and he soon returned the sack and soil with a rough reminder never to try and cheat him again. However, much of the "under the counter" type of commercial activity was based on mutual trust and respect; information of availability was spread by word of mouth so depended to a certain extent on who knew who and perhaps more accurately who could pay most.

People coped with the situation by looking for food in places other than shops. They bartered for things like flour or pasta with other commodities; for example, a certain Mr Miller who didn't smoke, swapped 80 cigarettes from his ration for a bag of flour so that his wife could make some tagliatelle, which she did. However, in a cruel twist of fate, that night his sister and her 9 children were bombed out of their house, and the tagliatelle, so carefully dried overnight had to be shared among many and, as he put it, *"Baħħ it-tagliatelli!".* An aunt of mine who lived in Sliema during the war used to cycle all the way to Birkirkara to visit the market there, as vegetables were reputed to be a little better and possibly more abundant. She then had to cycle back, balancing purchases and herself, along bad roads risking air raids and all sorts of things – just in the hope of buying some extra vegetables. Some people went to the pasta factory in Balzan and bought up any surplus production – sold at a high price of course, just as certain farmers are said to have sold their extra produce for gold coins or silver trinkets. Some country people even collected carob pods, usually used for fodder and sold them as food at a penny each, or ate them themselves when all else failed.

This situation suited the besieging forces perfectly; the hungrier the Maltese became the more likely they were to surrender. German pilots

returning to bases in Sicily strafed fishermen to try and put them off fishing and supplying islanders with fish, similarly they turned their guns on farmers, shoppers and other ordinary people going about their day. One of my aunts remembers the day a German pilot pounded the main street in Rabat, Gozo with his machine guns – narrowly missing one of her sisters who was there shopping and had to take shelter in a narrow doorway – he then turned his guns on a large herd of sheep and goats grazing in the valley that led down to Marsalforn. "At least we had some meat for a while!" she said with a smile although that particular herd certainly stopped producing vital milk.

As food supplies dwindled further, the government decided to set up "Victory Kitchens" and the first one opened at Lija on January 3rd 1942. They were supposed to ensure a fair and efficient distribution and use of rations and save on kerosene used for cooking. The number of Victory kitchens all over Malta and Gozo rose to 200 during the worst of the siege and thousands were served one meal a day that cost sixpence. Unfortunately, although the system was well intentioned, the meals were quite unpopular and while menus sounded almost decent the reality was quite different. Consider the list below; each meal was all that was on offer each day and the portions were small, watered down and cooked with the poor supplies available.

A typical week's menu on offer at the Victory Kitchens is as follows:
Monday and Saturday: Macaroni with tomato sauce
Tuesday: Balbuljata (made with powdered eggs)
Wednesday and Friday; Minestra or herrings
Sunday and Thursday; stewed meat or corned beef
with tomatoes and baked beans or peas

People took a container with them and queued up at the Victory Kitchen once a day to collect their meal which was ticked off their ration card. There was some jostling and pushing as queues were long and people were tired and hungry, however they would collect it and take it home to eat. Some people had something extra at home to add to it while other, less fortunate ones had to make do. Sometimes the spaghetti was simply boiled and given out and people had to take it home to add some sort of sauce of their own, possibly some watered down *kunserva* or something similar.

Mrs Pisani from Ta' Xbiex who lived in Hamrun during the war remembers miserably thin *minestra* with strange bits of meat floating in a thin, greasy liquid. Sometimes there was some short pasta called *żibeġ* in it and her mother would carefully fish them out to warm up for the evening meal with some powdered egg and possibly a little corned beef mixed in when supplies permitted. Corned Beef, popularly known as bully beef from the French *bouilli* meaning boiled, was very much a siege food which may explain some people's aversion to it – my father for example refused to have it in the house, let alone eat it.

Another of my aunts, who helped manage the Marsalforn Victory kitchen for a while, said that the system was quite simple. The Communal Feeding Department in Rabat, Gozo would ring up with the day's order; for example how much spaghetti to cook per person or how many slices of corned beef to dole out per person. The Victory Kitchens stored certain foodstuffs like pasta, tinned beans, corned beef or tinned tuna which the manager would issue, but when minestra or "meat" stew was on the menu fresh vegetables were sent in from the central office and the cooks would simply have to do their best with the ingredients sent in.

Circular No. 150 issued by the Communal Feeding Department to Sub-Managers on 29th July 1942 and entitled "Amendment of menus" starts off with the words "Owing to the shortage of certain supplies..." and goes on to explain how to amend the menus with recipes attached. The short note emphasises how important it was to strictly follow the standard recipes for preparation and service of meals at the Victory Kitchens so that the same meals were served at all Victory Kitchens in an attempt to minimise complaints.

The same note explains that although some of the recipes contained instructions for frying the cooks had to follow the stewing recipe until frying utensils were issued to the kitchens which might explain why there were many people who complained that meals were watery and inadequate or as one lady from Rabat, Malta described the stew, "The portion for three persons offered in one plate consisted of a piece of skin with a good layer of fat and a shadow of meat on top, six tablespoons of sauce and five peas." Or a Sliema lady who remembers the minestra was roughly made, "the vegetables were cut in big chunks, half a turnip, big pieces of long marrow with skin, turnip leaves and stalks in quantity, a shadow of pumpkin and tomatoes, just to give a hectic colour, a few *żibeġ* swimming in water, pure water. Ġużè Cassar Pullicino wrote that "they vented their displeasure in a series of triplets, or groups of three lines, sung on an old folk tune such as the following verse:

Baked pasta in trays and people in array at the Victory Kitchen.
Minestra and sardines, pasta and beans at the Victory Kitchen.
What a treat on New Year's Day! They made us eat sardines at the Victory Kitchen.
Their legs are so fat, they eat so much grub, the girls at the Victory Kitchen.
Lipstick-laden maidens with polish on their nails at the Victory Kitchen.
Their hair set all wavy to flirt with boys in the navy, the girls at the Victory Kitchen.
The kitchen staff were not slow to retaliate by saying We served you
goat's meat, which you had to eat from the Victory Kitchen."

Those who could, cooked at home on a *spiritiera* or small stove using precious paraffin which was in short supply and rationed. When paraffin ran out, my mother-in-law remembers her mother cooking on an improvised stove made from a large paint can or large round metal container called a *patalott*. It was converted into a stove in the following way: first, a tinsmith cut little hole into the side of the patalott, next, an empty bottle of Martini or something similar was put into the middle of the can and then straw was piled into the space around the bottle and pressed down to form a solid mass. This, in fact, is the part my mother-in-law remembers enjoying as a

child, jumping up and down on the straw to compact it as much as possible. Then the bottle was pulled out of the straw, taking care not to dislodge the straw and the hole filled with bits of paper which were set alight and a pot of soup, stew or other food was put on the top and set to simmer. As the straw was packed in so tightly it would burn away very slowly and often last for up to two or three hours allowing food to be cooked fairly sucessfully. Although a *patalott* smoked dreadfully and burnt and stung the cook's eyes, it offered an ingenious solution to a situation where there was no paraffin, barely any wood and absolutely no coal, but of course, it could only work in areas with easy access to farms where straw was available or somewhere next to carpentry shop for sawdust.

But, however ingenious and brave people were, until the Santa Maria convoy arrived on 8th August 1942 Malta was in dire straits so much so that it is said that the Islands were 10 days away from absolute starvation as opposed to near starvation. What made all of this deprivation so much worse was that the people suffered all of this dreadful hunger and deprivation amid the misery of tons of bombs falling hourly from the skies, crumbling and smoking buildings, in smelly and crowded rock-hewn, dark shelters, lost homes, disease and death. We were indeed a George Cross island – most other nations would have given in and surrendered.

BALBULJATA

During the war this would have been made with powdered eggs
that were nowhere near as good as the real thing. Everybody likes
a *balbuljata* made their own way – I like it with less tomato than
others who add far more – it is a matter of personal taste.

To make enough for 4 (not wartime sized portions)
8 eggs
1 small onion
4 small tomatoes or 2 big ones
A little fresh mint or parsley (optional)

Finely chop the onions and fry gently in a little olive oil. In the mean time chop the
tomatoes, then add them to the pan and cook gently. While they cook beat the eggs
with a little salt and pepper and then add them to the pan and stir them around gently
until they are cooked but still creamy. Serve sprinkled with the chopped herbs if using.

"PORK" WITH TOMATOES AND BAKED BEANS

Recipe taken from circular no 150 dated 29th July 1942.
For 100 portions:

17 ratal or rotolos pork (1 ratal = 800g)
10 ratal rotolos tomatoes or 1 ratal rotolos tomato paste
16lbs baked beans in tomato sauce
2 ratal onions

Place meat and onions in cauldron with ½ an inch of water to cover bottom of cauldron. Place cauldron on fire and allow to broil for 30 minutes. Add tomatoes or tomato paste and allow to simmer for a further 20/30 minutes.

Now cover meat with water and continue cooking till meat is cooked. Remove meat from gravy. Add beans to gravy, boil for 5 minutes and serve.
Service: portion of meat and 2-3 tablespoons of tomato and beans.

STEWED BONEY PORK

A modern version of the recipe – made tastier with a few added ingredients

1 rack pork spare ribs
250 ml tomato sauce
1 large onion
Olive oil
Rosemary
1 glass red wine
Tinned beans

Fry the onion till soft. Add the ribs and cook till brown, then add the rosemary, red wine and tomato sauce. Simmer till tender and serve with the beans.

POTATO BREAD

Prepare the dough as follows:

500g plain flour –"00" or other soft grain flour

2 tbs olive oil

½ sachet instant yeast

½ tsp sugar

A pinch of salt

150g boiled, peeled (hamra cara or bajda)potatoes, lightly mashed

Tepid water

Heap the flour, instant yeast, salt and sugar up on a work surface and make a well in the centre. Add the oil and the potatoes and a little tepid water and begin to knead into dough, adding water as you go. The potatoes make the dough soft and moist so add less water more slowly than usual or you may end up with sticky dough. Once the dough is ready knead it for approximately 10 minutes to ensure a good rise then dust the dough with flour and leave it in a warm place till it has doubled in size.

LITTLE ROLLS

Then either cut it up and shape into little buns – possibly fill them with mozzarella and Parma ham – or some anchovies mashed with chopped fennel and garlic, and leave them to rise again until doubled in size then bake it in the oven at gas mark 7/210ºC for 25 minutes or until golden.

FOCACCIA

Otherwise knead the dough again and shape it into a foccacia, drizzle it generously with olive oil, sprinkle it with salt and rosemary sprigs and bake as above. Then serve it cut into wedges with some olive oil blended with fresh rosemary and fresh fennel fronds to dip. *This quantity makes 1 medium foccacia or 6 medium rolls.*

CAROB COFFEE AND POTATO BREAD

During the Second World War when food supplies were scarce carobs regained their popularity as a food and were sold for a penny each. The seeds found inside the carob pods were ground along with the very few coffee beans available to make up quantities and extend the flavour – much as French people used acorns during the same war.

A description of Malta with a sketch of its history and fortifications written in 1792 translated from the Italian in 1801 by an officer resident on the island

Aquilina, Joseph, *Maltese-English Dictionary*

Ashby, T.H., *Roman Malta*

Blondy, Alain, 'A Treasure of 18th Century Malta: The Maltese Orange', in *Treasures of Malta* Vol. X No. 1

Blondy, Alain, T*he Commerce of Oranges in the XVIII Century*

Blouet, Brian, *The Story of Malta*

Bonanno, Anthony, *Distribution of Villas and some of the Maltese Economy in the Roman Period*

Bonello, Giovanni, *Histories of Malta Vol. I, Deceptions and Perceptions*

Borg, Joseph, A., *Woodland Walk from Xemxija to L-Imbordin*

Bradford, Ernle, *Mediterranean, Portrait of a Sea*

Brincat, Joseph, M., *Malta 870-1054 Al-Himyari's Account and its Linguistic Implications*

Brockman, Eric, *Last Bastion*

Brydone, Patrick, *A tour through Sicily and Malta: in a series of letters to William Beckford, Esq. of Somerly in Suffolk* (1st ed. 1773)

Callus, P., *The Rising of the Priests*, 1961

Caruana Galizia, Anne & Helen, *The Food and Cookery of Malta*

Cassar, Carmel, *A Concise History of Malta*

Cassar, Carmel, *Fenkata; An Emblem of Maltese Peasant Resistance*

Cassar Pullicino, Ġużè, *Il-Kitba bil-Malti sa l-1870*

Cassar Pullicino, Ġużè, 'Antichi Cibi Maltesi' in *Melita Historica: Journal of the Malta Historical Society* 3 (1961) 2 (31-54)

Cavaliero, Roderick, *The Last of the Crusaders*

Colt Hoare, Richard, *A Classical Tour through Italy and Sicily*

Dalli, Charles, *Malta, The Medieval Millennium*

de Boiseglin, Louis, *Ancient and Modern Malta*

de Piro, Nicholas, *Occasions, Social Events and Occurrences in the Palace*

de Piro, Nicholas, *Lost Letters*

Del Amo Garcia, Julio, Fiorini, Stanley & Wettinger, Godfrey, *Documentary Sources of Maltese History Part III Documents of the Maltese Universitas*

Din L-Art Ħelwa, *Walks Red Tower/Foresta 2000*

Durrell, Lawrence, *Prospero's Cell*

E.L.V., *Ctieb Tal Cchina*, Second Edition 1908

Epigram XXXVI, *A Jar of Olives*, Book XIII

Fiorini, Stanley, 'Carnj per lu Carnivalj' in *Melita Historica*, 9 (1987) 4 (311-314)

Fiorini, Stanley, *The Mandati Documents at the Archives of the Mdina Cathedral, Malta 1437-1539*

Freller, Thomas, *Malta and the Grand Tour*

French Angas, George, *A Ramble in Malta and Sicily in the Autumn of 1811*, 1842

Galea, Victor J., *Qwiel u Qaddisin*

Gambin, Kenneth, Buttigieg Noel, *Storja tal-Kultura ta' l-Ikel f'Malta*

Ganado, Herbert, translated by Refalo, Michael, *My Century Vol 1 (Rajt Malta Tinbidel)*

Ganado, Herbert, translated by Refalo, Michael, *My Century Vol 3 (Rajt Malta Tinbidel)*

Houel Jean, *Voyage Pittoresque en Sicile*, 1784

Hulme-Beaman Ardern, George, *The Story of My Life*

Luke, Sir Harry, *Malta an Account and an Appreciation*

Luttrell, Anthony T., *Approaches to Medieval Malta*

Luttrell, Anthony T., *Girolamo Manduca and Gian Francesco Abela – Tradition and Invention in Maltese Historiography*

Mallia Milanes, Victor, *Descrittione di Malta anno 1716*

Mercieca, Michele, *Libro di Secreti per Fare Cose Dolci di Varii Modi*, 1748

Mifsud-Chircop, George, *Past Carnival and New Year's Eve Drama in Malta*

NLM Lib. Ms. 1 with thanks to Liam Gauci, *The Journey Of Don Ignazio Saverio Mifsud The Grand Tour Of A Maltese In 1746. All The Places He Touched Upon*

NLM Lib. Ms. No. 1953 Archives of the Order of Malta

Petronius, Arbiter, *Trimalchio's Dinner*

Sandys, George, *A Relation of a Journey begun in Anno Domine 1610*, 2nd Edition 1621

Savona-Ventura, C., *Outlines of Maltese Medical History*

Schermerhorn, Elizabeth, *Malta of the Knights*

Sørensen, Sven and Schiro, Joseph, eds., *Malta 1796-1797: Thorvaldsen's Visit*

Spiteri, Stephen C, *The Great Siege*

Trump, D. H., *Skorba, Excavation carried out on behalf of the National Museum of Malta 1961–1963*

Trump, David H., *Malta: Prehistory and Temples*

Vella, Philip, *Malta Blitzed but not Beaten*

Wettinger, Godfrey, *Slavery in the Islands of Malta and Gozo Ca 1000-1812*

Wignacourt, John, *The Odd Man in Malta 1914*

INDEX